MIDDLESEX WATER COMPANY

A BUSINESS HISTORY

MIDDLESEX WATER COMPANY

A BUSINESS HISTORY

11/30/94

For Bill Scott,

With many thanks for your interest - It was good meeting you.

BY

Very best regards,

Mark Lender

MARK EDWARD LENDER

METUCHEN THE UPLAND PRESS *1994*

Published by the Upland Press
91 Upland Ave.
Metuchen, NJ 08840

Cataloging Data

ISBN: 0-9642916-0-6

Printed in the United States of America

This book is dedicated to the
past, present, and future employees of the
Middlesex Water Company
and to their families:

"We are people serving people."

and, with love, to
Shannon Rebecca Lender

MIDDLESEX WATER COMPANY:
A BUSINESS HISTORY

TABLE OF CONTENTS

Illustrations

All photographs courtesy the Middlesex Water Company, Newark Public
Library, Walter Choroszewski, Anthony Ferraro, and Leon Silakoski.

FOREWORD

THIS BOOK IS THE HISTORY OF a water company. More precisely, it is a history of the Middlesex Water Company.
Incorporated in 1897, the company originally sold water to industrial customers along Staten Island Sound, largely in Carteret, New
Jersey. Today, it is one of the largest investor-owned water companies in the state, and it provides water service for residential,
commercial, and municipal users in three counties. From modest
beginnings, Middlesex Water has emerged as a mainstay of the
infrastructure of one of the most developed and economically
important sections of the eastern United States. Its story is important, for it stands as a case study of how utility companies across
the nation, which usually operate out of the public eye, have fostered economic growth and the public welfare. Without safe and
reliable water supplies, modern society as we know it could not
exist.

This narrative relates the progress of the Middlesex
Company from its founding to its current position as a mature and
successful public utility. It also provides an accounting of that
progress; that is, it asks why the company evolved as it did, and
how it interacted with the major economic, social, and political
developments of its times. Put another way, my goal was to write
a corporate biography that examined Middlesex Water in the context of regional history.

A century is a long time in the life-span of any American business. In the case of the Middlesex Water Company, a hundred years saw its service area evolve from a pastoral rural district into a commercial and industrial powerhouse. As a consequence, the passing years saw the company grappling with a series of daunting challenges as it marshalled capital, deployed new technologies, and developed sources of water supply—all of which was essential if the communities and industries of central New Jersey were to sustain economic growth and the public safety. The nature of doing business also changed dramatically over the decades. Those who incorporated Middlesex Water conducted their affairs with little regard for government intervention in company operations. Yet the advent of state regulation early in the century set a new course for the entire utilities industry; indeed, during the 1920s the company's battle against regulation attracted national attention. Yet Middlesex made its peace with the regulators, and ever since, in the economic equivalent of high-wire walking, the company has sought to strike a balance between regulatory guidelines, the needs of its service area, and the expectations of shareholders.

Finally, the people changed. Early managers and employees were remarkably dedicated to the water business, but they usually came to the business without specialized training or experience, and they learned their roles as they went along. Changing technologies, financial requirements, and legal conditions, however, compelled an increasing focus on human resources; today, those who work at Middlesex Water are a highly skilled and integrated team, constantly retraining to maintain stringent standards of service performance and water quality. Thus if the product—pure water—has remained the same, dealing with it has changed enormously over the years; and the history of the Middlesex Water Company's role in these changes has been the history of the water business in microcosm.

A word is in order on my approach to the subject. As narrative history, this volume is little concerned with some of the more theoretical or abstruse perspectives on business development or

history. The Middlesex Water Company, because of the nature of
its business and its size, never evolved or structured itself after the
fashion of, say, U.S. Steel or General Motors. Thus it reflected little of any of the models of corporate growth or operations
explored by some business historians, who generally have focused
on large industrial or financial concerns. In fact, the vast majority
of water companies, so critical to the national infrastructure, fall
under the federal government's definition of "small" businesses.
Case studies of small companies, however, are the building blocks
of future, broader works on the history of the utility industries in
America. On that basis alone they are worth pursuing; and certainly the history of the Middlesex Water Company illustrated
more than a little about the importance of such companies to
American economic and social well-being.

* * * * * *

In writing the history of the Middlesex Water Company, I
received the encouragement and assistance of dozens of individuals along the way. At the company, I enjoyed the full support of
everyone I dealt with. Nancy Essig compiled an extremely helpful
list, including background sketches, of current and retired employees willing to be interviewed. Marion F. Reynolds, company Vice
President and Secretary-Treasurer, gave me unrestricted access to
the corporate archives and offered invaluable help in locating particular record groups. She also explained a good deal about company financial operations and offered some helpful and lengthy
comments on a draft of this manuscript. Ernest (Ernie) Gere,
Senior Vice President, did the same and provided some valuable
information that significantly enhanced my understanding of company developments between the 1960s and 1980s. Over the
course of the project I met periodically with the Middlesex
Chairman of the Board and President, J. Richard Tompkins, and
Vice President for Administration Walter J. Brady. Both were
enthusiastic about the book and provided perceptive and helpful
critiques of the manuscript. While proud of the company and con-

cerned for its well-being, neither man ever told me what to write or how to portray particular events or individuals. I was always free to draw my own conclusions and I always appreciated that scholarly freedom.

A dozen individuals were kind enough to talk with me about their years with the company. Carolina M. Schneider, who joined the company in 1948 and was still active as Secretary-Treasurer when we spoke (she remains a director), provided a detailed overview of corporate affairs, a wealth of revealing anecdotes, and some very perceptive observations on management. Edward Bastian, who retired in 1982 as Senior Vice President and served as a director until May 1991, managed to make details on engineering and water treatment operations understandable. I hope I did his explanations justice in the text.

Henry (Ted) Grundmann, who was hired in 1947 and eventually became Manager of Engineering, was one of the best sources of information on daily operations, especially during some of the difficult periods of the 1960s. Arline J. Rask, active since 1947 and Manager of Customer Accounting, offered an inside view of life at Middlesex Water and explained a good deal about customer service efforts. Louis H. Rask worked from 1953 to 1986 as a vehicle mechanic, and saw first-hand the development of shop and yard operations, all of which he described for me at length. Louis Plisko, retired Shop Superintendent who worked at Middlesex from 1948 to 1986, recounted what it was like to work in the company shops and conveyed a real sense of the morale of those who made the company work on a daily basis. Anthony (Tony) Ferraro started work in 1935 and retired as Distribution Superintendent in 1981. He remembered any number of incidents from the field, and discussed in detail what it took for crews to get mains into the ground in all kinds of weather and in the face of often difficult conditions. He provided a number of wonderful photographs of field work from decades ago. George Devlin spent over three decades at the company (1939 to 1972) as a chemist, and he recalled vividly the efforts to maintain water quality at the

Robinsons Branch Reservoir, as well as steps necessary to establish laboratory operations at the Carl J. Olsen Water Treatment Plant. While he was active, no water company had a more vigilant guardian of water quality. Ambrose Mundy, the third President of the Middlesex Company, was recalled fondly by family members Barbara Reusmann, Carmen Mundy, Stephen H. Mundy, and Marian Sanborn. They gave a very human dimension to a man who was virtually the embodiment of Middlesex Water for most of his professional life. I interviewed Leon Silakoski, Sr., three times. In his fifty plus years at the company, he met everyone and saved everything; he is a treasure trove of company lore, and his clipping files and photographs are a record group unto themselves. He was of enormous help to me. All of these individuals are mentioned in the book, and all have my thanks for their time and assistance. Talking with them was one of the most enjoyable aspects of my research.

There was also plenty of help from outside of the company. At Kean College of New Jersey, Charles Kimmett, then Vice President for Administration and Finance, first encouraged me to undertake this project; my secretary, Frances Siburn, has followed its progress ever since. In the Nancy Thompson Library at Kean, Library Director Barbara Simpson opened all necessary doors for me and encouraged my use of the New Jersey Collection; Mark Ferrara cheerfully handled any number of reference questions; and the staff at the East Campus Library gave me carte blanche in the New Jersey Collection (they also made excellent coffee). Faruque Chowdhury, Bursar at Kean College, did considerable research for me on modern New Jersey water policy and kindly allowed me to draw from his unpublished work. Jane Kelly guided me through the collections at the New Jersey Utilities Association in Trenton. Sarah Collins, then Library Director at the New Jersey Historical Society, was equally helpful; she was able to locate some obscure titles by Frank Bergen, the company's founding President. Bob Burnett, then Editor of Publications at the Society, read sections of the manuscript and always had good editorial advice. At Rutgers

University, Ron Becker dug some useful materials out of Special Collections. Also at Rutgers, Penny Booth Page, Library Director at the Center of Alcohol Studies, located a number of useful works on the history of water treatment technology. Ms. Page is also my wife, and every time I undertake another project, I am reminded of how essential it is to marry one's reference librarian.

The Newark Public Library held collections indispensable for my research. In particular, the clipping files of the old Newark News, in its day one of the finest newspapers in the country, were placed at my disposal. Paul Stellhorn, Charles Cummings, and Marilyn Kussick, all good friends, worked generously to gather scores of clippings on Middlesex Water. They have my genuine gratitude.

All of these individuals, and many others at smaller libraries and historical societies, have my thanks. They did their best to help me with this history; and if the book has any errors, they are mine alone.

Mark Edward Lender
Kean College of New Jersey, 1994

CHAPTER

1

Industry, People, and Water: Middlesex County to the 1890s

OVER THE LATER NINETEENTH century, the industrial revolution gradually changed the face of much of New Jersey. Since the colonial period, New Jersey was famed as an agricultural keystone of the Middle Atlantic region; the province was blessed with good soil and plentiful water supplies, and its produce enjoyed ready access to the markets of New York City and Philadelphia. From the earliest years of settlement, travelers remarked on the bounty and diversity of Jersey farms, and important harvests of corn, grains, vegetables, fruits, berries, and livestock buoyed the state's economy. After the 1860s, science and education added their support to the state's farmers as the Agricultural Experiment Station, at Rutgers College in New Brunswick, helped pioneer new crops and techniques.[1] But even as manufacturing and commerce came into their own in the years after the Civil War, agriculture remained the chief occupation of most of the populace. New Jersey had fully earned its popular name as the "Garden State."

Yet the last quarter of the century increasingly saw the advance of industry and commerce. By the 1850s, New Jersey already had an impressive array of industries, and its mills, machine shops, and factories were exporting goods to most of the nation. Newark, for example, already one of the country's most important centers of the insurance industry, also sent saddles, harness, shoes, and other leather goods to the agricultural South. Paterson was a manufacturing center of national importance. After the Revolution, the Society for Establishing Useful Manufactures (which listed Alexander Hamilton as a founding member), impressed by the water power generated by the falls of the Passaic River, had selected the town for industrial development. By mid-century, Paterson was a major center of textile production, and its locomotive works turned out some of the period's most highly regarded railroad engines. Other cites, notably Camden, Newark, and Jersey City, also had growing industrial plants. Mining, banking, insurance, and transport industries were firmly established as well.[2]

Transportation was particularly important in this period, and New Jersey was home to some of the earliest and most innovative developments in canal and railroad operations. In the northern counties, the Morris Canal connected Newark with Phillipsburg on the Delaware. Engineers considered its construction across the rugged terrain of north Jersey as one of the technological marvels of the nineteenth century. The Delaware and Raritan Canal, which carried barges across the central part of the state, was built primarily to bring Pennsylvania coal to New York markets. Coal and other bulk cargoes travelled both canals well into the twentieth century, long after the rail lines had captured the lion's share of commercial traffic. New Jersey railroads were developing rapidly well before the Civil War. In fact, the Garden State's Camden & Amboy line helped pioneer commercial railroading. By mid-century, then, the seeds of industrial expansion were in place throughout the northern portions of New Jersey.[3]

The Civil War added a major impetus to commercial and manufacturing development. While thousands of New Jerseyans marched off to war, many thousands more marched to work. Textiles, agricultural processing and distribution, construction, heavy manufacturing, and other industries boomed as businesses responded to military contracts. Urban population increased as workers and their families moved into the newly industrialized towns, and while the distribution of wealth was uneven, most New Jersey residents enjoyed a purchasing power unparalleled in the past. The new affluence and industrial capacity added substantially to New Jersey's heavy manufacturing base and carried economic expansion into the post-war years. Despite some setbacks in the depressions of the 1870s and 1890s, before the turn of the century New Jersey had emerged as one of the most industrially advanced states in the Union.[4]

State government also played a major role in fostering this development. Successive legislatures courted business with some of the most liberal incorporation laws in the nation, and the state was generous in granting special franchises and other favors to influential companies. State officials saw to it that railroads and certain utilities operated under especially advantageous tax structures and were able to set fares and rates without government interference. Consequently, some of the largest corporations in the country did business under New Jersey charters. Eventually, certain of these close corporate-government relationships became a source of political outcry, but there was no denying that the favorable business climate brought considerable development and investment into the state.[5] If New Jersey was still the "Garden State," there was now, as historian Leo Marx once put it, "a machine in the garden."[6]

MIDDLESEX COUNTY WITNESSED some of the most pronounced social and economic changes as New Jersey industrialized. But unlike some of the northeastern counties where change came relatively quickly, the evolution from a rural countryside to a bustling industrial and urban region came slowly in much of central New Jersey. In fact, the process took well over two centuries, and as late as the early 1900s, when much of northeastern New Jersey was heavily industrial, Middlesex remained largely agricultural. Industrial growth in most of central New Jersey, then, came

3

in midst of a still prosperous farming economy. In fact, shops and factories rose next to farms that dated from the colonial era.

Economic change began with the arrival of the first European settlers in the mid-1600s. Originally, Holland claimed all of what became New Jersey as part its New Netherlands colony; but the Dutch never settled the province in any significant numbers. Their largest settlement was Bergen, on the site of modern Jersey City in northern New Jersey, and they established no permanent villages in the future Middlesex County area. In the 1650s, Dutch investors expressed an interest in the region, and especially the later site of Perth Amboy—they called it Ompage—but any intentions to settle never moved beyond the planning stage. European immigration did not begin in earnest until after the British conquest of the Dutch colony in 1664. (In 1673, a Dutch fleet briefly regained the colony, but a peace treaty in 1674 restored it to Great Britain.)[7]

The British established the county in 1682, naming it after Middlesex County, England. It was one of the four original counties of the province—the others being Bergen, Essex, and Monmouth—and it was huge. Borders ranged from Staten Island Sound (also called the Arthur Kill, which separated New Jersey from Staten Island) in the East and westward over much of central New Jersey. The early county lines changed over the years as population growth spurred the creation of new counties or prompted adjustments in old borders. The first major change came in 1688, when the colony carved out Somerset County. Royal and state governments then made other territorial transfers through 1858, when the state gave part of Woodbridge Township to Union County. In its final form, Middlesex County occupied some 340 square miles, about a third of its original extent.[8]

The original towns actually predated the county. Woodbridge, across from Staten Island, was chartered in 1669, three years after the founding of Piscataway, which was farther toward the interior up the Raritan River. By 1682, Woodbridge may have had some six hundred residents and Piscataway far fewer. Settled largely by Puritan immigrants from New England, both were thinly populated agricultural districts which retained their rural character for almost two centuries.

Perth Amboy, however, on Raritan Bay, was a town of real importance. The proprietary government of East Jersey (there were two colonies, East and West Jersey, until the crown unified the provinces in 1703) founded "Ambo" Point, one of the original British names for the Dutch Ompage, a "sweet, wholesome, and delightful place," and designated it their capital in 1686 under the name of Perth Amboy. The new name honored the Earl of Perth, who assisted Scotch immigration to the town. By this time, the population numbered several hundred Scots, Dutch, English, and French Huguenots, and the town was a small but prosperous commercial and shipping center. Growth was slower in the rest of the county. It would be over a generation before another Middlesex town, New Brunswick, home to a scattering of British, Dutch, and French Protestants, was of sufficient stature to receive a charter in 1730.[9]

The colonial county reflected the agricultural economy of the rest of the province. The ground was gently rolling and much of the soil was fertile and generally well watered. The Raritan River drained Middlesex from west to east, and served as an artery to the sea for the county's produce. The Millstone River bounded the county in the southwest and supported a rich agricultural district, and many other small streams offered water for stock and fields. Well before the Revolution, New Brunswick, Piscataway, and Woodbridge were thriving agricultural towns; crops of corn, oats, wheat, and hay, as well as butter, brought prosperity to the region's farmers. County produce and dairy products routinely supplied New York tables, and as the colonial age came to a close, Middlesex was a mainstay of the Middle Atlantic region's agricultural economy.[10]

During the War for Independence, however, both the prosperity and location of Middlesex County brought residents some of the worst of times. The locality saw considerable action as British and American armies maneuvered against one another during 1776 and 1777, and then raided back and forth until the end of the war. Rival units foraged heavily across the county, and regional crops were a valuable prize of war. The cost was high: The troops of both sides had struck hard at the agricultural economy. Middlesex property owners and public officials reported some 655 cases of damage to farmhouses, crops, barns, churches, and other public and private buildings. Commercial farming revived slowly after the conflict, hindered by a 1786 wheat crop devastated by an insect plague. Matters began to improve only near the end of the decade.[11]

While agriculture struggled to recover from the war, other economic sectors showed initial signs of activity. Farming, even in its depressed state, remained predominant, but the late eighteenth and early nineteenth centuries offered some hints of the region's later economic diversity. Copper mines, opened in the New Brunswick area around 1751, proved to be a disappointment, although the prospect of striking a profitable vein of ore continued to intrigue investors for decades. A number of quarries, also dating from the colonial period, produced a distinctive red sandstone that went into local buildings. By the late 1770s, early entrepreneurs began to work the extensive claypits around Woodbridge and Perth Amboy, and their efforts produced a growing number of profitable brick-making, terra cotta, and other clay product operations. The county was also home to scores of small businesses supporting agriculture and the needs of the small towns. As the numbers of mills, general stores, blacksmiths, masons, contractors, and other trades and establishments expanded, they in turn broadened the base of the region's financial strength. These early industrial and commercial foundations developed steadily, if slowly, over the decades. They were important, but they only gradually altered the rural nature of antebellum Middlesex. As late as the early 1880s—almost a century later—a survey of New Jersey business activity still characterized Middlesex County as "largely agricultural."[12]

Yet there were elements that pointed toward an increasingly industrial and commercial future for the county and for central New Jersey generally. Indeed, simple geography favored economic development. Its central location made Middlesex one of the earliest crossroads of New Jersey. Since the early 1680s, travelers between East and West Jersey had used a ford across the Raritan River at what became New Brunswick. In 1686, John Inian opened a ferry service at the same location, and by the early 1700s, the crossing generated enough business to support a small village on the south bank of the river. One of its first names was hardly prosaic: Prigmore's Swamp. Residents changed that to Inian's Ferry in 1713, and adopted the name of New Brunswick when the town received its official charter in 1730.[13] As road networks developed in the later colonial period, the main routes between New York and Philadelphia spanned the length of the county, continuing to cross the Raritan at New Brunswick. Before the Civil War, regular interstate stagecoach service followed the established route, which became one of America's most active commercial thoroughfares.[14] Significantly, more than people traveled these roads; agricultural produce and other merchandise moved as well.

Advances in transportation technology worked to the county's advantage. By the 1830s, it was possible to ship goods in and out of Middlesex in greater volume and at greater speed. The local economy enjoyed a brief boom when the Delaware and Raritan Canal opened in 1834. The waterway ran for fifty-six miles, traversing most of the county while connecting eastern and central New Jersey with Bordentown, on the Delaware River. New Brunswick was one of the most important stops along the way. There were also new rail links carrying goods and passengers to the New York ferries; and competing steamboat services connected New Brunswick directly to New York, with a stop at Perth Amboy on Raritan Bay.[15] While colonial New Jersey had developed no major ports, there had been an active coastal shipping trade. Small craft out of Woodbridge, Perth Amboy, and New

Brunswick plied coastal waters trading locally and with New York. By the mid-1800s, many areas along Staten Island Sound had wharf and storage facilities for goods moving across the Sound to New York or to parts south. In Woodbridge, at least, some entrepreneurs wanted to expand port facilities to accommodate transatlantic shipping.[16] Wherever they lived in the county, however, Middlesex residents, farmers and businessmen alike, knew the economic value of living and working in close proximity to some of the state's key transportation arteries.

The fact that Middlesex lay astride the main routes of communication between New York and Philadelphia encouraged trade with two of America's wealthiest markets. Proximity to New York alone would have spurred regional growth, and the county's chief towns grew substantially over the last half of the nineteenth century. The state's general industrial expansion after the Civil War accelerated the growth of Middlesex, and that growth slowly assumed new dimensions. The area's small shops, factories, and mills remained, and even turned out an increasingly diverse range of goods. Larger manufacturing and other industrial operations, however, gradually moved into the region, and residents of Middlesex towns found themselves in a social and economic milieux that was becoming more complex and varied. The county was not about to challenge northeastern New Jersey for industrial leadership; nor was agriculture ready to concede its economic importance to industry. Yet after the 1850s, "big business" finally was making an impact.

New Brunswick, for example, the county seat, continued to flourish as a transportation hub. It was easy to ship goods to and from the town, which evolved as the county's first significant manufacturing center. The three largest rubber companies in the nation located there, including the pioneering works of Horace Day and Christopher Meyer. The rubber factories employed hundreds, and hundreds more found work in New Brunswick's leather goods firms, carpet, and wallpaper companies. There were also several shipyards, a carriage plant, cotton mill, and machinery works.[17] As businesses multiplied, the town also became the county's banking and financial center.

Other towns prospered as well. Woodbridge and Perth Amboy, with their nearby clay pits, were national centers of brick, clay pipe, white ware, and terra cotta production. Entrepreneurs had worked the pits since the revolutionary period, but the late nineteenth century saw over two dozen firms shipping products to

Clay pits, Woodbridge, New Jersey, 1890s. The pits supported a large number of brick-making, terra cotta, and other businesses, many of which became early Middlesex Water Company customers.

national and international markets. The local Perth Amboy and Woodbridge Railroad connected the two larger towns with outlying villages, which tied even the smaller population centers to wider markets.[18] Perth Amboy also had important rail facilities and served as the eastern terminus of the Lehigh Valley Railroad; the Camden and Amboy had similar yards in South Amboy. By the 1880s and 1890s, the Woodbridge area boasted some of the East's most significant copper refining and chemicals operations. As these enterprises expanded, localities along Staten Island Sound—notably the Sewaren and Carteret areas—developed their waterfronts, adding wharf and dock complexes to facilitate the shipping requirements of the new companies. Regional business leaders, especially in Carteret (which had a manufacturing base in paints, machinery, and fertilizers by the 1890s), even revived older hopes of bringing major ocean-going vessels into local ports.[19] As it was, coastal shipping became more important than ever.

The smaller towns also felt the lure of development, and local Boards of Trade actively touted the virtues of their municipalities as commercial or industrial centers. Piscataway, Metuchen, Port Reading, and South Plainfield, still largely farming towns late in the 1890s, did their best to make land available to business developers at attractive prices. South Plainfield was only typical when it promised that "land will be sold at especially low figures to those contemplating the erection of factories."[20] By the turn of the century, then, it was no surprise that Middlesex County was among the nation's most rapidly developing business and manufacturing regions.

It also had a growing population. Business and commercial development created jobs, and employment opportunities attracted a stream of immigrants and the native born over the later years of the nineteenth century. Hungarians, Germans, Poles, Czechs, Danes, Russians, Italians, Irish, and other immigrant groups became increasingly visible in New Brunswick, Perth Amboy, Carteret, South Plainfield, and other towns.[21] Population figures reflected the shift toward a more urban and industrial county. Between 1860 and 1905, as its businesses multiplied, New Brunswick's population more than doubled, climbing from 11,256 to over 23,000. Perth Amboy, home to thousands of Irish and other European arrivals, surged from 2,302 to almost 26,000 people over the same half century. Woodbridge, with fewer than 4,000 residents in 1860, counted over 10,000. The general county population presented the same picture, moving from 45,029 in 1870 to 52,286 in 1890; by 1905 it neared 100,000, and it had topped 114,000 by the 1910 census.[22] There was a ready supply of labor for new industries, and as the twentieth century dawned,

Middlesex had a growing population with a diversity hitherto unknown in its history.

WATER ALSO PLAYED A KEY ROLE in the industrial growth of Middlesex County. Central New Jersey was fortunate in its natural water supplies, a fact which had a great deal to do with its early agricultural prosperity. Average annual precipitation in the county (as of the 1890s) was about 46.9 inches; and there was no dry season, as rainfall was spread almost equally over the calendar. Settlers found plenty of surface water in the region's streams and rivers. The drainage system feeding the Raritan River was one of the most extensive in the state, and its numerous creeks and streams easily supported abundant fields and herds of stock, as well as a number of water-powered milling and light manufacturing operations. The smaller watershed of the Rahway River supplied the northeastern corner of the county; while just below this, Woodbridge Creek and its tributary streams, which flowed into Staten Island Sound, provided more than enough water for the extensive farming district around Woodbridge.[23]

Ground water was generally available as well. Much of the county lies within the geologic Piedmont Plain, characterized by underlying formations of trap rock, shale, and sandstone. Trap rock usually holds little subterranean water, while shale formations and sandstone have better potential, including some aquifers with major reserves.[24] The shales along Staten Island Sound, for example, often yielded only meager flows of ground water, a fact which made little difference before the growth of regional industries. But in much of the Raritan water shed, the red shales and sandstones often trapped water between layers of stone, which protected the supplies from pollutants and helped keep the water table high enough to allow home owners and early industries to drill wells. In the red shale sections of Middlesex, artesian wells between 33 and 97 feet generally produced a good supply.[25] Wells constituted the normal source of water for residential use throughout the eighteenth, nineteenth, and early twentieth centuries.

The geologic Atlantic Coastal Plain province lies south of the shale district, on a line running roughly southwest from Woodbridge Neck, on Staten Island Sound, to the Raritan River near New Brunswick. The Middlesex areas within the plain are composed of drift formations left over from the last glacial period and gravels from more recent ocean activity. The important clay pits lay in these formations, and the clays and gravels held considerable amounts of ground water.[26] As a rule, then, no one went thirsty or faced water shortages in pre-industrial Middlesex County.

Until at least the mid-nineteenth century, and in some places for much longer, available surface and ground water were sufficient to support the local economy. Most of the county had no formalized, centralized water supply systems until well after the Civil War, so farmers, town residents, and businesses drilled wells, built cisterns, or pumped water from surface sources.[27] Manufacturing operations, which could require relatively large amounts of water, often sought riverside locations. Its location on the Raritan River, for example, helped make New Brunswick an attractive site for tanning and rubber manufacture. The clay-based businesses in the Perth Amboy and Woodbridge areas offered one of the best illustrations of manufacturing concerns operating with available natural water supplies. By the 1820s, some of the clay works boasted extensive Plants, and their operations used huge amounts of water in casting various clay products. The lack of commercial or public water utilities in the Woodbridge locale, however, compelled individual enterprises to make substantial investments in wells and water storage facilities.[28] Fortunately, enough water was at hand.

Yet if water resources assisted regional development, they were also a limiting factor. In fact, concern over the supply and quality of water sources grew steadily after mid-century. By the 1880s at least, it had become clear that ground and surface water sources, abundant by pre-industrial standards, could not always sustain the expansion of the county's industrial base.

12

There were several aspects of the problem. Perhaps the most obvious was the steadily climbing population. More industry, as we have seen, meant more people, and the urban population put new demands on available supplies. People, in fact, used more water than businesses. As housing densities increased, water consumption rose as well, especially as indoor plumbing and toilets became more common. Among New Brunswick residents, for example, annual per capita water use went from 57 gallons in 1882 to 79 gallons by 1894. And New Brunswick was only typical: Across the state, a Geological Survey study reported an average 33 percent per capita increase in water use during the same period.[29]

Industry, however, also put a great deal of pressure on regional water supplies. It was more than a matter of additional manufacturers moving into the county—although by the 1880s and 1890s, the sheer number of industries were making enormous new demands on water supplies. Rather, the manufacturing processes of many of the plants necessitated particularly heavy water use. The chemical industry, for example, which developed steadily in the Carteret and Woodbridge areas, often used over 100,000 gallons of water to produce a single ton of certain products. Metal refining, a major enterprise in the Carteret section of Woodbridge, could use nearly 100,000 gallons in turning out a finished ton of metal. New Brunswick's rubber plants were major water users as well; and to the extent that many of the new businesses relied on steam-powered heavy equipment, water use increased still further.[30] Problems went beyond the matter of supply. By the 1870s, water quality also had become a matter of real concern in New Jersey's urban areas. In 1877, the State Geologist declared that the wells from which over half of Newark's residents drew their water were contaminated. Drinking water was rife with biological organisms from garbage and human waste leeching into the soil—and then into ground water—from innumerable dumps, outhouses, and cesspools. A decade later, Camden and Jersey City faced similar problems.[31] In Middlesex County, the deterioration

of water quality through biological contamination was not immediately so severe, although regional development brought other
pollution concerns. Intensive agriculture and continuing industrial
and residential construction exposed vast surfaces of the local red
sandstone formations to erosion. The result was an increase of red
mud leeching into ground and surface water sources, imparting a
vile taste and turbidity to the water and making it unfit for many
domestic, farm, and industrial uses.[32] In order to keep pace with
residential and industrial demands for pure water—and in
quantity-wells frequently had to go deeper into the county's sandstone and shale formations, which made water supplies more
expensive.

Responses to water pollution were of varying effectiveness in the late nineteenth century. Chemical and biological analyses were sensitive enough to detect foreign substances in water
supplies, but not always reliable in determining which organisms
or other pollutants were harmful to humans or animals. Without
accurate data, warned Cornelius C. Vermeule, an engineer working
for the State Geological Survey in the early 1890s, officials had to
use their common sense in evaluating the safety of water sources,
avoiding those "repulsive to the natural instincts of intelligent per-
sons." In other words, "sight, smell and taste" were tests as good
as any in the absence of "thorough and conclusive" scientific
proof on the quality of a water supply. Filtration through beds of
sand and settlement—sometimes assisted by the addition of alum
to the water—could remove considerable turbidity and sediment.
In some cases, Vermeule's report noted, artificial aeration of
cloudy water could improve clarity and taste, although neither of
these processes was always reliable. The best guarantee of good
water, Vermeule concluded, was the protection of water sheds, as
"nothing can take the place of original purity of the source of supply."[33]

While concerns over pollution were genuine, however, the
chief concerns in the last half of the nineteenth century remained
those of quantity: Would Middlesex factories have access to

enough water to sustain their operations? Would the growing towns have sufficient supplies for residential use, fire protection, and municipal needs? In some areas, these questions were pressing by the 1880s, and high stakes hung on the answers. This was particularly true along Staten Island Sound, an area with considerable development potential. Real estate and business promoters predicted a bright future for properties on the Sound: The location was accessible to shipping, rail connections, the New York markets and financial centers, and New Jersey's ample supply of skilled and unskilled labor.[34] The area actually saw appreciable growth into the late 1880s, by which time, however, water supplies came into question and developers hesitated.

In fact, industrial operations were largely dependent on ground water, which, as experience revealed, was adequate only to the needs of a limited number of plants. There was too little ground water to support extensive industrial growth along the Sound, and as new companies moved into the region, their demands on water reserves threatened to overtake available supplies. Established businesses experienced periodic water shortages, and by the 1890s, some otherwise prime industrial real estate fronting on the Sound was "unsalable" because of unreliable water supplies.[35] In 1901, the state *Industrial Directory* reported that a great deal of waterfront property was very cheap; and as late as 1918—long after formalized supply systems were in place—the town of Carteret actually was willing to *give* certain factory lots away in an effort to spur development.[36] By the turn of the century, then, the business and residential growth of Middlesex County was pressing hard against the limits of regional water supplies.

MIDDLESEX COUNTY FACED an age-old problem—moving water from sources of supply or storage to areas where people and businesses needed it. This issue was neither new nor unique to the county; at one time or another, most of the industrial or densely populated regions of the state found themselves in similar circumstances. In the late 1880s and early 1890s, there was plenty of water in New Jersey, although many of the most abundant supplies lay twenty or more miles away from the key urban regions opposite New York. If companies and towns along Staten Island Sound found local water sources insufficient, cites in Hudson, Union, Bergen, and Essex Counties periodically labored under similar difficulties. Larger cities such as Newark, Trenton, Hackensack, Paterson, and Elizabeth had to pay particular attention to the limitations on growth imposed by available ground and surface water. The water situation in Middlesex, then, was a microcosm of circumstances elsewhere in industrializing New Jersey.

New Jersey never experienced an initial burst of water supply construction. Rather, the process of laying mains began slowly, beginning in areas where growth came early, reliable or pure water sources were especially scant. Some towns installed systems even before the turn of the nineteenth century, with Trenton taking the lead in 1783. Morristown followed in 1799, and then Newark in 1800. The works in Newark, the state's largest city, were substantial. By 1850, however, only two more towns, Burlington in 1804 and Mount Holly in 1846, had built supply systems; and a decade later, a total of only twelve towns were supplied. Serious utilities construction began only after the Civil War, especially in the industrializing northeast. In 1894, the State Geologic Survey counted eighty-one towns with commercial water systems, which included most towns with over 1,000 residents.[37]

The various water systems differed in their sources of supply. Of the 81 towns, 48 relied on wells to fill the mains, while 22 pumped water from convenient rivers. The Delaware, for instance, supplied 8 cities and towns along its banks, while the Hackensack supplied the pumps of 10 regional towns. The Passaic, Rahway, and Raritan each supplied several towns as well. Eleven other towns also tapped nearby rivers, but were able to use gravity-fed mains. Only 12 supply systems employed any water treatment, mostly filtration through sand or aeration, a situation the State Geologist usually found disturbing. He wanted more active efforts to safeguard the quality of municipal water supplies.

16

On the other hand, he was at least pleased that formal water systems were supplying more localities by the early 1890s.[38]

The majority of these supply systems began as private ventures, usually corporations with state charters. Like all companies, they were subject to the whims of business cycles, the decisions of managers, and their abilities to attract investors. Some survived to become mature water systems while others disappeared entirely (occasionally without laying any mains) or merged with stronger companies. Historical archives around the state contain a surprising number of early water company records—all that remain of enterprises that failed the test of longevity.[39] Even some ultimately successful utilities got off to rocky starts. The Hackensack Water Company, for instance, founded in 1869, and which emerged as one of the largest in northern New Jersey, went through bankruptcy and reorganization before showing a profit. Others, like the Elizabethtown Water Company, took advantage of larger urban customer bases and quickly proved successful.[40]

In any case, it is important to note that private enterprize eventually responded to water supply needs when a locality appeared capable of supporting a profitable system. The Newark Aqueduct Company, which put in some of the first Newark mains, vigorously promoted its stock and attracted both large and small shareholders.[41] In the Paterson area, the Society for Establishing Useful Manufactures chartered several water supply companies, intending them as independent business ventures and as part of a utilities base to support further industrialization. They had installed mains in Paterson by the late 1850s, Montclair after 1887, and in nearby areas *via* the East Jersey Water Company beginning in 1889.[42] In fact, corporate records make clear that, in the last decades of the nineteenth century, water utilities (and utilities generally) were attracting an increasing number of investors. So were water rights, and investors looked hard at properties with good water supplies. In southern New Jersey, for example, entrepreneur Joseph Wharton acquired large tracts in Burlington, Camden, and Atlantic Counties as possible water reserves for

17

Philadelphia.[43] As a consequence, the importance of water companies in the state's industrialization loomed ever larger as the century drew to a close.

None of this activity was lost on state government. From time to time, the reports of the State Geologist would remind Trenton of the importance of reliable and pure water supplies to New Jersey's economic and physical health. Partly with these reports in view, and also because of calls by investors for a simpler incorporation process, in 1876 the state passed legislation meant to facilitate the formation of water companies. Prior to this, the legislature had issued individual corporate charters as investors came forward with their plans. The process was both slow and fraught with politics, especially when competing groups of investors expressed an interest in the same service area. Under the new general incorporation act, however, water utilities filed appropriate corporate papers with the state in order to receive a charter to operate. After this, they were free to negotiate service franchises with towns and businesses.[44] The act, as intended, vastly simplified the creation of new companies, and served to increase the appeal of water supply as an investment.

The interest in water companies, and the new water company legislation, was of a piece with broader business interest in utilities of all kinds. By the last quarter of the nineteenth century, the state had chartered hundreds of water, gas, sewer, and traction (street car) companies, and would do the same for electric utilities a few years later. The utilities were popular investments and, as with the water companies, the successful utilities made handsome profits. Even marginal companies were attractive targets for consolidation with other companies; in 1903, for example, such a merger resulted in the formation of Public Service Corporation, the largest and wealthiest utilities firm in the state.[45] The utilities existed in a symbiotic relationship with New Jersey industry: The growth of industry (and the urban population that served it) provided the utilities with a customer base; the utilities supplied the power, water, and transport that kept the wheels of industry turning. The two enterprises depended upon a common prosperity.

Despite the state-wide interest in utilities investment, however, water companies got off to a slower start in Middlesex County. Even around Carteret, Middlesex had better natural water supplies than many other industrializing sections of New Jersey, and there was little early interest in laying mains. New Brunswick installed a system in 1861, but as late as 1893, Perth Amboy and South Amboy were the only additional Middlesex towns to have mains. Woodbridge, Carteret, Metuchen, Port Reading, and other municipalities which would have prominent roles in the county's industrial history remained without supply systems.[46] Given the situation near Staten Island Sound, however, and the pressure exerted on natural supplies by continued residential and industrial growth, Middlesex County, especially its eastern sections, became a logical site for a water distribution system. In fact, as the 1890s began, investors began to express an interest, and the stage was set for significant changes in the management and use of regional water supplies.

CHAPTER
2

Enterprise and Organization:
Frank Bergen and the First Companies

WHEN THEY FILED THE FIRST CORPORATE CERTIFICATE in 1896, the intention of the founders was to secure a reliable supply of water for the industries located near Staten Island Sound. Their primary concern was an area extending south from the Carteret section of Woodbridge almost to Perth Amboy. These rather direct intentions aside, however, the path from corporate filing to functioning public utility was fraught with unexpected turns. Problems of finance, organization, and geology, as well as an occasionally uncertain economic climate, all complicated matters beyond expectation and challenged the resources and ingenuity of the early investors. Indeed, these issues frustrated any hopes that one company could immediately supply the region's water needs; instead, the modern Middlesex Water Company evolved from three corporate roots in a process that took almost a decade. Yet the joining of those roots in a single corporation, however difficult, revealed a great deal of the administrative and financial tasks inherent in organizing a successful public utility during the late nineteenth and early twentieth centuries.

THE INITIAL MIDDLESEX WATER COMPANY was founded on April 20, 1896. Principal investor and first president, William H. Corbin, filed a corporate certificate with the New Jersey Secretary of State and announced his intention to supply water to the northeastern section of Middlesex County. Corbin hoped to find a source of supply, lay mains to the existing factories along Staten Island Sound, and expand his customer base as the promise of reliable water service attracted additional industries into the area. The new company opened with a stock offering of a thousand common shares at one hundred dollars per share.[1] Investor interest in industrial development along the Sound, as well as the need for a water supply, were well established by the mid-1890s, and Corbin's initiative appeared to hold real promise.

Corbin's leadership in forming the new water company was itself an inducement to investors. Corbin (1851 - 1912) was a native of Union County but spent most of his career in nearby Jersey City. In 1881, he joined his older brother's Jersey City law firm, Collins and Corbin, and his legal practice flourished along with his involvements with other local businesses. Over time, Corbin was active in real estate, banking, and other investments, and he was fully in touch with the regional economic climate. He was active politically as well. A life-long Republican, Corbin served in the State Assembly from 1885 to 1887, including a year as G.O.P. Assembly leader. After completing his term, Corbin was counsel for a number of legislative committees, and in 1896 he drafted the general incorporation act that allowed the organization of most of the state's modern corporations. In addition, he sat on numerous local boards and commissions, and his years of service afforded the opportunity to build friendships in both political parties. Even fiercely partisan Democratic Governor Leon Abbett—a fellow Jersey City attorney—thought well of Corbin, placing him on the state commission to arrange a memorial for New Jersey veterans of the Battle of Gettysburg.[2] In short, Corbin was well-connected politically and in business, a man accorded the respect of his colleagues and whose judgment commanded attention.

Part of Corbin's background included considerable experience with water supply. By the 1880s, Jersey City faced a growing problem in supplying water to its populace and industries and in maintaining the purity of the water that was available. Searching for a solution, the city acquired a reservoir site in Boonton, some 20 miles from Jersey City, and contracted for the building of an entirely new water works. Corbin managed the legal affairs of the company that built the water works, and received his share of public credit when the effort proved a success. He also came away from the effort with an appreciation of the potential of the water business.[3]

He also knew the state of business activity along Staten Island Sound. The existing industries constituted the potential customer base of his water company, and by 1896 he had reason to be encouraged by the course of regional development. Indeed, he had waited some time for good economic news. Over the late 1880s and early 1890s, industrial growth had been unspectacular; in addition to unreliable water supplies, manufacturers had contended with an ailing economy. In fact, the malaise was national. A business slump had begun in 1892 and quickly developed into the worst depression the nation had ever experienced. Hard times gripped the entire country for several years, and the Garden State, which had a major industrial base, suffered acutely. New Jersey manufacturing activity fell a full third below 1892 levels, a development with catastrophic effects even on non-manufacturing and service businesses. Unemployment and social misery reached tragic heights.[4] But the crisis had eased by the middle of the decade, and with the economy rebounding, business expansion eastern in Middlesex County accelerated. By 1896, the county listed some impressive firms, including several engaged in heavy industrial operations and employing hundreds of workers.

Corbin was most interested in the manufacturing concerns in Woodbridge Township, especially in the Carteret and Chrome sections (Carteret would become a separate municipality in 1906, calling itself Roosevelt; it later reverted to the name of Carteret).

23

In 1881, the Williams & Clark Company, of New York, had located in Carteret, and in the early 1890s merged with the American Agricultural and Chemical Company. The consolidated firm erected a second plant, the Liebig Works, in neighboring Chrome; and the two plants constituted one of the largest fertilizer manufacturing operations in the nation, employing some six hundred men. They turned out 175,000 tons of fertilizers annually, a level of production requiring about 63,000 gallons of water per day.[5] Other fertilizer companies, notably the Armour Company, a division of one of America's largest meat packers, also built factories near the Sound.[6]

By the late 1880s, a number of heavy machinery and refining companies also had located in the area. In Carteret, Wheeler Condensing and Engineering employed some two hundred workers in the manufacture of water towers and iron products. The De Lamar Copper Works, in Chrome, helped establish Middlesex County as a national center of copper refining. A number of other refining operations and steel works, attracted by the area's excellent rail connections and coastal shipping facilities, moved into the region by the early 1890s. All of them needed large amounts of water to maintain production; the De Lamar Works alone, for example, used over 350,000 gallons per day. Moreover, the clay-product companies of the Woodbridge area continued to thrive, and the larger ones—M.D. Valentine & Brother Company, Mutton Hollow Company, Anness & Potter Company, among others—used thousands of gallons of water each day. These three companies, all of which later became Middlesex Water Company customers, probably used a combined total of almost 57,000 gallons daily. In all, these figures were indicative of why Corbin and other investors found the water supply business so appealing.[7]

Over the late spring and early summer of 1896, Corbin was in contact with many of the industrial firms in Woodbridge Township, and he persuaded a number of them to sign service contracts pending the water company's ability to develop a source of supply and to lay mains. Several of the clay-product firms, as well as Wheeler Condenser and Engineering and a few other manufacturing plants, came aboard; other companies expressed an interest but were unwilling to make commitments until Corbin could actually guarantee water service.[8] The first Middlesex Water Company, then, seemingly had a great deal in its favor. A mending economy, an astute and experienced president, and a potentially lucrative customer base augured well for the success of the enterprise.

Yet the new company lived only for a year—and only on paper at that. It never laid a water main; it never drilled a producing well. Corporate records do not reveal exactly what went wrong, although years later, Frank Bergen, one of Corbin's closest friends and business partners, recalled some of the problems. The chief impediment was that of a water source: Corbin never found one. He was defeated by geology along Staten Island Sound, for the area had little ground water and all of the test wells were disappointments. Moreover, the company never found a source of water elsewhere which could have supplied the Sound via pipeline.[9] Had these facts alone determined the situation, one could have predicted the quick demise of Corbin's hopes. In fact, however, the rescue of his venture was close at hand.

CORBIN MAY HAVE HEDGED A BET on the early success of his company. Certainly he knew that prospects were thin of finding a water supply along Staten Island Sound, and there is room to question whether the first Middlesex Water Company was sufficiently capitalized to allow the acquisition of an inland water source and the construction of a pipeline. While the company's stock had a paper value of $100,000, little of it was sold when the firm opened and there was no initial operating capital in the corporate treasury.[10] With the laying of mains in doubt, the real worth of the corporation lay only in any contracts it might negotiate with companies to supply water service. Corbin may have concluded (and quickly) that the lack of a ready water source would discourage investors, and within a month of the incorporation of the

Middlesex Company, he was involved with yet another venture in the water business.

On May 25, 1896, six investors incorporated the Midland Water Company. The group included Corbin, future New Jersey governor Foster M. Voorhees, Elizabeth attorney Frank Bergen, and Elizabeth businessmen Meline W.Halsey, Edward C. Woodruff, and Edward M. Wood. The directors elected Bergen president of the company and announced their intention to sell water in Union, Middlesex, and Somerset Counties. They offered two thousand shares of common stock at a hundred dollars per share and, significantly, started business with $50,000 in working capital in the till.[11] The Midland Water Company did not have the Middlesex Company's business connections along Staten Island Sound, but otherwise it opened its doors with at least as much promise.

The first order of business for the new board of directors was the acquisition of an adequate water supply. They resolved the matter quickly, formalizing an arrangement very likely agreed upon before incorporation. At only their second meeting (in July 1896), the board voted $25,000 to buy a site at Brooklyn Mills, in the South Plainfield section of Piscataway Township, for a water pumping station.[12] The transaction was with Frank Bergen and his wife, and included acreage with proven reserves of ground water. The Bergens had purchased the property some years previously as an investment, and the sale enabled the Midland directors to actively seek customers and map plans to develop the water resources in South Plainfield. In taking title from the Bergens, the new company had dealt easily with an issue that the early Middlesex Water Company was never able to resolve.

By mid-1896, a curious situation had developed in Middlesex County. Where there had been none at the beginning of the year, there were now two water companies sharing some of the same directors and an interest in serving the eastern part of the county. One of them, the Middlesex Company, was actively nego-tiating with customers; the other, Midland, had a water supply. It

Frank Bergen, founding president of the Midland Water Company, and then of the consolidated Middlesex Water Company.

Foster McGowen Voorhees, an original incorporator of the Midland Water Company and a director of the consolidated Middlesex Water Company. Voorhees was an old friend of Frank Bergen and Governor of New Jersey from 1898 to 1902.

took no leap of genius to conclude that competition between the companies made little sense; and even before the end of the year, it is likely that Corbin and Bergen had begun to talk about merging the firms. By the following spring (1897), the directors of the Midland Company set the legal process of amalgamating the corporations in motion. At their May meeting, they voted to buy shares in the Middlesex Water Company and to guarantee performance on all contracts that Middlesex Water might conclude with industrial customers.

The final legal steps in the consolidation of the two companies came in June and July of 1897. The respective boards agreed on June 23rd to convey all corporate assets to a new company, which would retain the name of Middlesex Water Company, a decision ratified at a stockholders' meeting on July 17th. A new certificate of incorporation was filed with the state three days later, July 20th, and the first meeting of the consolidated board of directors followed on the 22nd. The board was, in fact, the old Midland board, with the single addition of Harry G. Runkel, a businessman from Plainfield in Union County. They quickly approved new corporate by-laws, voted the issue of two thousand shares of common stock (five hundred shares based on old Middlesex Company stock, and 1,500 shares derived from Midland) at a hundred dollars each, and elected Frank Bergen president.[13] The new Middlesex Water Company (referred to in corporate records as the "consolidated company") was now a functioning reality.

FRANK BERGEN WAS THE GUIDING HAND on the new board of directors. The formation of the consolidated Middlesex Water Company had been chiefly his idea and, to an even greater extent than William Corbin, he was an established authority on virtually all aspects of the water business. Bergen had served on the board of directors of the Elizabethtown Water Company for many years and, since 1890, as president of the Plainfield Water Supply Company. At one time or another, he had dealt with most of the other regional water companies on business matters. Few men were in a better position to offer leadership to a new company, and he would remain at the helm for almost two generations.

Bergen did not come easily to success. He was the son of old New Jersey stock, descended from Hans Bergen, the first of the family to reach America from Bergen, Norway, in 1633. Hans settled first in Dutch New Amsterdam, and his grandson, Evert Bergen, became one of the original settlers of Somerset County. Two centuries later, Frank Bergen was born there, in Hillsboro Township, on December 1, 1852. Raised in a family of only modest means (his father, Peter, was a Hillsboro merchant), he attended the Somerville public schools. Unable to afford college or law school, he read law in the office of his uncle, Isaiah N. Dilts of Somerville. He joined the bar himself in 1873, and from that point on Bergen's professional rise was meteoric.[14]

Bergen launched his career in the growing city of Elizabeth. He practiced law independently until 1880, when he helped form the new firm of Cross, Bergen & Noe. In 1881, Elizabeth named him city attorney, and the young lawyer quickly established a state-wide reputation as a skilled and eloquent advocate of the city's interests. Some of his cases were bruising affairs. The most important was a victory over municipal bond holders, who had sued to recover $7,500,000 in principle and interest when the city defaulted on its debts. Elizabeth had gone bankrupt in undertaking street improvements, and creditors wanted to seize city property to make good their claims. Bergen prevented any such action in court, and then helped frame state legislation to protect cities and property owners from confiscations on behalf of creditors. He then played a vital role in reorganizing city finances and returning Elizabeth to economic prosperity, which included an equitable settlement with the bond holders. It was the most bitterly contested legal fight in the city's history.

Another suit was less acrimonious, but even more protracted. In 1889, Bergen began court action on behalf of the city against the Central Railroad of New Jersey, seeking to eject the railroad from lands Elizabeth claimed along Staten Island Sound. Bergen left his post with the city in 1903, but he continued to represent the municipality without charge as the case dragged though the courts until 1910—when the State Court of Errors and Appeals found in favor of the city. The case earned the tenacious lawyer considerable public acclaim and, in its early stages, afforded him the opportunity to learn a good deal about developments near the Sound. He was no stranger to the area when, as a water company executive, he had to do business there.

It was during his years in Elizabeth that Bergen formed his appreciation of central New Jersey's industrial potential, and especially of the prospects for utilities. Indeed, by 1890 he was willing to invest personally in a water company: he spent two hundred dollars for two shares of stock in the Plainfield Water Supply Company. The Plainfield firm had struggled along since 1869, staying in business but failing to develop water sources or capital enough to become really prosperous. Bergen changed all of that. His regional stature was such that the Plainfield Water Supply stockholders elected him president of the company in August 1890, and he quickly arranged financing to secure an adequate water supply and to expand the company's service area. Over the years, he built Plainfield Water Supply into an important company, ultimately merging it (in 1906) with the Union Water Company to form the Plainfield-Union Water Company.[15]

Bergen's business and legal careers blended comfortably. His regard at the bar was considerable, including a reputation as a learned and aggressive litigant, and he deployed his talents forcefully on behalf of his business interests. As president of the Plainfield and Middlesex companies, he followed court actions and state legislation touching on all aspects of water supply; and his peers generally conceded that he knew as much as anyone about the legal aspects of water in New Jersey. In fact, he was an authority on utilities law generally. In 1903, he left his position with the city of Elizabeth and joined the newly-organized Public Service Corporation as general counsel. Public Service was the largest utility in the state, combining gas, electric, and traction (street car) operations, and it quickly became politically influential. Bergen was among its most articulate spokesmen and effective advocates. For a generation, he labored to defend the prerogatives of utilities generally—and Public Service and his water companies specifically—against what he characterized as the unwarranted attacks of critics and social and political reformers. He remained general counsel until 1933 and a Public Service lawyer until his death a year later.[16]

Although he never ran for public office, Bergen was prominent in civic and political affairs. He was a stanch Republican and served actively on campaign and other party committees, and he was a frequent speaker on public questions. While Bergen fiercely resisted legal efforts to regulate or otherwise intervene in the affairs of utilities companies, he had lively interests in aspects of court reform, the preservation of historic sites and park lands, and support for higher education. An avid student of history, he served as an active board member of the New Jersey Historical Society and he wrote widely on early America.[17] Mentioned as a candidate for Congress, Bergen demurred, preferring his executive and legal roles. For the same reasons, in 1899 he declined appointment by President William McKinley as chief judge of Puerto Rico, which the United States had captured in the Spanish-American War. In 1906, he turned down an offer of a seat on the New Jersey Supreme Court.[18] By any measure, then, Frank Bergen was a considerable public figure in his native state.

The Bergens lived graciously in the style of the period's business and social elite. Frank Bergen was anything but the wealthiest man in New Jersey, but his legal practice and business involvements—which including banking (he was a director of the Union County Trust Company) and real estate in addition to utilities—provided for more than common comforts. He married Lydia M. Gardiner in 1887, and they maintained an elegant home in Elizabeth as well as a country estate in rural Bernardsville. They were a cultured and popular couple, entertaining frequently, enjoying classical music, and generously supporting a number of philanthropic causes. The Bergens had three children: a boy who died in infancy; another son, Francis, killed in an automobile accident shortly after graduation from Harvard Law School; and a daughter, Charlotte. Charlotte Bergen ultimately inherited her parents' estate, including their interests in the Middlesex Water Company. As a major stockholder, she was a familiar figure at the company for many years after her father's death in 1934, and company veterans remembered her as a pleasant eccentric. Her passion was orchestral conducting, and annually she rented Carnegie Hall, with a full symphony, in order to conduct a concert. Upon her death in 1982, the family wealth went into the Frank and Lydia Bergen Foundation, which continues to support musical performances and education.[19]

A reprise of Frank Bergen's career also illustrates something of utilities management at the turn of the century. The Middlesex Water Company president—in his wealth and professional prominence, his political and business connections, and his public involvements and visibility—was fairly typical of the period's utility executives. Generally, they had no training as engineers or in fields related directly to power, water, or streetcar systems; but they were men with successful careers in established professions and were positioned to take advantage of promising investment opportunities. Bergen knew little, for example, of the mechanics of drilling wells when he first became interested in the water business. But over his years at the company, events would demonstrate Bergen's ability to reach the right people within his professional network to secure financing for corporate projects and to move through the complicated thicket of legislation that surrounded utilities operations in New Jersey. He could hire people who knew how to drill wells.

Similar situations existed in the majority of other utilities companies. Thomas N. McCarter, for example, the founding president of Public Service, had done legal work for the various utilities he finally organized under the Public Service umbrella. His expertise was not in the mechanics of generating and transmitting electricity; but his background as a lawyer, a major voice in the Republican Party, a former New Jersey attorney general, and member of a bank board gave him undeniable advantages in the utilities business. His legal skills and political contacts afforded unparalleled advantages in negotiating for franchises and in influencing legislation favorable to his company; his business connections allowed him easy access to critical financing arrangements.[20] At Middlesex Water, Bergen and Corbin were not alone in their legal and professional connections: Foster M. Voorhees also was an invaluable board member until his death in 1927. He maintained his corporate participation even as he served as a state senator and as governor (from 1898 to 1902), and he shared banking investments with Bergen and Corbin as well. At the Elizabethtown Water Company, the Kean family had similar relationships with the political, banking, and legal communities, and the same was true of the principal investors and founders of the Hackensack Water Company.[21] In short, the early utilities owners and managers included a substantial number of New Jersey's social and political elite.

There is no question, however, that Bergen and most of his contemporaries were active executives. They simply were not in a position to invest and then turn their companies over to professional managers, for there were virtually none to be found. At the turn of the century, utilities were relative newcomers to the industrial scene. Unlike mature industries—the railroads, steel, textiles—the utilities lacked a cadre of technically trained specialists, and this was particularly true in the water supply business.[22] There were several consulting firms with expertise in various aspects of water treatment, but there were few managers with long-term experience, let alone careers, in the field. Eventually, there would be plenty of them, but over the initial decades of corporate development, most utility company founders literally had to manage for themselves—a fact that Frank Bergen fully accepted.

THE CONSOLIDATED MIDDLESEX water company quickly got down to business. In fact, Bergen had begun negotiations for service agreements and planning mains even before the consolidation. Over May and June of 1897, the Midland Water Company secured franchises to lay pipes in Piscataway and Raritan Townships, authorized the construction of a water works at the South Plainfield pumping station, and took the first steps to start construction of a twelve-inch pipeline from South Plainfield toward Staten Island Sound.[23] There was a foundation in place, then, as the new company addressed its two initial goals: to develop the water sources in South Plainfield and to transport that water to the Sound.

Bergen oversaw every step of the construction effort, revealing himself as an executive happy with the minutia of business affairs, intolerant of waste and mistakes, and possessed of a dry if caustic wit. He hired a superintendent to handle daily operations, a Robert M. Kellogg, but he retained personal control of company affairs. As president, he arranged work schedules and equipment purchases, reported frequently to his fellow directors, and loosed fusillades of abuse against anyone he saw as impeding the company's work. This included his own employees. For example, during construction of a standpipe at Bloomfield Hill in Raritan Township (needed to maintain water pressure in the trunk main), he decided that Kellogg was taking too long and was spending too much. He judged that the problem lay with digging unnecessarily deep footings, and the superintendent caught the sharp end of a classic Bergen rebuke. "Unless there has been a change in the laws of nature recently," he told the hapless man, "it is a sheer waste of money to put a foundation on the hill suitable for Washington's monument."[24]

He was even less subtle with critics of the pipeline. In October, he discovered that one Thomas Doud of Plainfield, for reasons unknown, had charged "that the pipeline of the Middlesex Water Co. is badly constructed, with leaks in many places." Bergen's combative nature surfaced immediately: "These state-

35

ments are entirely incorrect," he wrote to Doud, whom he then implied could expect all of the legal trouble he would ever need if Bergen heard so much as another word from him "about the company's affairs."[25] Bergen did not suffer fools lightly.

By 1898, the company had pushed the main fifteen miles to the Sound, and then another three miles along the shore to reach water-starved factories. Thus the consolidated company completed the job that had frustrated Corbin's original venture: water service had reached the Sound. Moreover, the company successfully drilled a field of wells at South Plainfield. By the early 1900s, the field grew to twelve wells, which ultimately yielded nearly a million gallons per day through suction (compressed air later would increase the daily flow of these wells to over a million gallons).[26]

With a water supply and a trunk main in place, Bergen could turn his efforts to building a customer base. The first customers were the industrial firms along the Sound brought under contract with Corbin's original company. Williams & Clark Fertilizer, Wheeler Condenser & Engineering, and American Lucol in Carteret and Chrome connected to the main in 1898, and other manufacturers followed. As the century turned, most of the metal and chemical companies and railroad facilities near the Sound had become Middlesex customers as well, as had a number of the clay-product operations in Woodbridge Township. The two largest accounts were the De Lamar Copper and Chrome Steel Companies, which between them used well over half a million gallons of water per day.[27]

For almost ten years, the Middlesex Water Company built on this customer base and improved its works and supply system. Over time, it completed the standpipe at Bloomfield Hill, put in a storage facility at Metuchen, and purchased some real estate with promise as a water source at Bonhamtown (later part of modern Edison Township). In addition to the trunk main, the company also laid distribution mains in communities along the trunk. Residents in South Plainfield, Metuchen, and Woodbridge Township (which then included Chrome, Carteret, Port Reading, and Sewaren) gradually connected to the distribution mains. Bergen, however, was anxious to encourage new business, and urged Kellogg to send residents in the vicinity of the mains "a catching sort of circular." It might bring a few more customers, he wrote, and reminded that "we need all [of the customers] we can get."[28] He was right, because none of the continuing work was cheap; by 1905, the company had spent almost $206,000 in construction costs.[29]

As the system expanded, however, Bergen never relented his personal drive to get the most out of his people and resources. In late 1900, when work slowed in laying a main from South Plainfield to Woodbridge, Bergen fired off a typical missive to the contractor. "Why in the world don't you send some 12 inch pipe to South Plainfield?," he asked a Mr. Conlan of Newark, "so that your men can do something besides sleep in the grass all day. If you carried on your business with common intelligence it would not be necessary to charge twice as much as it is worth, in order to keep afloat." Late with an assignment, Mr. Kellogg got more of the same: "I notice," Bergen wrote to his superintendent, "that in matters that save money for the company you do not seem to be half so alert as you do in respect to schemes to plunder the treasury."[30]

Bergen may have been a difficult taskmaster, but he got results. The distribution mains increasingly brought new residential and industrial customers into the system, and some of the added accounts were important. Soon after its organization in 1903, for example, Public Service Corporation, with Bergen serving as general counsel, established a large facility in Metuchen, which quickly became one of the company's most profitable accounts. Fire hydrants in Woodbridge, Metuchen, and Carteret, added income as well. Steadily, the young company prospered. Income during 1901 was over $38,000 and corporate assets placed at $314,477; by July 1907, annual income was over $56,000 with assets well above $400,000. Significantly, the company was pumping over 1,330,000 gallons of water per day.[31]

WHATEVER THE LEVEL PUMPED, however, it was not enough. After the turn of the century, the company was expanding its system as quickly as demand and finances allowed. But water use gradually pressed against the limits of available supply as more customers connected with the mains, and the company pondered conservation measures and how it might sustain adequate levels of service. As early as October of 1897, Bergen had wanted to install water meters in the plants of all industrial customers; and he became as concerned with controlling waste as he was with assuring accurate billing. By 1903, worries over waste had become acute, and some customers had voiced complaints over low pressure in the system. The board of directors ordered frequent inspections of its largest accounts in order to correct leaks and other problems, and ordered Kellogg to cut off service to any customers refusing to comply with water-saving recommendations.[32] Thus, even as the system expanded, the makings of the first corporate crisis loomed.

While the water situation was serious, the corporate board acted before the advent of any major disruptions to the system. In July of 1903, the directors appointed a special committee to look into "the increasing demand for water" and the means to keep service up to standard. Over the following year, special meetings of the board of directors discussed drilling additional wells at South Plainfield and authorizing the metering of more industrial customers. In January of 1905, the company decided to meter all customers, including private homes, and voted to issue bonds in the amount of $16,000 to pay for the project. Later in the year, the directors ordered improvements in the South Plainfield pumping station intended to increase water flow in the system and to maintain pressure.[33] The board was active, then, in the face of the developing concerns over the water supply; but it was clear that a real solution would depend on more than stopgap measures.

Years later, a memo by Bergen recalled that by "1907 the business had outgrown the source of supply." This was something of an overstatement, as the Middlesex system managed to keep customers supplied.[34] Yet Bergen's note did express growing urgency as Middlesex County industrial and residential development brought more connections to company mains. In any event, the company decided as early as 1905 that it could no longer depend exclusively on ground water, and that it would have to develop alternative resources in order to forestall a crisis. Even as it drilled new wells and improved its pumping capabilities, the company determined that it would have to build a reservoir if it was to guarantee uninterrupted service into the future.

The site the directors had in mind was Robinsons Branch of the Rahway River. Robinsons Branch is the north fork of the Rahway; it begins in Ash Brook Swamp in Union County, about four miles northeast of the South Plainfield pumping station, and flows roughly two miles to the east, where it joins the Rahway River at the city of Rahway. The course of the Branch takes it through formations of glacial drift, which—at the turn of the century—held ready supplies of ground water and offered a reliable and generally pure recharge for the stream.[35] The corporate records are silent on who suggested the acquisition and development of Robinsons Branch, but both Robert Kellogg and Foster Voorhees owned property along or near its banks, and they probably suggested its potential to the board. The directors commissioned a study of the site in late 1905, which reported favorably on the project. The engineering firm of E.W. Harrison found that a dam across the Branch would produce a major supply supported by a good watershed. In addition, contacts with businesses in Carteret indicated that if a reliable water supply was assured, they might be willing to enter into long-term water service contracts.[36] On that basis, the Middlesex board decided to move ahead.

The task in front of the company was considerable. It entailed the acquisition of over four miles of shoreline around Robinsons Branch, including enough land—about 150 acres—to protect the watershed. Plans then called for the construction of a dam in Clark Township, about a mile above Rahway, which would create a reservoir about forty-five feet above sea level. The height of the supply was critical: it would provide enough water pressure to allow a low-pressure pumping station to maintain the flow in an eight-mile cast iron pipeline to Staten Island Sound, terminating at the works of the Chrome Steel Company. Laying the new main would require negotiations for rights-of-way with Rahway, Woodbridge, Roosevelt (Carteret), and private property owners. In addition, the company would have to install water treatment facilities at the reservoir, a standpipe about half way to the Sound in order to maintain pressure in the pipeline, and build a bridge over the reservoir to replace a local road.[37]

None of this would be cheap, and the company already had its funds committed to existing operations. Faced with the prospect of a major new expense, the directors acted to avoid further debt. Instead of borrowing, in December of 1906 they voted to increase the Middlesex capital stock from its original limit of $200,000 to $500,000 (the new issues included $50,000 in common shares and $250,000 in preferred stock, all at $100 per share). A month later, Bergen announced a major coup: he had negotiated a contract with the Elizabethtown Water Company worth about $10,000 per year. Elizabethtown was pressed to maintain reliable service in Union County, and Bergen, as a director of Elizabethtown and president of Middlesex, saw a chance to help both companies. Under the agreement, Middlesex would sell its neighboring company large supplies at favorable rates as soon as the new reservoir came on line. With these financial arrangements in place by early 1907, the company actively began the Robinsons Branch project.

The effort moved in a number of directions, beginning with the acquistion of real estate around Robinsons Branch. The company made outright purchases and, when necessary, went to court in condemnation proceedings. At the same time, Bergen arranged the purchase of new pumping equipment from the Plainfield Water Company (of which he also was president), while Kellogg bought a site for the standpipe. Finally, in July of 1907, the company purchased the entire water plant of the Sewaren

Improvement Company. This was a major step, which secured not only needed equipment but also extended the Middlesex service area further to the south along Staten Island Sound.

Expenses mounted quickly as these activities gathered momentum—probably more quickly than Bergen and the rest of the board had anticipated. By June of 1907, Middlesex had spent almost $24,000 on various charges associated with the new reservoir, which did not even include actual construction costs. The purchase of the Sewaren Improvement plant alone accounted for another $7,500.[38] Moreover, there had been a serious disappointment in negotiations with some of the water company's bigger customers. Since 1906, Bergen and Kellogg had been meeting with representatives of De Lamar Copper, Chrome Steel, and Wheeler Condenser, trying to reach long-term agreements on price and supply (similar to the contract negotiated with the Elizabethtown Water Company). The Middlesex directors had counted on increased business with these companies to help finance the expansion of the water system, including the new reservoir. Multi-year contracts, however, failed to materialize, and this setback, coupled with rapidly mounting costs, once again raised questions about the financing of the Robinsons Branch project.[39]

The answer this time was the organization of an independently financed corporation, the Consumers Aqueduct Company. The new company, incorporated on March 25, 1907, would attempt the sale of $200,000 in stock and handle the actual construction of the reservoir. If all went well and the reservoir became a reality, the new and old companies could merge; if the project failed, then at least the Middlesex Water Company would not have to bear the entire loss. Bergen was the chief shareholder in Consumers, while three other directors, including Voorhees, formed the board; and Corbin took care of the legal work. In all but name, the new venture was a division of the Middlesex Water Company.

The arrangement worked quite well. The new company

was able to sell $10,000 of stock, and Bergen, as an officer of the Union County Trust Company, saw to it that Consumers Aqueduct was able to borrow another $15,000. Shortly thereafter, the Consumers board voted to issue $200,000 in bonds, which found a ready market before the end of the year. With enough capital in hand, the work went quickly. The board gave a contract for the construction of the dam and other reservoir facilities at Robinsons Branch to the firm of Edlow Harrison; he was to complete the work for a sum "as near Forty-five thousand dollars as possible." A second contract went to the W.T. Kirk Company to build a bridge over the new reservoir.[40] Before the year was out, the dam was finished and a sixteen-inch main had connected the reservoir with the Middlesex distribution mains in Woodbridge. Finally, in May of 1908, water began to flow from the newly-named "Corbin Reservoir" into the mains of the Elizabethtown Water Company and to Middlesex customers. At least in its construction phase, the reservior project had been a resounding success.

Even before the completion of the Corbin Reservoir, however, it was clear the various financial and construction arrangements were going well. Costs would continue to mount—a filtration plant, for example, would be installed after the reservoir went on line—but the Middlesex board was convinced that the Middlesex and Consumers corporate debts were reasonable. In fact, Bergen calculated that the value of all Consumers Aqueduct Company assets far exceeded "the par value of securites issued to pay" for them. By the fall of 1907, then, it seemed appropriate to merge the two corporations, and the consolidation took place on October 3rd.[41] Consumers Aqueduct had served its purpose.

THE OPENING OF THE CORBIN RESERVOIR, at least symbolically, closed the initial chapter of the history of the Middlesex Water Company. It had been an important decade; the company had progressed through a rather complicated organization to a successful expansion of its plant and customer base. Founded to sell water to industry, after ten years the account books

Aerial view of the Robinsons Branch Reservoir (actually named the Corbin Reservoir after William Corbin, a founding director of the company). The picture dates from the 1950s, and shows Middlesex Water Company facilities as well as post-World War II residential development. The Garden State Parkway crosses the reservoir at the top of the picture.

reflected this fact: almost exactly two-thirds (67%) of the Middlesex customers were industrial, with the remaining third residential. The company was also profitable, posting an income of over $22,000 for the first half of 1908 despite continuing constuction expenses, and paying shareholders dividends of three percent on the par value of their stock.[42] By virtually any business measure, then, the Middlesex Water Company was a going concern.

The first decade also had demonstrated the importance of effective corporate leadership. In all likelihood, men such as Bergen, Corbin, and Voorhees, already successful, would have done well enough based on their prior business experience. But the performance of the Middlesex Water Company derived from more than experience: the professional network of the directors was a crucial factor as well. Bergen's ability, for example, to arrange equipment purchases from his Plainfield company, and his key position as a banker able to expedite financing for Middlesex, were enormous advantages (for that matter, Corbin and Governor Voorhees also were bank officers). So were Corbin's legal connections, which got Consumers Aqueduct off the ground so quickly, and the prestige of having a state governor as an active director and an inducement to investor confidence. It was not by chance that the company could sell stock as easily as it issued bonds to finance the Corbin Reservoir. Middlesex leadership, well-connected as well as talented, had every reason to look ahead with confidence to their company's second decade.

CHAPTER
3

Progress, Profits, and Problems:
Company Operations through 1920

D URING ITS FIRST FULL DECADE OF OPERATIONS, the Middlesex Water Company had devoted most of its attention to matters of internal organization and the expansion of the system. Issues of administration and finance, establishing sources of water supply, laying the mains, and building a customer base necessarily left Frank Bergen and other officers time for little else. Yet it was time well spent. After the completion of the Corbin Reservoir, the Middlesex Company steadily became an asset critical to the economic growth of Middlesex County. Specifically, the extension of the water mains supported, and even helped to make possible, the expansion of industrial and residential development within the company's service area. Civic and political leadership agreed that company operations played a key role in making eastern Middlesex County an increasingly attractive place to live and to do business. Thus for a time, the interests of customers and investors were in harmony.

The rise of Middlesex Water to regional influence, however, hardly guaranteed that the next stage of company development would be tranquil. In fact, the pace of corporate development placed unprecedented demands on management, and while Frank

Bergen continued to shape events, after 1908 other individuals would assume prominent roles in company affairs. Moreover, the expansion of the mains and the service area raised important issues involving water quality, the performance of the distribution system, and corporate finance. In short, getting water from sources of supply to customers became an increasingly complex matter; accordingly, during its second and third decades, the company had to undertake increasingly complex projects to maintain service.

External developments, however, had an equally significant impact on Middlesex Water Company operations. Of particular concern in this regard was the advent of state regulation of the utilities industry. After 1911, management decisions—once the prerogatives of Bergen and his fellow directors—became entangled with questions of public policy. Clashes between the new State Board of Public Utility Commissioners and the company generated considerable friction, and the situation eventually complicated Middlesex efforts to resolve some particularly difficult problems. By 1920, questions on how to finance vital improvements to its distribution system, and on how to cooperate with other companies in heading off a regional water shortage, both loomed as genuine crises—for the company and for its customers. In attempting to address these questions, however, the directors found their actions severely circumscribed by government regulators and public opinion. Clearly, the era of relatively unimpeded enterprise, which had fostered the early growth of the company, had ended; and the changing rules of doing business brought consequences for water service that neither the company, the state, nor the public could predict.

THE MIDDLESEX WATER COMPANY had been a successful business since its inception, and the completion of the Corbin Reservoir held out the promise of better things to come. With an adequate water supply assured, the company could concentrate on extending its mains and attracting new customers. This was relatively easy as the population of Middlesex County had grown steadily since the turn of the century. Census reports noted 79,762 Middlesex residents in 1900, about 114,400 in 1910, and some 130,000 by 1920. Population growth within the Middlesex Water Company service area reflected the broader county trend. Between 1900 and 1910, Woodbridge went from 7,681 people to 8,948, and Roosevelt (later renamed Carteret) climbed from 4,500 to 5,786. The combined populations of Piscataway, Metuchen, and Raritan (later called Edison)—smaller towns also with Middlesex Water service—climbed some 16 percent, up to 8,368 people. Industrial and residential construction paced the census figures, especially as new plants appeared along Staten Island Sound. Thus the potential for new company business was substantial.

Nixon Eborn, in a horse-drawn wagon, about 1910. Eborn, then a meter reader, was a long-time company employee.

In fact, business was good. By 1911, three years after the completion of the Robinsons Branch project, the Middlesex Company served almost 1,600 industrial and residential customers. The vast majority of them (72 percent) lived or did business in the more populous and industrial towns of Woodbridge and Roosevelt. At this point, water service depended on a distribution system with 56 miles of mains, including the original pipeline from South Plainfield to Staten Island Sound. Over the decade, crews digging trenches and laying Middlesex Company mains were a familiar sight along county roads and in the streets of new neighborhoods. The mains grew by well over two miles per year, and by 1921 they totalled more than 81 miles.[1]

Laying mains was a tedious business. Laborers had to dig trenches by hand, which was no easy task given the shale formations just beneath the top soil in much of central New Jersey. Leon Silakoski, a fifty-year Middlesex Water Company veteran who began his career as a water boy to the digging crews, recalled the pick and shovel work of the years before World War I: If the ground was considered "good digging," the foreman would mark off eight lengths of a shovel handle for each member of the crew; the laborer was expected to start digging at 8:00 A.M. and to finish that distance in a 9-hour work day. "Bad digging," meaning a stretch of difficult ground, meant as little as four shovel lengths; but "good" or "bad," the digging had to go down at least three feet to guard the mains against winter freezes. This activity went on six days a week, for which a laborer received the princely sum of fifty cents per hour.[2]

Laying pipe with a pick and shovel. Note the log used to hold the pipe.

During the work day, the crews stuck to

their jobs. There was a half-hour break for lunch, but that was all. Nor was talking among crew members encouraged; in fact, the foremen used a novel means to keep the men at their trenches. Before 1920, most of the crews were composed of recently arrived Hungarian and Italian immigrants. They knew nothing of each other's language and not very much English, and foremen took advantage of the fact by alternating Hungarians and Italians along the digging line. The theory was, of course, that the men would lose little time in talking to a fellow worker they could not understand anyway. As insurance in this regard, the foremen also issued short-handled shovels—nothing long enough to encourage leaning.[3] Thus did early foremen contribute to the productivity of the American worker.

Once the trenches were ready, the crews would lay the pipes, often simply man-handling them into place. This was the norm when laying smaller distribution lines—those used to feed water out of the large trunk mains—or making connections direct to a consumer. The company generally used 6-inch and 4-inch cast iron pipe in these cases, and sometimes even 2-inches was enough. When dealing with trunk or larger distribution mains, however, installation by hand was largely out of the question. These lines used pipes of between 10 and 16 inches, and their weight was such that workers had to rig scaffolding from timber, or even from trees, and use block and tackle to lay the pipe. There was a lot of this heavy work: of the system's 56 miles of pipe in 1911, for example, some 28 miles consisted of pipe 10 inches or larger.

The demand for residential and industrial water service was such that the company had little trouble in running mains when and where necessary. Bergen usually acting through the company superintendent, did try to accommodate local officials if they expressed a preference for a particular route. This courtesy even extended to private individuals, although there were limits in this regard. One John Leisen, however, went beyond the limit. Leisen operated a clay pit in Woodbridge, and in late 1913 he had received township permission to dig a bed of clay which extended across a local highway. In return, he was to build a temporary road and restore the original route within three years. In the course of exploiting the clay, he dug up to the Middlesex Water trunk line supplying Woodbridge and Roosevelt. The company then obliged Leisen by shifting the main out of his way (many of the clay pit operators being good Middlesex customers). But Leisen kept digging, and in August 1915 he undermined the main, which collapsed. The company moved the main again, whereupon Leisen announced his intention to keep digging toward the pipeline—and asked for yet another shift in the main. At this, Bergen had a court enjoin Leisen from making further disturbance. The company had shown "unusual. . complaisance," observed the Newark Evening News, but had "favored [the] Woodbridge clay digger long enough."[4]

KEEPING WATER IN THE MAINS REQUIRED the company to undertake a series of major capital projects. The most pressing was an effort to assure the quality of the water supply at Robinsons Branch. In 1908, a laboratory report on the new reservoir indicated the need for anti-pollution measures. Chemist Herbert B. Baldwin, of the Newark Department of Public Health, found that the water met safe drinking standards, but that it had "a rather high turbidity and color," a high nitrite content, and enough bacteria and colon bacilli to raise concern for the future.[5] The directors reacted quickly, approving the purchase of a water filtering system from the Continental Jewel Filtration Company of New York. Including construction, the new system ultimately cost some $42,000; and in 1920, the acquisition of a chlorination unit for the reservoir added another $1,200 to water purification costs.[6] These measures were not cure-alls—water pollution was a source of constant concern for water companies—but they did reduce any immediate biological threat to the reservoir.

Yet the decision to install anti-pollution systems, especially the water filters, entailed a certain amount of uncertainty. Purification technology was still young, and not all water utilities were convinced of its effectiveness. In fact, by the turn of the century most American water systems used no filtration at all, and the chlorination of water supplies began only in 1912.

As late as 1901, the New Jersey State Geologist considered that a water shed protected from pollution offered a better guarantee of water quality than any method of purification.[7] But the case for filtration was strong. It had proved its worth in European water systems, and a growing number of American water companies and publicly-owned systems had decided in its favor. The city of Elizabeth had installed the nation's first gravel, sand, and charcoal water filters in its municipal system as early as 1855; and by the late nineteenth and early twentieth centuries, other American systems, including several in New Jersey, began to install sand filters.[8]

Even so, there remained a debate over the best filtration procedures. Most of the argument centered on two filtration approaches: One urged the slow filtration of water through a thick field of sand, with a field that might extend to some 15 acres (although it was normally less). If you had enough acreage, this method was relatively cheap. The second method relied on pretreating water with coagulants in order to remove most sediments and organic materials, which would allow rapid filtration as water was pumped under pressure through small sand filters enclosed in concrete or metal containers. This method was faster, and the savings in space was a major advantage for systems near urban and industrial areas. But constructing the filter containers, chemical feeding equipment, and a sedimentation basin where coagulated impurities could settle to the bottom, was expensive. So was maintaining the more complex system. Rival engineering companies touted the merits of various rapid filters, and the final choice fell to individual utilities.[9]

Fortunately, Middlesex Water directors could look to the experience of other regional companies in making their decision on a filtration system. Only six years earlier, in 1902, the East

Jersey Water Company installed a Continental-built rapid filter at its Little Falls, New Jersey, water works. The following year, after considerable deliberation, the Hackensack Water Company contracted for a similar filtration system. Both installations were expensive, but the systems worked and even won recognition as model water treatment operations. The Continental Jewel system, which used pumps to force water through the filter containers, was similar to the designs selected by the East Jersey and Hackensack companies. The municipal systems of Asbury Park and Atlantic Highlands, New Jersey, also utilized Continental-Jewel equipment.

Thus, in a period when water treatment technology was still young, the Middlesex Water Company directors at least had the benefit of previous New Jersey experience on the subject—and some reason for faith in their expensive new filtering system. With improvements over the next several years, the company filter plant consisted of twelve horizontal cylindrical steel pressure filters, 20 feet long and 8 feet in diameter, each with a daily capacity of 500,000 gallons.[10]

The acquisition of the filtration system was a significant step, but it was only the first of many. Two others, launched in 1916, stemmed from the negotiation of contracts to sell water wholesale to the Elizabethtown and Plainfield-Union Water Companies. The Elizabethtown Company, already the largest Middlesex Water customer (the existing contract with Elizabethtown had helped make construction of the Corbin Reservoir possible), paid a discounted rate of $.22 1/2 per 1,000 cubic feet.[11] Supplying the water-starved Elizabethtown Company was potentially so lucrative that Bergen renegotiated the arrangement, agreeing to provide the sister utility with water for another four years at $32.50 per million gallons. Elizabethtown promised to purchase a minimum of 700 million gallons per year, which meant that Middlesex could plan on substantial receipts long into the future. The Plainfield-Union Water Company, also with water supply problems and of which Bergen also was president, subsequently received substantially the same terms.

To meet the new contract demands, Middlesex Water had to substantially expand its pumping and distribution capabilities. To initiate new construction and equipment acquistions quickly, Elizabethtown Water advanced $89,000 upon signing the contract with Middlesex. With this new capital in hand, Bergen promptly had contractors and company personnel at work. In April 1916, considering the twelve wells at the original field in South Plainfield (in Piscataway Township) inadequate to meet new demands, the directors ordered the drilling of additional wells on a 70 acre tract about a half-mile away, at Park Avenue, also in South Plainfield. The new drilling ultimately gave the company a total of twenty-seven wells. At the same time work began on a new pumping station at Park Avenue, and on a twenty-inch main to connect Park Avenue with the mains of the Elizabethtown Company, more than two miles away. The new station, including land, construction, necessary equipment and tools, finally cost some $120,000—a major expenditure for those years. But it came on line quickly, and in late 1916 the combined capacity of its three pumps reached 8.5 million gallons per day, enough to handle alone all immediate demands on Middlesex supplies. Park Avenue performed so well that the company was able to close the old South Plainfield wells in 1917.[12]

The new projects proved a major success. By the end of 1916, Middlesex was able to divert almost 70 percent of the 6.6 million gallons it pumped each day into the mains of the Plainfield-Union and Elizabethtown Companies. This figure would fall to 44 percent within several years; nevertheless, these contracts established Middlesex Water as one of New Jersey's most successful water wholesalers. By 1920, wholesale receipts from Elizabethtown alone would total more than $91,000, and few other water companies in the state could boast such a steady source of income.[13]

Further efforts steadily added to the physical plant through the early 1920s: additional standpipes at Bloomfield Hill in Raritan Township (later renamed Edison), in Chrome, and in

Park Avenue pumping station. The original pumps were coal powered, with coal reserves piled outside (lower right).

Rahway; general work shops, a meter shop, wagon sheds, engine shop and a 1.75 million gallon per day pumping station, and office space, all in Woodbridge; and extensive improvements to the pumping and maintenance facilities at Park Avenue and Robinsons Branch. With all of this, of course, came provisions for appropriate tools, furniture, and the other minutia of a growing business. By early 1920, the company estimated the worth of its property at almost $1.1 million—with everything either paid for or financed on terms well within the means of Middlesex Water revenues.[14]

With these various improvements and projects in place, the company's water supply resources rested on three legs. It is worth summarizing them at this point, as they provide an important context for assessing company performance over the next several years:

The Corbin Reservoir, with about 280 million gallons of storage capacity, relied on two main coal-fired steam-powered pumps which, together, could send 10 million gallons per day into the mains. Later, after problems with water pressure in the system, the company installed a 4 million-gallons-per-day pump to reinforce pumping capacity. The reservoir was to remain the only Middlesex Water surface supply until the 1960s.

The main ground water supply was at the Park Avenue site in South Plainfield. By 1922, it consisted of fifteen 10-inch wells and an additional 6-inch well, all drilled about 300 feet deep into a shale formation. The station's three main pumps, assisted by three vacuum pumps, were now capable of pumping over 9 million gallons of water per day by direct suction from the wells. (Airlift methods would later assist the pumping.) The water was unpolluted and entered the company's mains without filtration or other treatment.

Finally, there were the company's original wells at South Plainfield, located a half-mile from the Park Avenue pumping station. With the completion of the reservoir at Robinsons Branch and the development of the Park Avenue facilities, the company was able (as noted earlier) to close the original well field in 1917. But by 1922, the demands of the Elizabethtown and Plainfield-Union contracts led to the renovation of pumping facilities, the reopening of the twelve original wells, and the drilling of a thirteenth. A suction pump drew about 750 thousand gallons per day, all destined for Elizabethtown and Plainfield-Union mains.

By 1920, it was clear how important these sources had become to the east-central New Jersey region. With only the supplies at Robinsons Branch and Park Avenue on line, the company pumped some 8.6 million gallons of water each day, which represented about 25 percent of the combined daily total for the Middlesex, Plainfield-Union, and Elizabethtown companies. However, fully 53 percent of Middlesex water went to fill wholesale contracts outside of the system (44 percent) or for industrial purposes within the service area (9 percent). Elizabethtown and

55

Plainfield-Union respectively devoted only 26 percent and 1.6 percent of the water they pumped to similar purposes. The Middlesex figure rose to 70 percent a year later, making the company a linchpin of regional industrial prosperity.[15] If the Middlesex Company ever faced supply or distribution problems, the ramifications would reach far beyond the corporation's immediate service area.

THE EXTENSIVE CHANGES IN THE SYSTEM entailed management changes as well. Frank Bergen was still very much in charge, but over time the growth of the company, and especially the initiation of the various capital projects, made daily operations an increasingly complex and time-consuming affair. The president, who had delighted in the details of the firm during its early years, no longer could afford the time. Busy with his work in connection with Plainfield-Union and Public Service, Bergen's efforts on behalf of Middlesex Water gradually shifted away from direct management of the system. Rather, he focused more on external business affairs: negotiations with larger customers, financial matters, and, after 1911, relations with the BPUC. Moreover, he devoted considerable time to regional water resource planning, often in conjunction with the management of other water companies. Thus, well before the 1920s, Bergen concluded that he could not continue to function simultaneously as president and manager.

What Bergen wanted was a superintendent capable of running operations more or less independently, without the president becoming involved in routine matters. Robert Kellogg, the original superintendent, was not the man. He had been active in company affairs, holding over a hundred shares of stock and serving as an organizing director of Consumers Aqueduct. Company records indicate that Kellogg did good service on the Robinsons Branch project; and, in fact, the directors had elected him treasurer in 1906. It also appears, however, that his relationship with Bergen was not the best. Certainly Bergen felt compelled to criticize his superintendent's performance on occasion, sometimes without bothering to veil his sarcasm. It was perhaps no surprise, then, when Kellogg resigned in October 1908.[16] However, the directors hired his replacement within two weeks—and in Ambrose Mundy, Bergen found the general manager he wanted.[17]

Ambrose Mundy, hired as superintendent by Frank Bergen; he was later the third president of the company.

57

Mundy would work at the company for over fifty years, becoming its most visible officer for many of them and eventually serving as its third president. Born in 1876, he was a native of Metuchen, where Mundys had lived since colonial days. Several ancestors of Ambrose bore arms during the Revolution. His father had farmed, and Mundy grew up on the family property. The Mundy's, however, were hardly well-to-do. Young Ambrose and his father, Alfred Mundy, trapped to earn extra income and hunted local game to put food on the table. Ambrose's formal education consisted only of elementary classes attended in a one-room school house; his teacher allowed him to miss school if he trapped a mink, which, because of its value, had to go to market quickly. Yet Mundy was active and his backround had instilled the value of work; and sometime after the turn of the century (no one is sure exactly when) he secured a position with the A.B.C. Elevator Comapny in New York City.

Apparently, it was while commuting to New York that he met Frank Bergen on the train. According to family members, it was a chance meeting; but the two men fell to talking and Mundy, living in Metuchen, a town in the company's early service area, certainly knew about Middlesex Water. He sufficiently impressed Bergen as an intelligent and decisive young man (he was 32 in 1908), and the job offer followed.[18]

The new superintendent quickly established himself as competent and, no doubt to Bergen's relief, careful with operating expenses. His financial reports, which he began compiling in 1908, were not models of accounting technique, but they offered the directors a clear view of what it cost to run the company. Bergen also approved of Mundy's work routine: the general manager worked long hours, seldom took vacations, represented the president at meetings, and handled most relations with customers and contractors. Aside from his family, Middlesex Water became the central focus of his life. Unlike Robert Kellogg, he received no needling letters from Bergen urging him to work more quickly or at less cost.

In effect, Mundy had emerged as a successful manager of what, in terms of its number of employees, was a thriving small business. Even as the system expanded and revenues grew, Mundy worked with a limited staff. By 1908, Middlesex Water had only about twenty employees, and this had increased to fifty-six by 1915. About fifty men operated and maintained the pumping stations, worked on the mains, and repaired water meters at a shop in Woodbridge; Mundy had a secretary and occasionally two or three clerical and accounting personnel in his office (also in Woodbridge); and a full-time blacksmith kept Middlesex Water Company horses ("Charlie" and "Dick") ready to transport supplies and equipment. Work crews undertook repairs to the mains and other facilities, and occasionally they laid new mains.[19] But the company increasingly relied on contractors for most heavy construction and most professional services, including engineering. With no real corporate bureaucracy to support daily operations—the Middlesex Water Company never needed or developed a large corporate structure—Mundy's "hands-on" management role was crucial to company success. This was true not only from an operational perspective, but also in that Mundy's effectiveness allowed Bergen the time to look after broader matters.

IF FISCAL PERFORMANCE WAS ANY TEST of management, Middlesex Water got high marks as the system delivered profits and dividends almost as well as it delivered water. Excellent financial performance continued uninterrupted from roughly 1908 through the 1920s, even in the face of an alarming development just before the completion of the Corbin Reservoir. A severe, if short, national recession rocked New Jersey: Remembered as the Panic of 1907, the economic slump reduced industrial orders 35 percent in a year, and terra cotta operations, an important Middlesex County business, were hit especially hard.[20]

Yet even in hard times, people and industry needed water and the company performed well. In 1908, with the state and nation still in recession, company gross earnings stood at $49,255 (down from a prerecession $56,000), which netted $23,616 after deducting for wages and other expenses. These earnings allowed payments of $6,993 in preferred stock dividends. The economy recovered by 1909, and Middlesex profits reflected the fact. The following year (1909), the respective figures were $63,029 and $31,938, with $14,000 in dividends; and by 1911, the gross was up to $107,928 with a net of $35,627, and the company paid almost another $14,000 in dividends.[21] Middlesex Water had demonstrated the ability to weather a sharp economic depression (a trait it shared with most other established New Jersey utilities) and to emerge stronger than ever.

Unfortunately, Middlesex Water management did not use standardized accounting techniques until 1911, and even for several years after that, entries in company books did not always accurately reflect some aspects of operations.[22] Thus we can only form generalizations on profitability from summary information in various company records. Still, it appears that virtually all measures of corporate fiscal performance were positive (if not always stellar) well into the 1920s. In a review of company operations, one auditor noted that Middlesex Water "has at all times been able to meet its operating expenses and taxes, to satisfy its fixed charges; to apply income to capital purposes, [and] to declare stock dividends."[23]

In fact, dividends were especially attractive. The company had issued common stock four times between 1907 and 1920, including 500 shares offered in consideration for the property of the Consumers Aqueduct Company upon consolidation. By 1920, there were 3,400 shares of outstanding Middlesex Water Company common stock valued at $340,000. Shareholders received dividends of 9 percent in 1913, and then between 6 and 8 percent down to 1920, when the company declared an 8 percent dividend in additional stock. Preferred stock, also issued first in 1907, totalled 2,500 shares by 1922 and was valued at $250,000. The stock faithfully paid 7 percent in each year since 1907.[24] Over time, then, all shareholders did well, and the original shareholders did especially well; certainly no stockholder saw any reason to regret his investment.

Significantly, the company was able to sustain its financial performance without increasing rates. In fact, the rates in effect until 1920 were those Frank Bergen had announced at the company's founding. Residential or small business customers paid $2.50 per 1,000 cubic feet of water, with a $2.50 per quarter minimum charge in Woodbridge and Roosevelt ($1.50 per quarter elsewhere). Large customers paid a cut rate of $.55 per 1,000 cubic feet, and negotiated rates were established for special customers. The Plainfield-Union and Elizabethtown Water Company, the largest accounts, paid a wholesale price of $32.50 per million gallons, while a 1917 agreement with the federal government provided water for the Raritan Arsenal at a $1 per 1,000.[25] There were also various fees for connections to the mains for certain industrial uses and for service to fire hydrants. Until American entry into World War I, when massive government spending fueled inflation, the steady expansion of the customer base generated volume sales that made up for any deficiencies in the original water rates.

FINANCIAL SUCCESS, HOWEVER, and the steady expansion of the system could not mask a number of looming problems. In fact, trouble came from several directions at once, triggered by events beyond the immediate control of the company. The most serious matter was a regional water shortage which, by 1917, was too pressing to ignore. Coupled to this were certain financial difficulties complicated, as Bergen saw events, by the involvement of the State BPUC with the water crisis. These issues were interrelated, complex, and manifested in the worst service interruptions—and the most difficult customer relations—the Middlesex Water Company ever encountered.

It is important to note at the outset that the Middlesex Company itself did not have a supply problem. The Corbin Reservoir and the Park Avenue station produced enough water for the immediate Middlesex Water service area. But the

Elizabethtown and Plainfield-Union Companies did have supply difficulties; even before World War I, residential and industrial development had put considerable pressure on both systems. After the war, it was clear that the more than twenty towns dependent on the two companies were growing so rapidly—up to 50 percent per decade—that new supplies would have to be found. In the meantime, both corporations installed meters and investigated leaking mains as quickly as possible in order to conserve water. Still, consumers aired periodic complaints about dry faucets, and local governments expressed genuine alarm over the prospect of "inconveniences and dangers" to the public and a "retarding influence upon general industrial development."[26]

This situation was fraught with trouble for Middlesex Water as well, given its contractual obligations to supply the other companies with wholesale water. The diversion of water outside of the Middlesex system made many local residents and businesses nervous, and they were vocal in their concerns. All of the town governments and several industrial spokesmen within the Middlesex service area complained (at one point to the BPUC) that the company could not sell water wholesale without imperiling local service.[27] This may or may not have been true, but the company's ability to support its own expanding system while supplying Plainfield-Union and Elizabethtown had become at least problematic.

Critics of the Middlesex Water Company wholesale activities seemingly had a point. When diversions to the mains of the other water companies began, local service did appear to deteriorate. Middlesex customers steadily increased the frequency and urgency of complaints about service problems; but, significantly, their concerns focused not on any lack of water—Middlesex Water Company kept water in the mains—but with poor water pressure. Thus, in Bergen's view, there was no connection between pressure problems and the contracts with Elizabethtown and Plainfield-Union.

This is not to say that conditions attributable to poor water pressure were not serious. Complaints were astonishing in their variety, and they were well founded. Wheeler Condenser, one of the company's largest corporate customers, and one of the Staten Island Sound companies that Middlesex Water had been organized to serve, was strident in its appeals for better service. Pressure was so low at times, plant personnel noted, that they had to turn off the water in sections of the factory in order to get enough water to maintain operations elsewhere. Faced with water pressure too low to fill boilers for heating or to allow the flushing of toilets, a public school in the Fords section of Woodbridge had to send its students home for days on end. In Carteret, a Doctor John Reason maintained that he had to shave in his basement; the water would not reach the first floor of his house. The Metuchen fire department reported difficulty in fighting several fires; there was "plenty of water," the fire chief noted, but not enough pressure behind it. In Woodbridge, the fire department had to watch a former mayor's house burn down because Middlesex mains lacked enough pressure to fight the blaze. As one can imagine, the press gave such incidents wide and prominent coverage.[28]

These incidents derived largely from the expansion of the system. That is, as the mains spread into new areas, the system eventually had difficulty sustaining water pressure, especially at points more distant from the pumping stations. The larger the system became, the harder it was to pump water through the mains. The problem was a matter of physics, or more precisely, of hydraulics: With enough pressure behind it, water could travel considerable distances, reach the top floors of multi-storied buildings, allow the quick delivery of mass volumes required for industrial purposes, and produce a strong flow out of hydrants for fire protection. But the unpleasant fact was that the Middlesex Water Company system—as it existed about 1916—was no longer capable of generating enough water pressure.

Generally, there were two ways to maintain water pressure in a system. The first was to maintain an elevated source of supply; the gradient would then sustain a flow of water strong enough to maintain (or to help maintain) pressure in the mains. In part, the company's four standpipes were intended to serve exactly this purpose. Each of the standpipes stood on high ground which, combined with the height of the pipes themselves, could release water into the system with considerable pressure behind it. (Not incidently, the standpipes also doubled as water reserves for emergency fire-fighting purposes.)

In addition to gradient pressure, most water systems also relied on pumping. Enough pump strength could maintain pressure through main force: If a system lacked pressure, simply pump harder. This, in effect, was exactly what Middlesex—which pumped virtually all of its water—was doing when it improved pumping capacity at Park Avenue, South Plainfield, Woodbridge, and Robinsons Branch. Too great a dependence on pumping, however, had major fiscal disadvantages. The equipment was expensive to buy, to install (it required a pumping station), and to maintain. Of the Middlesex Company's net estimated worth in late 1919, for example, over 17 percent was allocated to pumping equipment and related buildings and fixtures.[29] In addition, the pumps needed fuel. Middlesex used coal to power all but one of its pumps, and the price of sending water through the mains, and therefore company profits, depended in some measure on the price of coal. Not surprisingly, it was a cost that company managers followed closely.

Lacking a sufficient grade or pumping capacity, distance alone could work against water pressure. Water moving down the mains generated friction, which slowed water flow, and thus lowered pressure in proportion to the distance traveled. Corroded mains, or mains relying on small pipes to carry water long distances, were prime sources of friction, and thus of poor water service.

In fact, pipe size was a particular problem in the Middlesex system. The branch mains, mostly of six, four, or two-inch pipe, and the trunk mains, mostly of twelve and sixteen inches, were adequate when laid. But after the system's expansion, a report by Nicholas S. Hill, Jr., one of the nation's most eminent hydraulic engineers, concluded that pumping capacity and pipe sizes prevented the company from getting appreciably more water to its customers. Warren Fuller, another engineer, stated flatly that the "pipe lines from the pumping stations" were too small, and that water pressure was dissipated "in overcoming friction and other losses. . .and it is not available to the consumers at the other end of the line." All engineering reports stressed that the company would need larger mains and larger pumps—preferably both—to overcome low water pressure.[30]

And the pressure was low. The company's pumps generally sent water into the large trunk mains at pressures between 90 and 95 pounds per square inch, which dissipated over distance and as water entered smaller mains. This was normal, and adequate service through four or six-inch pipe for such tasks as fire protection or getting water to the upper floors of buildings usually required at least 35 pounds per square inch (psi). By the late nineteen-teens, however, Middlesex Water Company four-inch lines often delivered less than 25 psi. When four-inch mains ran for a mile or more, as they did in some parts of the system, water could arrive at only 11, 8, or even 2 pounds per square inch.[31] There was simply no overstating the gravity of the situation.

The company conceded as much, and never denied that its customers had suffered serious inconvenience. Indeed, Ambrose Mundy publicly expressed his displeasure with the fact that pressure problems occasionally were so bad that the standpipes were empty or only partially filled. Bergen even told the BPUC that the Middlesex system was "saturated," and he fully agreed that the transmission system needed strengthening before pressure problems ceased.

Nor would there be any quick fixes. Putting the old South Plainfield wells back into service in 1922, for example, kept water moving to Elizabethtown and Plainfield-Union, but did nothing to alleviate pressure difficulties. Bergen understood as well as anyone that the company faced a major job in improving its pumping capabilities and the capacity of its mains. He also knew that putting things right was going to be expensive, and that for parts of the Middlesex service area, things were going to get worse before they got better. In this regard, accumulating low pressure incidents forced the company to make some difficult decisions. By 1922, they reluctantly decided that they could not extend mains into certain developing sections of Carteret and Woodbridge. These districts were too far from the pumping stations to guarantee sufficient water service.[32] Never had the company had such a difficult time with its system; never had relations with consumers been so strained.

ALL OF THIS PUT FRANK BERGEN in a dark mood. It was not controversy he minded as such; rather, he objected to unnecessary and wasteful controversy, which was exactly how he characterized the flap over the Middlesex Company's water service and the regional water shortage. Stoking his resentment was the fact that he considered that technical solutions were at hand for both problems, which, by 1920, had become parts of a single "water crisis" in the public mind. The frustrations of Bergen and the public, however, need some explanation:

In Bergen's view, the solution to the Middlesex Water pressure question was no mystery. In fact, he considered that improving water pressure in the system was no more challenging a project than previous company efforts. All engineering studies agreed that booster pumps at Robinsons Branch and a new 24-inch main from Park Avenue to Woodbridge would alleviate transmission problems; better pumping capacity and the larger main would yield plenty of water pressure. The problem then, Ambrose Mundy told the BPUC, would be to keep the standpipes from overflowing.[33] The project would be expensive but technically within the expertise of the company.

A solution to the regional water shortage would be even more expensive. But this too, Bergen was positive, the three water companies could handle. Indeed, they already had undertaken considerable planning and work. Since 1904, the Elizabethtown

Water Company and two of its subsidiaries—the Piscataway and Raritan Water Companies—had sought to run a 36-inch main from the watershed of the Raritan River, around Somerville, to Elizabethtown. Legal problems had sidetracked the plan in 1911; but by 1914, the Elizabethtown Company had laid about 18 miles of the main between Piscataway and Linden, and acquired a site for a pumping station and treatment plant at the junction of the Raritan and Millstone Rivers in Somerset County. The plan was to develop the Raritan-Millstone property and to complete the pipeline.

The cost of the undertaking was too large for one company, however, and the project languished for several years. But in 1918, the water crisis brought the effort back to life as a consortium of the three large water companies. Considering their close business relationships, and the fact that they served consumers in contiguous areas, the Middlesex, Plainfield-Union, and Elizabethtown Companies agreed to share project costs and to jointly exploit water resources. Bergen was a major force in reaching a decision on the matter, and he represented all three companies in legal proceedings before the New Jersey Board of Conservation and Economic Development. Late in the year, the Board granted permission to divert up to 20 million gallons of water per day from the confluence of the Raritan and Millstone Rivers. Work then began again, with the three companies committing about a million dollars to the project.[34]

At this point, however, matters took a serious turn. The city of New Brunswick, having designs on the Raritan's waters for its own use, sued to block the project. Additional litigation arose with the North Jersey Water Supply Commission, which coveted the business of the towns served by the three water companies. Bergen again carried the legal battle for the allied companies, but the litigation slowed the work, and in November of 1919, the companies publicly notified the twenty-six towns within their service areas that the prospects of water shortages were quite real. In June 1920 the courts ruled decisively for the companies; by then, however, even more serious complications had arisen. The World War, now over for more than a year, had left a pronounced economic legacy: it had ignited an inflation that raised construction prices drastically. Bergen, citing two examples, noted that cast iron pipe that used to cost about $25 per ton before the war now cost around $80; coal had gone from $3.35 to $7.59 a ton. Wages, taxes, and the costs of other materials had increased similarly. To complete the work, Bergen estimated that the companies would need at least another $5 million; he also said that the companies did not have that kind of money, and that their chances of raising it were slim. Once more, work in Somerset County ground to a halt.[35]

The timing of this interruption could not have been worse. It happened at precisely the time when public alarm over water problems—involving all of the allied companies—was crystallizing. As the work stopped, the companies once again told their consumers of the gravity of the situation, stressing that without new financing they could not proceed at the Raritan-Millstone site— and that site offered the only source of supply capable of meeting regional water needs. The municipalities, all twenty-six of them, responded with the formation of a standing conference committee to investigate the situation. They retained hydraulic engineer George W. Fuller, whose comprehensive report on the regional water supply eventually (1922) sustained the warnings issued by the companies, as well as their views on the value of the Raritan-Millstone project.[36] In addition, the conference committee expressed its alarm to the BPUC, which added a volatile new dimension to the situation.

The Public Utility Commissioners were well aware of the problems facing the customers of each of the three companies. Political and industrial leaders, as well as private citizens, had barraged the commissioners with a litany of justifiable complaints; the new communications from the committee of municipalities only added further detail to an already dark picture. Consequently, on June 8, 1920, the BPUC issued a memorandum with orders involving all three companies. In the eyes of the regulators, individual corporate problems were now officially part of what the Commissioners saw as a single disaster in the making.

The BPUC orders were comprehensive. They directed Plainfield-Union and Elizabethtown to install meters as a conservation measure, and told Middlesex to install booster pumps at Robinsons Branch and to report on efforts to finance the new main from South Plainfield to Woodbridge. The memorandum went on to state that since "the water supply to the whole area south of Elizabeth, east of Bound Brook and north of the Raritan River has to be considered as one large problem," that the three companies consider merging. In any case, the Commissioners wanted the development of Raritan-Millstone pressed. All of the companies were to report on their joint and individual progress by October 1920.[37]

Reactions to the BPUC memorandum sent matters rapidly out of control. Bergen exploded. Any consolidation of the companies, he retorted, was the business of the corporate directors and not of the BPUC. Furthermore, in his opinion, only one thing had prevented MWC and the other companies from securing the capital required to make necessary improvements: the politicization of the water issue by (as Bergen saw it) a meddling and even hostile BPUC. His argument was brutally direct, and he accused the BPUC of ruining the credit of the water companies. Private investors, Bergen claimed, would not provide capital for companies regulated by outside bodies. Such companies were not creditworthy inasmuch as they could not set their own rates and were not free to conduct vital aspects of their business, such as initiating capital projects or issuing stock, without approval from the regulators. Moreover, practice since 1911, when the BPUC set up shop, demonstrated that approvals entailed lengthy hearings and, if litigation rose, final decisions could be delayed for years. All of this, Bergen proclaimed, made investors shy away, making it all but impossible for utilities to raise the funding necessary for large capital projects. And it was the inability to raise money, the Middlesex president told the public, that caused low pressure in company mains and threatened a regional water famine.[38]

Bergen was equally insistent on another point: rate increases, even if approved in timely fashion, would not generate enough revenue to finance work of the scale facing Middlesex, Plainfield-Union, or Elizabethtown companies. In law, Bergen pointed out, the BPUC lacked the power "to grant rates to sustain water works not built"; it could rule only on increases to support existing operations. Even the BPUC admitted its limitation in this regard, and in one case it specifically noted that it did not consider the requirements of future capital projects when formulating rates.[39]

And even if the BPUC did consider capital needs in rate-making, Bergen argued that any rate increases would be too small. The Commissioners worked with an eye toward popular opinion—such as the remonstrances of twenty-six towns—and were unlikely to grant increases large enough to support large capital ventures. In this, he argued from experience. In March 1920, Middlesex, citing increases in operating expenses, requested a new rate. Approval took three months, coming only in June 1920, with a further adjustment in July to account for a dramatic increase in the price of coal. The BPUC considered the increases to be "material"; the company considered them "meager and insufficient," providing as they did for a uniform base quarterly charge of $2.50, graded charges by volume for metered service, and a surcharge of 15 percent on all water bills until the price of coal dropped below $8.50 ton (since 1908, the price of coal had more than doubled).[40] The new rates would support normal operating expenses, but not capital ventures in need of millions of dollars. Nor, in Bergen's view, would they allow the fiscal stability that would attract the outside investments—bank loans and the sale of stocks and bonds—that had traditionally financed utilities.

The Utility Commissioners responded with equal vehemence. For a decade, they pointed out, regulated companies had managed to raise capital. Only recently, the Board president pointed out, the Middlesex Water Company had successfully issued $100,000 in bonds. And if regulation largely eliminated "the opportunity to enjoy speculative profits," the fact that regulators could prohibit stock manipulations and other risky business practices generally would assure a "bona fide investor. . .a reasonable return on investments honestly made." The argument that regulated utilities were not credit-worthy, the BPUC retorted, "would not be regarded as worthy of discussion, but for the position of the [Middlesex and Plainfield-Union] companies."[41]

The Commissioners made their reply out of conviction, although, without question, Bergen would have enjoyed forcing them to define such terms as "bona fide investors," "speculative profits," and "reasonable return." Upon such definitions turned many of the arguments over the case for regulation. But the Middlesex president saw no reason to split hairs when he thought he had a concrete case. Selling $100,000 in corporate bonds was not the same thing as borrowing, or otherwise raising, up to $5 million—and this in a period of high prices and post-war economic instability, and in consortium with other companies, each with individual problems requiring additional financing. Under the circumstances, Bergen thought the Board's censure unreasonable.

In this, the Middlesex president was not alone. Indeed, state courts, upon appeals from utilities, had found that some BPUC decisions were detrimental to corporate finances. The order of June 1920, compelling Plainfield-Union and Elizabethtown to install meters was a case in point: the New Jersey Supreme Court set the ruling aside "on the ground of the companies' financial inability to comply." The estimated cost of that project had been under $400,000, but the court found the companies unable to raise a tenth of that figure. Shortly thereafter, litigation by the City of Elizabeth to reduce water rates, and then to acquire the mains of the Elizabethtown Company for use as a municipal system, in Bergen's view, so rattled investors that the water company was unable to enter the credit markets. Even the Conference of Municipalities, which had voiced its skepticism of company claims about the water crisis, concluded that Bergen's position was essentially correct in this instance. "Capital to com-

71

plete the [Raritan-Millstone] project was not obtainable," an Investigation Committee of the Conference reported, "due first to war conditions and later to a series of erratic and unreasonable decisions of the Public Utility Commissioners." Private "capital," the committee observed, "does not seek investments requiring protection by lengthy law suits."[42] Such comments had the ring of pure reason to Frank Bergen.

Moreover, the Middlesex president was dismayed by BPUC accusations that he had done nothing to help solve the water crisis. Indeed, the Board strongly implied that he had actually fostered the problem through his opposition to regulation. The facts, he argued, were otherwise. Bergen pointed repeatedly to his record as an advocate for the Raritan-Millstone project, his detailed warnings to the towns about the gravity of the regional water situation, and his work to further a public understanding of the importance of long-range planning in water resource management. He was active on any number of fronts; and in statements for the press, in speaking engagements, and in correspondence, he publicly called for water conservation, the location of new supplies, and the construction of new reservoirs and systems. Two generations before it was finally built, for example—on exactly the plan he proposed—Bergen advocated the construction of a major reservoir in Round Valley in western New Jersey.[43] Probably no one in the state did more to educate New Jersey citizens on water-related questions.

Besides, Bergen could also point out that he had led a corporate effort to solve the crisis outside of the purview of the BPUC. In December of 1920, the companies concluded that debate with the towns and the Utility Commissioners had, in effect, deadlocked, and that little good would come of trying to raise capital or continue work on system improvements under current conditions. Instead, they advanced a three-point plan for the consideration of the towns, any one of which offered an alternative to continued reliance on the companies for service. The first point suggested that the companies sell their works to the towns "at a price to be fixed by agreement, arbitration, or condemnation." Second, the towns could buy only the distribution mains within their respective borders, while the companies applied the proceeds of the sales to the development of new sources of supply. Finally, the towns could enter into long-term service contracts with the companies. This arrangement would guarantee stable rates, take the BPUC out of the picture, and end controversy and threats of litigation, all of which would restore the credit of the companies and enable them "to raise the money necessary to obtain more water."

Bergen was convinced that any of these alternatives offered a better approach to the problem than the orders of the BPUC; and while there were no immediate official responses from the towns—which, under these proposals, would themselves be faced with raising the money to buy, improve, and operate the water systems—the proposals did set local citizens to inquiring seriously into the merits of municipal ownership or other accommodations with the companies. Eventually (late 1922), these discussions went far enough to prompt legislative action on behalf of municipal efforts to act on the company suggestions. Two laws resulted: one provided the legal basis for the towns to jointly buy and operate company systems, the other authorized the towns to enter into long-term contracts with private utilities which would "enable the companies to obtain the necessary capital" to sustain adequate service. The BPUC, which saw these laws for what they were—a potential way to remove the dispute between the towns and the three companies from its jurisdiction—was perplexed, although it carefully noted that "it, of course, is not the province of this Board to question the wisdom or propriety of the Legislative action." No doubt the Board was further vexed to know that Bergen thought passage of the laws was a fine idea.[44]

BY 1920, THE MIDDLESEX WATER COMPANY was some twenty-three years old, and its last dozen years had been something of a paradox. Around 1910, relations with customers had been cordial, and government regulation was a thing of the future. The company's mains were growing and so were its revenues, which by 1913 had placed Middlesex Water Company among the twelve largest water utilities in the state.[45] Yet the end of the decade had brought turmoil. Even if the Middlesex Company had water enough for its service area, it was nevertheless part of a regional water crisis. Its distribution system was in trouble; its ability to finance new projects was questionable; and its relationships with the Board of Public Utility Commissioners were little short of venomous. Nor was there any end to the controversy in sight: Well into 1921, none of the towns had responded to Bergen's proposals, and the companies had ignored the BPUC reporting deadline set in January of 1920.

As Bergen pondered these developments, he saw nothing to suggest that he had miscalculated at any point. He had built two successful water companies which had fostered the growth of the communities they served. He had recruited capable managers to help him and had undertaken major improvements to his companies' water systems. By any reckoning, his reputation as an expert on the water business was second to none. Bergen was positively irritated that everyone could not grasp, as he intuitively did, the relationships between water service and water rates high enough to attract investment in water companies. Accordingly, he was genuinely offended when critics, notably those on the BPUC, accused him of impeding a solution to water service problems he honestly wanted solved.

Yet if Bergen considered his critics wrong, and sometimes terribly wrong, he was not willing to wait forever for them to come to their senses. Nor was he willing to do business under a constant threat of litigation or regulatory obstruction. If he must fight, he concluded, he might as well get it over with and fight to a finish. Thus, sometime in 1922—records do not reveal exactly when—Bergen decided to force the hand of the regulators who had stymied, as he saw it, reasonable efforts to address the problems of his companies and of regional water supply. Using the

Middlesex Water Company, he would attempt to force the BPUC to a showdown in the courts and, in effect, to dramatically change the nature of regulatory policy regarding the water business.

CHAPTER
4

Frank Bergen's Response: The Age of
Regulation and the Great Rate Case

A T THE BEGINNING OF THE TWENTIETH CENTURY, most Americans shared considerable ambivalence about the nature of business and industry and their places in society. The vast majority of the nation was committed to free markets and appreciated the merits of private enterprize, hard work, and profits. On the other hand, monopolies, or businesses large enough to effectively control a regional market or key services and resources, could offend popular perceptions of fair play. Any company or combination of companies amassing profits from noncompetitive enterprize generally aroused suspicion and resentment, even among other businessmen. Gradually, much of the public accepted the notion that government might intervene to restrain or modify business activities deemed contrary to the public interest.

This perspective on government's responsibilities *vis a vis* corporate America fueled some of the most intensive reform activity in history. A large measure of populist protest in the 1890s, for example, derived from objections to price-fixing by the railroads. Over the early 1900s, progressives widened the reform agenda to include warnings of the dangers inherent in price-fixing, monopolies, certain franchise privileges, and other noncompetitive business practices which tended to line corporate pockets at the expense of the public interest (or so progressives charged). Popular opinion never endorsed any single approach to dealing with these problems, or even agreed on the extent to which they *were* problems. By the end of the nineteenth century, however, it was equally true that plans for the regulation of certain business activity, in the interest of reforming the worst excesses of private enterprize, had become a familiar public issue.

This was the world in which Frank Bergen did business, although it was not an aspect of the world he liked. In fact, in Bergen one finds an unalloyed opponent of most economic reform, a man whose zeal on behalf of the old business order fully matched the progressive love for the new era of regulation. When regulatory reform pressure built in New Jersey at the turn of the century, he resisted with all of his considerable rhetorical and legal talent; and after the enactment of the New Jersey Public Utility Act in 1911, he did business as a regulated utility only under protest. Bergen never accepted either the efficacy or the ethics of any political body interfering with private property or companies—especially his companies.

It comes as no surprise, then, to find Bergen at crossed swords with the Board of Public Utility Commissioners over the problems of the Middlesex Water Company, or over the wider issues of the central New Jersey water crisis. What was remarkable was the vigor and extent of the counter-attack he finally launched. Over the 1920s, in a rate case that lasted almost as long as the Civil War, Bergen went after the BPUC's jugular vein: he called into serious question the very right of the Commissioners to determine rates for a utility. Without such power, the nature of utilities regulation would have been a profoundly different affair.

Thus, the stakes of Bergen's assault were high. He wanted nothing less than to roll back over a decade of regulatory policy, and if he had succeeded, then the powers of regulatory bodies across the nation would have been open to serious question. Consequently, the battle rightly attracted national attention and revealed much of the complex relations between reformers, public policy, and the regulated utilities industries. Moreover, what we can justly call the "Great Rate Case" offered one of the most articulate statements of contemporary argument against utilities regulation ever to go on the public record. In Frank Bergen, unfettered free enterprise had found one of its last great champions.

ANY EFFORT TO UNDERSTAND BERGEN'S position on utility regulation also requires some perspective on the forces arrayed against him. At the turn of the century, many businesses conducted their affairs in such fashion as almost to invite criticism; and in the eyes of much of the press and public, those who stood to challenge them often appeared admirable in comparison. In particular, the progressive critics, who rose to prominence over the 1890s and early 1900s, were articulate and animated by what they regarded as a public-spirited concern for the popular welfare.[1] They had a wide reform agenda and they took legislative aim at any number of graphic and highly visible targets.

One of the chief concerns of progressivism was the industrial work place. Too many workers toiled long hours in dangerous conditions in mines and factories for minimal wages; accidents on the job were numerous and worker discontent often surfaced in the form of strikes. Children not even ten years old worked full-time—which frequently meant a twelve-hour day—at looms and in mine shafts, to the detriment of health and education. Living conditions in tenement-ridden cities and poverty-stricken rural districts often were unsanitary, overcrowded, and bereft of even basic human comforts. Photographs of children working under horrid conditions, detailed reports on the wretched quality of life in the growing urban slums, and news of disasters such as the 1911 Triangle Shirtwaist Company fire, which took the lives of 146 young women workers, made a vivid impression on popular opinion.

So did the financial and other business activities of many banks and corporations. Periodically, there was public outcry as large companies and monopolies used means fair and foul to secure markets, often at the expense of small businesses and consumers. Charges of price-fixing and poor service by the railroads, large manufacturers, and various utilities provoked particular indignation across the nation. Literary "muckrakers," to use Theodore Roosevelt's pungent term, brought exposes of questionable (and sometimes outrageous) business and industrial conduct to popular attention. Upton Sinclair's *The Jungle*, to cite a classic example, exposed hideously unsanitary conditions in the meatpacking industry; Ida M. Tarbell revealed shocking abuses by the large oil corporations as they translated access to new markets and raw materials into vast economic and political power. Other writers and reformers offered scathing views of a veritable litany of abuses: banking policies that seemingly favored big business over small entrepreneurs; customers forced to pay inflated prices to monopolies; the ruin of investors through stock fraud; and the manipulation of state and national legislators to assure government policies favorable to business interests. Thanks largely to reforming progressives, much of the American public did not view the period spanning the late nineteenth and the early twentieth centuries as the finest hour of American capitalism.

It is no defense of such business conduct to point out that abuses could not have flourished so openly without a supportive social and political context. This, however, was the case. Even under the spotlight of progressive criticism, many state and local governments encouraged economic development while looking askance at its rougher edges. New Jersey was a prime example in this regard. After the Civil War, the legislature passed liberal incorporation laws, openly inviting major firms to bring their business to the Garden State. They did, and New Jersey earned handsome incorporation fees as it issued thousands of new corporate charters.

Leading politicians and businessmen also considered that the state's liberal incorporation laws helped stimulate impressive economic growth. New Jersey had, wisely in Frank Bergen's view, "enacted a series of statutes designed deliberately to give greater freedom to corporations than was enjoyed in former years; to invite capital to make its domicile here, offering security to enterprise and investment, and to render it forever unnecessary to resort to direct taxation to support the government of the state."[2] The state was the first to allow firms chartered under its laws to hold stock in other companies, and to issue stock in payment for purchases of property. Holding companies—trusts—became a common feature of New Jersey business, and of the nation's seven largest trusts, all held charters of incorporation from the Garden State. Certainly few business leaders saw anything wrong when reformers branded New Jersey the "home of the trusts."[3]

Probably the most influential New Jersey companies were the so-called "Three P's": Prudential Insurance, the Pennsylvania Railroad, and Public Service, Inc. They and their myriad subsidiary companies represented precisely the concentrations of economic and political power that the progressives so mistrusted. They were giants in their respective fields and they controlled substantial wealth, which many progressives did not consider wrong *per se*. Rather, reformers objected to the fact that the companies so blatantly used their influence in their own behalves. They actively courted members of the legislature to guard their interests against business or other rivals. Indeed, their corporate boards, and the boards of their subsidiary companies, listed former governors, state cabinet officers, members of the bench, and senior politicians of both major political parties, including members of the state's congressional delegation. The Three P's used lobbyists frequently and skillfully, and corporate officers contributed liberally to the war chests of both political parties in support of friendly candidates. Few states could point to such a powerful and seemingly secure combination of business interests.

Among New Jersey progressives, the litany of complaints against the influence of the Three P's, and for that matter, against other large industrial and business combinations, reflected a variety of concerns. Many reformers stressed what they feared was a perversion of the democratic process as corporate influence loomed larger in political affairs. Other complaints were more specific. Among urban reformers, resentments grew in the face of railroad political manipulations and graft to develop prime real estate, maintain rights of way, and assure favorable tax rates. They also took exception to the operations of utilities companies, notably Public Service. Like the railroads, the utilities paid only minimal taxes—two percent of gross receipts—and in any case functioned as regional monopolies. Franchise laws, which granted service areas to gas, electric, water, or other utilities in virtual perpetuity, prevented competition among utilities and left consumers little recourse against high rates and poor service. The situation came to symbolize a good deal of what reformers thought was wrong with corporate New Jersey.[4]

In the early 1900s, confronted as they were with these powerful and entrenched business interests, Garden State progressives watched as their ideological allies in other states came to grips with similar problems. What they saw was encouraging. Progressives in Wisconsin, Virginia, California, Ohio and elsewhere legislated reforms in municipal government and taxation, attacked monopolistic business practices, and began the regulation of railroads and utilities. The greatest promise of reform, however, came in 1907 when neighboring New York State passed the so-called Hughes Law. The new act created a state utilities commission with sweeping powers to regulate railroad and utilities activities, including the setting of rates and the authority to mandate the remediation of poor service. The Hughes Law drew applause from progressives across the nation and gave New Jersey reformers a model for emulation.

While reformers existed in many varieties in the Garden State, the most cogent voices were those of the "New Idea" movement. This was initially the progressive wing of the state Republican Party, generally led by State Senator George Record of Hudson County and a small circle of his G.O.P. allies. By 1905, the New Idea was a real force among Republicans, although it subsequently gained considerable bipartisan support. Step by step, the progressives marshalled their forces for a full-scale assault on what they saw as entrenched corporate privilege.

Their first major attack came in early 1907, when they entered a bill to create a "State Board of Commissioners of Railroads and Public Utilities." Led by Public Service, Inc., corporate interests rallied support in both parties to blunt the challenge. Thomas N. McCarter, the founding president of Public Service, never denied that there were some problems in the market place. Unregulated entrepreneurs, he insisted, had done a great deal of good, but "it is clear that they made mistakes too" when they watered stock and pursued other dubious schemes with investors' money. Nevertheless, McCarter—or Frank Bergen, for that matter—saw no need for mass public indignation; businesses could clean up their affairs by themselves, he believed, and existing laws were adequate to deal with those who did not.[5] Much of the legislature finally agreed, and the resulting law established a utilities commission empowered only to make recommendations on railroad rates and service. It had no authority at all over utilities companies. Legal experts considered the measure one of the weakest regulatory laws in the nation; in fact, progressives saw it as only the first shot in protracted war.

The New Idea and its allies refused to give up on utilities and railroad regulation. After 1907, periodic hearings on new regulatory proposals continued in Trenton, provoking heated controversy. The bitterest fight came in 1908, when the New Idea tried to enact a New Jersey version of New York's Hughes Law. On March 2, in testimony before a State Senate committee, Bergen spoke in his capacity of General Counsel for Public Service. Regulatory laws, in his view, were nothing but an assault on private property and honest business initiative. Such "bills, if they truly represent the dominant public sentiment of this country," Bergen warned, "would seem to indicate that we are entering upon a mild revival of the French Revolution. The wealthy and the prosperous are to be hunted and banished as enemies of the republic. . . .The Reign of Terror has been revived, and already extends over the industry and commerce of the country."[6] Bergen helped win this round for his allies, but their victory was brief.

IN 1911, THE ISSUE OF UTILITIES REGULATION came to a head with the inauguration of Governor Woodrow Wilson. Wilson had campaigned for a stringent public utilities act which, like the Hughes Law, would allow rate regulation. He pushed hard for just such a measure soon after moving into the statehouse, and again it was Bergen who emerged as one of his most vocal opponents. Such a powerful commission, Bergen warned, would stop "absolutely the investment of capital in the construction of public utilities, which we all know are so essential to the comfort and convenience of the people." Worse, he noted further, was the fact that "the mere anticipation" of strict regulation had "prevented the organization of a single" new utility in New Jersey over the previous five years. Using a line he would follow repeatedly over coming years, Bergen claimed that Wilson's proposed law would virtually drive private capital out of the utilities business.[7]

Bergen was not alone in his adversarial position. In fact, anti-regulatory opinion was articulate and organized across the state. While not sharing Bergen's fears of another French Revolution, there were those who thought that progressives were playing fast and loose with traditional constitutional protections of property rights, and that reformers were willing to see "the passion of today [become] the law of tomorrow." In Hudson County, a young New Jersey District Court Judge, William Henry Speer, urged the public to beware of "periods of excitement" and a demand for "reforms which would be subversive of the fundamental principles of government." "A government of passion," he warned only months after Wilson took office, "spells the end of this Republic."[8] At the time, Speer had no inkling that twenty-three years later he would succeed Bergen as president of Middlesex Water. Yet his sentiments neatly parallelled Bergen's, and they were typical of voices who rose as advocates of free

84

enterprise. This time, however, the reformers would not be denied.

On April 11, 1911, the Public Utility Act became law. It created a three-member Board of Public Utility Commissioners with full authority to set rates, conduct investigations, and govern a range of corporate financial activities including stock and bond issues. Governor Wilson—soon to be President Wilson—considered that he had given New Jersey one of the toughest regulatory bodies in the nation. Even his opponents agreed with that.[9]

The new BPUC wasted no time in setting up shop. The State Senate confirmed the appointment of Wilson's first three commissioners, and by May 1 they began to enforce the new regulatory legislation. Counsel for the Board was Frank H. Sommer, a prominent Newark attorney and New Idea Republican state senator. (Sommer would leave the BPUC within a few years and devote much of his practice to assisting utility customers in bringing complaints before the Board.) Anyone could bring a grievance against a utility to the commissioners, which then could initiate a wider investigation. Companies had to request permission to raise their rates, which triggered a protracted and frequently acrimonious hearing process. In setting rates, the commissioners considered general business conditions, the capital and other needs of the company, the nature and quality of services provided, and the value of corporate assets. The trouble was, however, that the BPUC and the utilities rarely agreed on how to value a company's worth, and proceedings could bog down for months on this point as the parties struggled to find common ground. Moreover, the board had to deal with hundreds of traction, gas, sewer, electric, and water companies—and there were some 126 private water companies alone in 1911—with tended to slow the Board's deliberations even more. The entire process could be painful for all concerned, and even some champions of regulation found the situation frustrating.[10]

Bergen watched these developments with barely concealed disgust. In his view, all of this activity was patent nonsense which slowed or crippled the pace of business and development and which did little or nothing to assure better service to consumers. At its worst, he considered regulatory activities as a mere first step toward socialism, which he opposed on principle. Early contacts between the BPUC and the Middlesex Water Company were minimal, however, and not especially intrusive: the first Board action was a 1913 order to connect one Ralph Kelly, of Woodbridge, with the system; and five years later, the commissioners actually complimented the company's operations as they approved a new stock issue.[11] But none of this assuaged Bergen's feelings. He clung implacably to the view that all regulators, even complimentary regulators, were inherently dangerous.

Bergen may have been the most obstinate of all of the PBUC's critics, or at least the most reluctant to compromise. Most other utilities executives came to terms with the Commissioners, especially when the BPUC proved anything but uncritical of those alleging corporate wrong-doing, and demonstrated a willingness to seriously consider the merits of industry positions. In 1915, in an effort to speak with a common voice in dealing with the Board, representatives of virtually all of the regulated companies formed the New Jersey Utilities Association. The NJUA met regularly, often hosting speakers from the BPUC, and the contact gradually helped reduce some of the early mistrust of utilities regulation. Yet Bergen was having none of it. While he was president, the Middlesex Water Company never joined the NJUA. Occasionally he would send Ambrose Mundy to a meeting, and years later he even addressed a meeting himself; typically, he used the forum to present a carefully-argued attack on BPUC rate-making policies.[12] At all times, Bergen remained the consummate anti-progressive, and it was this posture that shaped his perspective on the Raritan-Millstone issue and on the water pressure problems facing his company. It was not the outlook of a man trying to avoid a fight.

AS BERGEN'S ANGER GREW, SO DID HIS understanding of New Jersey's Public Utility Act. Like many important laws, the fine points of judicial interpretation took some time to emerge. A record of case law, however, eventually grew out of various hearings before the BPUC and, significantly, the federal courts. Indeed, Bergen helped establish this record. The key action was a 1921 Public Service suit brought against the Commissioners in the United States District Court. Public Service, with Bergen acting as general counsel, brought a suit arguing that the BPUC had illegally refused a request for an adequate trolley fare increase. The court issued a temporary injunction against the Commission and allowed the company to collect the higher fare while the case went back to the BPUC for review. What intrigued Bergen was not the fact that the court had required the Board to review the case while granting Public Service temporary relief. Rather, the salient fact, at least for the Middlesex Water Company president, was that the federal courts had agreed to hear the case at all, and that it had proved interested in looking at rate making by a state regulatory body.[13]

All of this led Bergen to consider another possibility: what if he could induce the federal courts—removed as they were from the passions of state politics—to actually assert a judicial supremacy over regulatory bodies and, even better, to issue a *permanent* injunction against BPUC rates? Best of all was the possibility that a federal court might rule on the constitutionality of BPUC rating-making procedures. Convinced as he was that utilities regulation was nothing more than an unconstitutional assault on private property, Bergen wanted nothing more than his day in federal court.

The basis for a constitutional attack on the Utility Commissioners, Bergen reasoned, lay in the controversies of the past several years. Hearing after hearing had elicited the same response from Bergen: if there had been occasional water shortages in Middlesex County, if the Raritan-Millstone project and the trunk main between Oak Tree and Carteret lay uncompleted, it was because of "the persistent refusal of" the BPUC to allow the Middlesex Water Company "to collect for its services sufficient income to. . .maintain, extend and enlarge its system of water works." And this, as Bergen had argued vociferously for years, prevented the company from attracting the new capital that would enable it to make the necessary improvements to the system. The enforcement of damagingly low rates was to destroy the credit and value of the company; and that, in Bergen's mind, amounted to the confiscation of the company and "communistic raids" on its treasury.[14] Good lawyer that he was, Bergen knew that there were constitutional safeguards against confiscation inherent in the Fourteenth Amendment, and he believed that they protected the water company from the BPUC. Therein lay the logic for an appeal to the federal courts; what Bergen needed was a case to get him there.

He found one in late 1923. After 1920, the Middlesex, Plainfield-Union, and Elizabethtown Companies all had spent a number of frustrating years trying to resolve differences with the BPUC over system improvements. For a time, Bergen became so pessimistic about the Board's attitude that he simply gave up filing for new Middlesex Water rates after October 1920. By late 1923, however, he decided to force the issue. On December 10, he submitted a schedule asking for a new base rate of $3.40 per 1,000 cubic feet of water up to the first 15,000 cubic feet; thereafter, the rate schedule changed to accommodate different industrial, residential, and municipal water needs. This was an increase of ninety cents per 1,000 cubic feet, or 36 percent, and Bergen suspected it would provoke a strong and negative response from the Board.[15] He was right.

As Bergen fully expected, the Board rejected the rate increase after a bitter and protracted hearing; the affair began on December 20 and finally ended only in July of 1924. The towns of Woodbridge, Metuchen, and Carteret, as well as the Carteret Industrial Association, all used Frank Sommer as counsel in fighting the company's request; and the clashes between the former New Idea senator and Bergen were not without drama. At one point, frustrated by Bergen's continued opposition, Sommer vented his anger in a stinging brief: He accused the company president of "agitation against the state policy of regulation of utilities," "unbridled condemnation" of the regulators themselves, stirring up public opinion against regulation, and blaming the water crisis on regulatory policies.[16] Bergen hardly appreciated Sommer's tone, but he could heartily agree with everything the man said.

Under Sommer's questioning, testimony also dragged out the old and familiar accusations of poor service. Bergen simply dismissed these matters as beside the point:

> The service is defective, I admit that, insufficient;
> has been for years; no doubt about that at all. I will
> say the company needs larger mains, more mains, more
> water, more trunk mains; has for years; no doubt about
> it at all; no use taking time to prove that. I admit it.
> ...The people in that neighborhood have been
> outrageously treated; I admit it; I admit it all.[17]

With sufficient revenue, the Middlesex Company president insisted, service problems would evaporate. In the meantime, dwelling on the matter obscured issues of more importance.

The real key to the problem, as Bergen saw it, was a fundamental financial disagreement with the Commission. Under BPUC procedures, a base utility rate derived in large part from the total value of a company's plant, equipment, mains, and other fixed assets; a rate was awarded, among other things, to give the company an annual percentage return on its total value. Over the various hearings of 1923 and 1924, Middlesex Water insisted that its plant and other assets were worth at least $2,500,000, while the commissioners accepted a valuation of only $2,190,200. The company claimed that the BPUC's figure was not only too low, but that a rate derived from it would yield an annual return of barely over 4 percent. To the contrary, the Commission argued that a base rate of $2.20 per 1,000 cubic feet would give the company over a 7 percent return; and at the same time, it insisted that the company rebate all bills 10 percent in consequence of poor service. On August 1, the BPUC closed the proceedings with a decision to that effect.[18] In fact, however, the Commission quickly found that the war had only begun.

When the Board rendered its decision, Bergen was ready with an unexpected counterattack. Instead of appealing again to the BPUC or to the state courts, Bergen followed the precedent set earlier in the Public Service case: within two weeks, he sought a permanent injunction against the orders of the BPUC in federal District Court. This was a first: no New Jersey utility ever had asked a federal court to permanently enjoin the action of the Board. To the dismay of the Commissioners, Judge John Rellstab chose to hear the case, agreeing with Bergen that there was a constitutional question involved. The embattled company president once again claimed that the BPUC rates were, in effect, confiscatory, and that the Board, in setting those rates, had violated the Fourteenth Amendment rights of the company. Rellstab appointed a special master, Trenton attorney Aaron V. Dawes, to take testimony from both sides, and new hearings opened in September.[19]

Bergen was now in his element. He attacked the constitutionality of rate-making procedures, arguing vigorously that no nonjudicial board, including the BPUC, had any power to fix prices. In compelling low rates and rebates, the Commissioners had acted illegally "to indict, try and convict the company" for service failures that were beyond its control. Any process was unconstitutional, he insisted, which failed to permit companies "to obtain sufficient income to meet their expenses and maintain their credit." The state could only protest that the legislature had, if only indirectly, granted the Board enforcement power, and once again assert that the lower valuation of Middlesex Company assets had been accurate and were not confiscatory. Clearly, however, important elements of public opinion thought that Bergen got the better of the argument. If Middlesex Water's service and rates were so bad, asked an editorial in the Newark Evening News, then New Jersey's leading newspaper, why had Middlesex County towns failed to take advantage of the laws enabling them to buy out the water company?[20]

In a report of May 26, Dawes sent his recommendations to the District Court. The special master found the Board's valuation of the company wrong and stated flatly that the suggested rate was "clearly confiscatory." While Dawes did not fully agree with the company's valuation figures either, he did recommend that the court allow the injunction against the BPUC-prescribed rates to stand, thus allowing the company to implement its own rate schedule. Dawes also said that the Board had not allowed the company a "reasonable opportunity" to solve its service problems, and he recommended that the court retain jurisdiction of the matter in case further disputes arose. Finally, in a bombshell, Dawes went to the heart of the entire affair, concluding that "rate making is not a function of the defendant board." Understandably, this finding left the BPUC utterly dismayed; and for the same reason, Frank Bergen was delighted.[21]

THE IMPLICATIONS OF THE MIDDLESEX WATER Company case were enormous. The entire confrontation had demonstrated the extent to which a federal court could supersede state regulatory authority. Bergen's appeal to Judge Rellstab had resulted in findings against the BPUC at virtually every point, "thus practically taking the power of rate making away from the state."[22] If a corporation could so simply appeal an adverse regulatory decision, then what power did state utility commissions really have? It was a question asked across the nation in late 1925 and early 1926—the *New York Times*, among other out-of-state journals, followed the case avidly—as both utility companies and regulators tried to fathom the full meaning of what had happened in New Jersey.[23]

Certainly the BPUC saw what was at stake, and the commissioners concluded within days that they would have to fight if they were to remain an effective regulatory body. As early as June 5, 1925, counsel for the Board was back in federal court objecting

to the special master's findings in their entirety and to his comments on the rate-making functions of the BPUC in particular. It
was the opening gambit in almost two more years of grueling
court appearances and commission hearings.

Frayed tempers promised wonderful material for press
coverage, and Bergen and Sommer (again counsel for the Board)
were in top form. At one point, the Middlesex president refused
even to examine certain Commission exhibits, disdained even
speaking to one Commission engineer, and finally complained that
if he could only sit down with anyone with "fifteen ounces of
brains" they could resolve the entire dispute. At another hearing,
Sommer exploded after a comment by Bergen and walked out of
the case—leaving a puzzled Ambrose Mundy sitting alone on the
witness stand in the middle of an unfinished cross-examination.
As the arguments continued, even the District Court judges eventually fell out; one of Rellstab's colleagues on the bench, Judge
William Clark, finally concluded that rate making in the federal
courts, while legal, was inappropriate. Such matters really
belonged, he felt, before local tribunals. The case was taking its
toll on everyone concerned.

In January of 1926 the District Court again rebuffed the
regulators. The judges, even those who wanted no part of fixing
rates, ruled that the Dawes findings were legal and that the injunction against the Board should stand.[24] The company immediately
put its new rates into effect. Unable to prevent the Middlesex
action, the Commissioners realized that if they wanted to fight on,
they had only one card left to play. They played it on April 5,
when they filed an appeal with the Supreme Court, asking for a
reversal of the District Court injunction against the Board's rate
schedule. Thus it was that a case begun before a state regulatory
body ended up before the highest court in the land.

Actually, given all of the fireworks at the state and
District Court levels, the Supreme Court appeal was something of
an anticlimax. On October 11, 1927, after waiting over eighteen
months, the BPUC won on technical grounds. The court refused

to look at the specifics of the case; had it done so, the action would have invited a flood of rate-case appeals. Instead, it ruled that the case belonged back in District Court, with any subsequent action going to the federal Court of Appeals. In effect, this decision gave the Board the chance to reopen the entire case. Fortunately, however, by this time few of the combatants wanted to start from scratch and most were looking for a way out of the legal quagmire.[25]

Indeed, signs of compromise from virtually all parties had surfaced as early as the summer of 1926. The municipalities and businesses within the Middlesex Company service area remained desperate for reliable service and pressed the Commission to resolve matters. The Commission itself felt besieged. Perhaps it would have maintained the tempo of battle against the Middlesex Company alone, but circumstances had changed. Bergen also had threatened a fight over Plainfield-Union water rates, and the Board already was locked in another struggle with the Passaic Consolidated Water Company. All of this had irritated the state legislature and other prominent politicians, who wanted the regulatory scene to calm down. Indeed, feeling the pressure, in July 1926 the Commissioners tried to organize a virtual peace conference between itself, the towns, and Middlesex Water. Bergen announced that he was willing to talk, but not to forgive or forget. The talks took place without yielding any immediate results. They did indicate, however, that well before the Supreme Court rendered its decision, the Commissioners were looking for a graceful way to come to an understanding with Bergen.

In fact, the Board finally brought the Middlesex president around later in the year. The key was a more sensible rate. Without ever conceding any original error, the Commissioners offered a new base water rate of $2.85 per 1,000 cubic feet; this roughly split the difference between the company's requested $3.40 and the original Board offer of $2.20. The arrangement also included provision for the company to collect a surcharge from its customers of $42,711 to off-set deficits it attributed to artificially low rates enforced prior to 1926. While grumbling that the company deserved nine times more than the additional surcharge, Bergen nevertheless took the deal.

If he had looked at the issue from a strictly personal perspective, Frank Bergen probably would have continued the contest with the BPUC. As a matter of principal, he never conceded the right of a political body to regulate the conduct of his business. But the perspective of a corporate president was another matter. The protracted litigation was expensive and time-consuming, and over the years it had cost the Middlesex Company some business opportunities. Negotiations to supply water to the borough of Highland Park, for example, a prosperous suburban Middlesex County community, had fallen through because the town fathers were uneasy about the regulatory controversies. On the other hand, by 1927 the company had collected excellent revenues for a year (at $3.40 per 1,000 cubic of water), and Bergen considered that the offered $2.85 rate promised a smaller but still adequate profit. He found that the Middlesex Company was even able to sell bonds again. Seemingly, the choice was between personal preference—that was, fighting on—and the larger good of Middlesex Water. Under the circumstances, Bergen chose to call off almost four years of sustained litigation. He settled, and when the Supreme Court announced its decision, it affected the situation not one iota.[26] For all practical purposes, the Great Rate Case was over.

HARD FEELINGS CAN LINGER FOR YEARS after a particularly bruising encounter of any kind. The Middlesex Water Company had fought one of the most protracted and bitter rate cases in the history of American utilities regulation, and certainly Frank Bergen never forgave his antagonists. Yet he had landed punches of his own. There was no doubt that he had put the New Jersey BPUC, and, for that matter, the entire progressive agenda of utilities regulation on the defensive. Of more immediate significance, however, was that in ending the war with the BPUC,

Bergen also had cleared the way for a resolution of several long-standing corporate problems.

Probably the greatest beneficiaries of the settlement were the company's industrial and residential customers. Bergen always had promised that Middlesex Water could deal with service problems as soon as it could generate revenues to finance system improvements. He was as good as his word. The company was ready to send out bids for the Oak Tree to Carteret trunk line as soon as Judge Rellstab's decision to sustain the Dawes report came down in early 1926.[27] Subsequent litigation afforded time to reconsider the trunk line issue, however, and despite continued state pressure to build from Oak Tree, the company decided on another route. By 1929, Middlesex had completed a transmission line from the Robinsons Branch reservoir to Carteret; and as Bergen predicted, even the BPUC found that the project corrected the existing supply and water pressure problems in the company's service area. There were further complaints about water quality, but improved coagulation and filtration efforts corrected most of these.[28] After almost a decade of controversy, the distribution system was never in better condition.

Other issues eventually disappeared as well. With the resolution of the water pressure problems, the BPUC no longer pressed the matter of corporate consolidation with the Elizabethtown and Plainfield-Union Companies. Middlesex continued to sell water to the other companies, but the state and the municipalities no longer saw any real purpose in merging the three systems. From time to time over the 1920s, Bergen discussed the possibility of consolidation with the other directors, and he commissioned careful legal and financial studies of the question. But by the end of the decade, with the company viable and healthy, the directors, like virtually everyone else, considered the issue moot and let it drop.[29]

Finally, the Raritan-Millstone project moved toward completion—but without the Middlesex Water Company. Bergen and Julian Kean, president of the Elizabethtown Company, pursued the matter over the early 1920s, although the lack of construction funds prevented the parties from doing more than talking. By 1927, Bergen—representing the Middlesex and Plainfield-Union Companies—and Kean had drawn up a lengthy contract for the formation of a proposed new Somerset Water Company. The Somerset Company would have built and operated the new water works for the three parent corporations. Yet Bergen and Kean could never agree on the final details and the contract went unsigned. Like the proposals to merge the companies, the Raritan-Millstone project seemed much less vital to Middlesex Water in the aftermath of the rate case and subsequent improvements to the system. Accordingly, Kean went ahead, and by 1930 Elizabethtown had largely completed the effort alone. At least it was done; and between labors of the two companies, the water crisis of central New Jersey largely dissipated for a time.[30]

The years of controversy also affected the management of Middlesex Water. In 1924, when the rate case began in earnest, Bergen already was almost 73 years old; he was 76 by the time the affair ended. His health remained excellent, and he maintained a full professional and social schedule. Yet he was slowing down, and the battle with the BPUC took up an increasing amount of his attention and energy. Consequently, he cut back on some of his duties at Public Service, and at Middlesex, he depended upon Ambrose Mundy to run the company with little if any supervision.

Mundy had enjoyed Bergen's confidence from the moment he joined the company in 1908, and early on his duties encompassed virtually all aspects of daily operations. Yet it is difficult to read the newspaper and official accounts of the various Commission and court hearings without concluding that the hardworking superintendent had become indispensable to Bergen. Mundy would not become president until 1959, yet his performance during the 1920s demonstrated a comprehensive knowledge of all aspects of company operations and policy, the needs and problems of the service area, as well as an ability to represent Middlesex Water before the public, the Board, and professional organizations. In effect, the experience of the 1920s, as bitter and difficult as much of it was for the company, had proved an effective school for a second generation of corporate leadership.

Middlesex Water Company headquarters building, 1930s. Originally a bank, the company acquired the building after the bank went out of business during the Great Depression.

Finally, the 1920s tacitly brought to a close a larger chapter of American business history. While the nation would never settle on any unanimous position on the regulation of utilities or other industries, most accepted at least some government oversight of private enterprise as a fact of business life. State laws throughout the nation conferred such authority on a variety of regulatory bodies, and federal courts eventually eschewed any desire to get involved with the minutia of rate fixing and other local actions. In its contest with the BPUC, Bergen and the Middlesex Water Company had waged one of the most intensive and, for a time, even successful counterattacks against regulation the nation had ever witnessed. In the end, however, one company, and one legal campaign, could not reverse a national trend with deep popular and political support. The Middlesex Water Company was better off as a result of its president's crusade, but regulation was in place to stay.

History, however, is replete with ironies. Events that inflame the passions of one era came seem tame and ordinary within years. The Great Rate Case will stand as a genuinely important chapter in the history of American utilities regulation and, consequently, in the history of the progressive movement. Certainly it attracted all of the attention it deserved from advocates and opponents of government oversight of business. Those who fought the battles did so with conviction. Yet only short years later the struggle over rate regulation seemed almost quaint; for by late 1929, economic survival itself was the central issue for the nation. The Great Depression had begun.

CHAPTER
5

Depression, War, and Reversals:
The 1930s to the 1950s

THE STATE OF THE NATIONAL OR REGIONAL economy never has reflected precisely the health of a particular industry or company. Over the years, economic adversity and prosperity have presented challenges and opportunities which, even for well-established companies, have run counter to general trends or prevailing business wisdom. Certainly this was the case with Middlesex Water Company operations between the 1930s and 1950s. The years that spanned the Great Depression and the era of unprecedented growth that followed World War II were among the most dramatic in memory. The fortunes of Middlesex Water, however, seemingly had only a tenuous connection to the economic performance of the rest of the region. During the 1930s, when most Americans faced one of the bleakest social outlooks in national history, the Middlesex corporation prospered; but over the 1950s it labored under the burden of daunting problems. For those who worked at the water company, these years offered an unsettling mixture of accomplishment and anxiety: They coped successively with the greatest economic disaster in American history, startling demographic changes, and mounting water supply and service problems. Finally, under genuinely adverse circumstances, they began a long-range planning process that set the stage for modern company operations.

THE LABORS OF FRANK BERGEN AND his fellow directors assured that the Middlesex Water Company would end the 1920s as a thriving and expanding concern. As bruising as it was, the Great Rate Case had allowed the company the means to improve the distribution system while earning a profit. The system was a lifeline to a region substantially different from the largely rural Middlesex County of the 1890s. By 1930, county population had climbed to some 212,208 people, over seventy-five percent of whom lived in urban or suburban areas. Business had flourished, and more than 36,000 wage earners worked in 379 companies. The familiar industries still dominated the local economy, and still supplied most of the Middlesex Water Company's customer base. Smelting and copper refining, chemicals, brick, tile and terra cotta, and oil refining all remained lucrative; the waterfront along Staten Island Sound bustled with more shipping and railroad activity than ever.[1] As the 1920s ended, the company and the county seemed poised for mutual prosperity in the coming decade.

Unfortunately, this was not to be. In October 1929, the stock market crashed and, shortly thereafter, the national economy followed. The country slid progressively into the Great Depression, and by 1933 over a quarter of the nation's work force was unemployed. In New Jersey, employment fell to under sixty-eight percent of 1925 levels, and payrolls dipped more than fifty percent. It was one of the grimmest and most tumultuous periods in American history.

In many respects, the situation in Middlesex County was an especially dire reflection of the national dilemma. The impact of the depression was devastating. By 1933, some 14,000 workers had lost their jobs as over 100 county businesses went under; county industrial payrolls dropped from 1929 levels of $48.2 million to about $19.6 million, and the value of industrial production plummeted from $563 million to just over $173 million. This was a truly catastrophic decline. Many families were literally in despair, and thousands of Middlesex County residents found no steady work for years. They consequently welcomed President

Franklin D. Roosevelt's New Deal, with its unprecedented governmental efforts to stimulate economic recovery and to provide relief to the unemployed. By the end of 1933, the federal Civil Works Administration (CWA) managed to offer at least part-time jobs to almost 2,000 people. Most government work was unskilled and poorly paid, however, and the total CWA payroll in the county came to only $138,000 for all of 1933.[2] This was important help for many of those who received it, but hardly enough to stave off destitution for many others. Middlesex County was the Great Depression in microcosm.

To an extent, the nature of its business offered Middlesex Water a cushion against the worst of the depression. Even in hard times, people and industries needed water, and with industrial expansion at one of the lowest levels in decades, the water distribution system could easily supply the service area. Moreover, the rates established in 1926 assured profitable operations during the 1930s, even if profits were lower than anticipated. In 1929, for example, before the Great Crash, the company reported a return of 13.3 percent on net plant cost; this dropped to 10.66 percent in 1930, and to 7.01 percent in 1931, perhaps the worst year of the depression. This was the lowest level of fiscal performance in Middlesex Water Company history. Relative to most American business and industry, however, even this reduced level of profits was substantial, and by 1935 the return on plant cost again had climbed above 8 percent.[3] If profitability—or at least the level of profitability—was something of a question in the early 1930s, actual corporate survival was never in doubt.

Work on the distribution system continued, although at a pace well below that of the booming 1920s. If the Great Depression slowed the expansion of the system, there was never a full halt. Between 1931 and 1933 the company added another four miles to the mains, which then totalled over 162 miles. In addition, crews answered repair calls and kept the pumping stations and meters working. Including several office workers, Ambrose Mundy supervised forty employees by 1933.[4] The company also

Leon Silakoski in company truck, 1934.

moved into new quarters in Woodbridge, a handsome brick building and former bank (a victim of the depression) fronting Main
Street. It would be home to Middlesex Water for over a generation.

Fortunately, those who worked at Middlesex Water found
the company a generally reliable employer over the difficult years
of the depression. Corporate records indicate no lay-offs, and
Mundy did most hiring based on personal recommendations from
employees who brought family members and other relatives to his
attention. Over time, the payroll included several networks of
brothers and cousins, and there was a sense of loyalty to the company that kept them working through those uncertain years.

At the same time, the company still reflected some of the
difficulties of the work place of the 1930s. If work was usually
steady, there were some drawbacks. Work weeks remained six
days; the work day was still nine hours long for the crews working
on the mains; and there was no work at all when the weather
turned bad, although workers were unlikely to find out until they
actually reported to the work site. There were no health benefits,
sick leaves, or paid vacations. When he asked for a vacation,
Leon Silakoski, Sr., learned that he could have one any time—but

it would be "permanent." Even so, there was little sentiment to unionize the company during the depression. Those employees who wanted to organize faced the opposition of Frank Bergen and Ambrose Mundy and they found little support among their fellow workers. In fact, across the nation depression-weary American workers placed a premium on job security rather than fringe benefits. Things were no different at the Middlesex Water Company.[5]

The early 1930s saw the culmination of a trend all but completed during the late 1920s. In effect, Ambrose Mundy had become the chief operating officer of the company, and Bergen had virtually no contact with daily operations. In April of 1932, the aging president suffered a serious heart attack; he was eighty-one by then, and his recovery was protracted, making it impossible for him to maintain his old business pace. He subsequently gave up his post as general counsel at Public Service, Inc. (he retained the title of "counsel") and devoted more of his time to civic and political affairs.[6] He still spoke and wrote widely on public policy, and he developed a passionate concern over national economic trends and the depression. It was a role he enjoyed and, with Mundy running Middlesex Water, a role he could afford.

Bergen's particular focus was Franklin Roosevelt's New Deal, toward which he evinced a grim and articulate animosity. No one should have been surprised. For years, Bergen had stood implacably against government interference with private enterprise, and in fighting the New Deal he simply continued the battle he had waged against the New Jersey Board of Public Utility Commissioners. Now, however, the stakes were even higher. In several articles and speeches, the old crusader denounced what he considered an abrogation of the Constitution. The reliance of the New Deal on massive deficit financing, government employment, and federal regulation of the economy was "unsound and dangerous," he warned, and had left "the country. . .in distress and the air tainted with Communistic sentiment." He genuinely feared that Roosevelt's answers to the Great Depression were bringing the nation to the verge of "anarchy." "This is the most dangerous

internal crisis which has confronted our country," he told one audi-
ence, "since the Civil War."[7] In that judgment, the company president was probably correct, although most of his fellow citizens,
especially those in heavily Democratic Middlesex County, failed
to appreciate his sour estimate of FDR and the New Deal.

IF FRANK BERGEN WANTED TO FIGHT the new deal the
way he fought the Utility Commissioners, he never got the chance.
He died of another heart attack early on the morning of November
12, 1934; he was almost eighty-three years old. His wife, Lydia,
and daughter, Charlotte, survived him. His will made generous
provisions for them, as well as several charities and institutions
including Yale and Rutgers Universities. Voting rights to all
Bergen stock in the Plainfield-Union and Middlesex Water
Companies passed to Charlotte, who for years afterward remained
a familiar figure to company personnel. (Lydia Bergen resided at
the family estate in Bernardsville until her death in 1948;
Charlotte died in 1982.)[8] And it may have been significant that
Bergen chose to keep the Middlesex stock within his family: He
had founded and built the company, and over the years he had
fought for it. Whatever else he left behind, one of Frank Bergen's
chief legacies was a strong and prosperous utility corporation, a
company that prospered even in the face of some of the most
adverse economic conditions in history. He was proud of this
accomplishment in life, and it would have surprised no one to find
that he wanted his association with the firm carried into the future.

Under any circumstances, the water company would have
felt the loss of its tireless and combative president. But the situation in 1934 was anything but normal. The Great Depression
showed no signs of abating, and while the controversy with the
BPUC was now several years past, the company remained wary of
the state regulators. For the time being, Middlesex Water could
look after its own finances; what it needed was a chance to rebuild
a relationship with Utility Commissioners and with local officials
within its service area. This meant a president who not only knew

the industry, but who also possessed considerable stature in the eyes of regional legal and political authorities. Very quickly, the company directors found their man.

The new Middlesex Water Company president was William H. Speer. Like his predecessor, Speer was a lawyer and a deeply learned individual; he once described himself as "a perfect fiend about reading" and he knew enough of the classics to doodle in Greek. He also had wide experience in utilities management. In temperament, however, Speer was remarkably different: Whereas Bergen brought a combative style to the job—he had refused offers to the bench in part because he relished the role of litigant—Speer was more of a diplomat. He was a highly respected judge, and his ability to see both sides of an issue trained him to deal tactfully with individuals in government and industry. It was a trait that would pay dividends for the company over the years.

Like Bergen, Speer was a New Jersey native with deep roots in the state. He was a descendent of the Brinkerhoff family, which settled in the region as early as 1650. The son of William H. and Eleanor C. (Brinkerhoff) Speer, the future corporate leader was born in Jersey City on October 21, 1868; he attended Jersey City public schools and Hasbrouck Institute before entering Columbia University. While an undergraduate, he rowed on the university's crew team and became an avid golfer, a game he enjoyed for the rest of his life. After graduating from Columbia Law School, he joined the New Jersey bar in 1891 and quickly established his own practice. By 1902, the young attorney was president of the Hudson County Bar Association, after which he served as county prosecutor from 1903 to 1908. At that point, Governor Stokes appointed Speer to the state Circuit Court for Hudson County, where he sat until 1922. By then, he had established a reputation, as the *Newark Evening News* once noted, as "one of the keenest and ablest" legal minds in the state.[9]

It was during his years in Hudson County that Speer developed his interest in the legal aspects of the utilities industry. He had been in law school with Thomas N. McCarter, the formida-

Judge William H. Speer, second president of the Middlesex Water Company.

ble lawyer and president of Public Service, Inc., and the men were close friends. It was through cases and related work involving McCarter and Public Service that Judge Speer met Frank Bergen professionally. Beyond personal acquaintances, Speer also fol-

106

lowed legal developments: Many of his cases involved the various utilities companies of the region, and he came to appreciate the potential for these firms as the economy of northeastern and central New Jersey expanded. In addition, the judge knew the water situation. His association with Bergen taught him much in that regard, while he also served on a special state canal commission which had major water-use implications. Eventually, the appeal of the utilities business overcame his love of the bench, and in 1922 he resigned from the Circuit Court to join Public Service.[10]

Speer was to remain with Public Service for twenty-five years as general attorney. In this position he emerged, along with Bergen, as one of the most influential men in the state on all matters related to utilities law. The judge was also an investor, however, and he had a pronounced interest in corporate management as well. In partnership with Bergen and others, he became actively involved in the affairs of a number of companies, notably the Plainfield-Union and Middlesex Water Companies. He became a director with both firms, and he quickly learned not only what it took to represent a utility in court or before the BPUC, but to actually review corporate business operations. By the early 1930s, Speer had participated as the Middlesex Water Company expanded its mains even in the face of the depression. He also took part in the intricacies of financing the company and, having assisted Bergen with legal affairs during the late 1920s, Speer was fully apprised of the strained state of corporate relations with the Utility Commissioners. Thus the judge was a seasoned veteran by the time he assumed the Middlesex presidency.

JUDGE SPEER QUICKLY PROVED HIS WORTH as chief executive officer. The company was sound financially and during the Great Depression Speer kept it that way. Residential and industrial customers still needed water service, and the company needed enough of a profit to support operations and attract continued investment. The new president balanced these needs, explaining to consumers and politicians the fiscal realities of keeping water in the mains while maintaining dividends for stockholders. And there were dividends. Middlesex Water Company preferred stock continued to pay 7 percent through the depression, while common stock returned 11.75 percent annually between 1932 and 1936. By 1937, as the headline of a local newspaper noted, company stockholders had every right to ask, "What Depression?"[11]

In 1937, however, good business was not necessarily good politics. Large industrial and financial concerns, particularly those with little or no competition in a given locale, came under increasing public scrutiny as the depression deepened. Utilities were no exception, and in New Jersey, as elsewhere, there were rumblings of discontent over allegedly high corporate profits in the face of an economic and social crisis. Rates agreed upon before the depression, so one argument went, were too high for most consumers during hard times. While most critics focused on rates, some voices, notably those on the left wing of the political spectrum, but also some moderates, saw a solution in public ownership of utilities. They cited the example of the New Deal's development of the Tennessee Valley Authority, which provided much of the upper South with cheap electrical power. In New York City, Mayor Fiorello La Guardia threatened investor-owned power companies with the construction of municipal generating plants unless electricity rates came down. By the mid-1930s, utility companies across the nation braced for what some political observers thought would be a major round of government takeovers or increased regulation.[12]

Yet in New Jersey, despite some criticism of the allegedly "almost monopolistic fashion" in which some Garden State utilities did business, demands for public ownership of utility companies fell largely on deaf ears. While there were plenty of municipal water systems, there was no evidence that they supplied better or cheaper service than investor-owned companies. Moreover, the experience of other utilities was fatal to calls for government ownership. In the mid-1930s, publicly-generated electrical power, for example, was some thirty percent more expensive than electricity from Public Service. Confronted with such figures, state government consistently shied away from encouraging local governments from building or buying any utilities; and there were serious proposals to sell municipal utilities of all types to private operators.[13] For New Jersey municipalities, the unwritten rule was to stay out of utilities enterprises if at all possible.

At the same time, however, utility rates could still be a touchy subject, especially in the politically-charged atmosphere of the Great Depression. In fact, the healthy dividends and profits of the Middlesex Water Company eventually did draw political fire. In late 1936, the Middlesex County Freeholders, responding to complaints from local governments throughout the company's service area, as well as from a number of industries, called for an investigation of water rates. Without dealing in specifics, and without accusing the company of any wrong doing, the county solicitor argued through the press that investors were reaping returns that were "not justified at this time." The charges were good politics and they received plenty of newspaper coverage; and in early 1937, with a $15,000 appropriation, the freeholders decided to launch a full-scale audit of the company.[14] Water service or quality was never mentioned: the action of the freeholders was politically-inspired and born of the desperation of depression-weary water users.

Had Bergen still held the corporate helm, an all-out court fight over the county's action might well have ensued. There were grounds to resist the freeholders. Company rates had derived from protracted public hearings and carried BPUC approval, and thus Middlesex Water had only collected legally-established fees for water use. While the BPUC could investigate a utility at any time, in this case the Utility Commissioners had not elected to do so. Moreover, the legal ability of the county to force company compliance with any audit or investigation was uncertain. A flat water company refusal to cooperate could have delayed matters interminably, or at least until the Utility Commissioners or the courts became involved. All of the elements were in place for a real confrontation.

This was Judge Speer's first real challenge as president, and it marked a departure in the company's relations with political and regulatory authorities. While the legal position of the company was sound, Speer understood that the county inquiry had political roots; under the circumstances, even a successful fight could have led to additional trouble in the future, and the judge wanted to avoid any long-term difficulties. Thus, he concluded that a fight would not be in the best interests of the corporation. The judge, like Frank Bergen, was a Republican, but he was tactful in dealing with Democratic Middlesex County. He was willing to give the New Deal a fair chance to work, and while active in politics, he was never as gloomy as Bergen about the nation's future political outlook. As a speaker, his tone was more that of a diplomat, and so was his approach toward the county. Consequently, when the freeholders chose the New Brunswick auditing firm of Arnold B. Rosenthal to delve into the company's books, Speer elected to offer all help short of compromising company operations.[15]

The wisdom of Speer's decision became clear as the investigation of the company's rates played itself out. The Rosenthal audit, which began in May of 1937, lasted almost a year. Rosenthal carefully documented company economic performance since its founding, reporting periodically to the freeholders as he went. The freeholders, of course, with as much fanfare as possible, reported the findings of allegedly high profits to the press. In the end, however, after thanking "the officers and employees of the Middlesex Water Company" for their cooperation, Rosenthal found little. In his final report of March 1938 (released in early April), he made a few inconsequential criticisms of company accounting practices and, in a less than dramatic finale, he recommended a relatively moderate rate reduction. Rosenthal's suggestions, if acted upon, would have brought a return on investment of over just seven percent down to about six percent. Hired by the freeholders, he could hardly have recommended less.[16]

Armed with these findings, the freeholders approached the BPUC asking for a rate reduction. The commissioners, who well remembered the rate case with Bergen, now found Judge Speer ready to negotiate. Speer, of course, had checked the Rosenthal report carefully, and in fact was convinced that the audit had improperly charged almost $300,000 out of capital.[17] The judge, however, chose not to raise the issue publicly, instead waiting to see how strong a stance the BPUC would adopt. As events developed, it became clear that the commissioners also wanted no part of another confrontation. Harry Bacharach, president of the BPUC, announced that he preferred to negotiate the matter with the company rather than go through formal hearings, and he was in no hurry to force the pace of negotiations.

In fact, talks progressed leisurely until May of 1939, when the company announced a rate reduction totalling less than $22,000 per year. Under the agreement, some 9,700 residential customers would pay $1.50 less each year, a cumulative savings of $14,600; large industrial consumers would share reductions coming to another $7,350. In effect, the settlement saw the company eliminate part of the surcharge approved at the end of the Great Rate Case.[18] There is no record of freeholder reaction to the agreement between the company and the BPUC, and perhaps the county officials considered it a victory of sorts. But if so, they kept quiet about it, and one suspects that they expected more political mileage out of the affair. In any event, the incident was closed without another acrimonious dispute with the Utility Commissioners or with Middlesex County.

In this fact alone, Middlesex Water considered the result highly favorable. For while the county freeholders looked to save local voters $1.50 per year, Speer had his eye on much larger stakes, and in this matter the good will of the BPUC was essential. Since 1937, Speer had wanted to refinance the bonded debt of the water company. Middlesex Water had $1,700,000 outstanding in such debt, $1,668,000 borrowed at 5.5 percent and $32,000 at 5 percent. The depression had forced interest rates considerably lower than this, and Speer was trying to call the old bonds. Two insurance companies, John Hancock and Mutual Benefit Life, were willing to refinance the entire debt at 3.74 percent, and the potential savings to the company over the years made the $22,000 rate reduction appear relatively insignificant. However, Speer needed the authorization of the BPUC in order to proceed with the deal, and the last thing he needed was a fight over water rates. In avoiding the battle, he received a routine approval of the refinancing.

Speer wasted no time in consummating the bargain with the insurance companies. The Middlesex directors voted their approval on August 10, 1939, only two months after concluding the rate reduction agreement with the Utility Commissioners. In an age when the refinancing of corporate debt was still a relative novelty, Speer had orchestrated a genuine coup. Even with the rate reduction, he had assured the continued prosperity of the company, and in 1939, dividends came to a very healthy $4.25 per share. Late in the year, the board of directors took the unusual step of voting a formal resolution of thanks to Judge Speer for his handling of the bonded debt. He had earned it; and the directors might well have added a thanks for the way Speer had dealt with the Middlesex County Freeholders. Certainly he had demonstrated that diplomacy and finesse could be as effective as litigation in dealing with key corporate issues.[19]

THE GREAT DEPRESSION CLUNG grimly to American life throughout the 1930s. It seemed almost impervious to government intervention, and while there were hopeful periods of increased industrial productivity and employment, there was no sustained recovery. Matching the bleak domestic scene was an equally unpromising international situation. While the United States grappled with the depression, much of the world drifted into war; and although there was considerable sympathy for the nations fighting Germany and Japan, there were few American calls to actually take up arms. To the contrary, American isolationist sentiments were strong and most of the public considered that they had enough to worry about at home. New Jersey residents were no exceptions in this regard; editorials, public opinion surveys, and religious, civic, and political leaders were generally united in their calls to stay out of combat. Until the Japanese attack on Pearl Harbor on December 7, 1941 forced the issue, the United States had no plans to join the Allies.

Yet this reluctance to fight did not preclude a willingness to prepare for the worst, and this meant a massive industrial program to rebuild America's armed forces. The industrial mobilization was unprecedented, and it moved into high gear during late 1938 and 1939 as Congress and President Roosevelt pumped hundreds of millions of defense-contract dollars into the economy. The impact on New Jersey was quick and dramatic. Hundreds of depression-idled plants opened their doors again, and hundreds of new factories, mills, shipyards, and other industrial facilities came on line. Ships, aircraft, military vehicles, munitions, and the vast array of other products necessary to sustain modern warfare poured out of New Jersey factories. By the end of 1939, defense orders had put some 433,000 unemployed Garden State residents back to work; it was the highest level of employment the state had seen in twenty years. This figure increased by 50 percent during 1940, while the value of New Jersey payrolls doubled. These trends continued through American entry into the war as the state experienced the most rapid period of industrial expansion in its history. The battle against the Axis lay ahead, but New Jersey finally had won the war against the Great Depression.[20]

This massive industrial effort had a major impact on the Middlesex Water Company and its service area. Chemicals, metal refining, and manufacturing boomed; so did construction as new plants and housing went up across the county. Middlesex Company mains kept pace, but only through a concerted effort. Between 1939 and 1941, the company added almost 41,000 feet of new mains to the supply system, which carried more water than ever. In 1939 alone, the Park Avenue station was pumping some

113

4,933,000 gallons per day, while Robinsons Branch supplied another 1,489,000 gallons. These levels rose as the system expanded and wholesale demands increased (Middlesex was still selling close to 30,000,000 gallons per month to Plainfield-Union). Pumping more water and laying new lines also meant adding to the work force, and by 1940 Middlesex Water employed over eighty people.

While the bulk of the customer base was industrial during the war, residential sales also grew quickly. The directors authorized Mundy to push the mains into new housing developments whenever he could connect groups of at least fifteen homes to the system. On this basis, the lines expanded steadily into new areas of Colonia, Fords, Woodbridge, and other towns. Ironically, this was a mixed blessing for the company, as extending water service into residential areas was not immediately profitable. A typical residence generated an annual income for the company of less than 12 percent of the costs of installing new lines and connecting the house to the distribution mains. While it took years for homes to generate a profit, cumulatively they placed immediate and increasing demands on the system.[21] Still, the expansion of residential lines continued as the nation moved closer to war.

Even as the company worked to support the industrial mobilization, however, it suffered a dramatic and tragic accident. At about 8:30 on the morning of November 12, 1940, a terrific blast leveled all but one of fifteen buildings in the Woodbridge complex of the United Railway and Signal Company. The sound of the explosion carried some twenty miles, shaking homes across the Arthur Kill (Staten Island Sound) on Staten Island and breaking windows in communities a dozen miles away. The firm manufactured railroad explosive signals, and was the immediate neighbor of the meter repair shop of the Middlesex Water Company and of a number of small buildings owned by A. Stanley Mundy, Inc. The force of the blast leveled the Middlesex meter shop, the Railway Signal factory buildings, and seriously damaged the A. Stanley Mundy structures. Tragically, it also killed outright or

114

mortally wounded thirteen people, mostly women working in the United Railway Signal shops. In the Middlesex facility, meter repairman Dominick LaPenta, sixty years old and the longest-serving company veteran, died instantly; several other employees, including Anthony Silakoski, received serious wounds from the blast and from flying glass, wood, tools, and metal. A cyclone fence between the water company and United Railway stopped considerable debris and probably saved Silakoski's life. It was the worst disaster in the Middlesex Company's history.[22]

Leon Silakoski heard the blast while preparing to leave home for work at the ill-fated meter shop. Driving toward the shop entrance, a police officer stopped him, saying that "there was no more water company." Beyond the policeman, Leon could see the leveled shop with meter parts and fittings thrown all over the

Wreckage of Woodbridge meter shop and other company facilities, November 12, 1940.

grounds. Only then did he learn that his brother, Anthony, was among the wounded. At least he had survived.

For a time, it appeared that the catastrophe might have national implications. The United Railway blast came within hours of explosions at two Pennsylvania munitions plants, a major fire at an Atlanta, Georgia, Army warehouse, and damage to the machinery of an important Navy dry dock facility in Seattle, Washington. Local, state, and national authorities all assumed that sabotage was responsible. In Woodbridge, United Railway did not have defense contracts, although both the Army and Navy were considering some of the company's manufacturing equipment for possible military use. This fact, plus a media emphasis on the possibility of foul play—the New York *Daily Mirror*, which published a sensational photo spread of the wrecked buildings, all but announced sabotage as an established fact—fanned area fears that a pro-Axis conspiracy was afoot. This was not totally wild speculation. Shortly before the United States entered World War I, German agents may well have set off several terrifying explosions at New Jersey munitions manufacturing and storge facilities. But lengthy investigations by the FBI, the county prosecutor's office, and the New Jersey Bureau of Explosives turned up no evidence to indicate that the Woodbridge tragedy was anything more than a sad accident. Slowly, the matter faded from the public eye.

Whatever the cause of the explosion, it certainly jolted the company. A week later, a stunned board of directors received a full report from Ambrose Mundy on the extent of the damage and learned of the plight of Dominick LaPenta's widow, who was left with seven children.[23] The board made provision for a voluntary contribution to Mrs. LaPenta, then quickly authorized the construction of new meter repair facilities and the replacement of damaged and destroyed equipment. In the meantime, the company used temporary space to keep meter repair tasks moving. The entire affair demonstrated how vulnerable complex industrial operations could be in the face of a serious accident, even a *neighbor's* accident, and the point was not lost. Until this juncture,

Middlesex Water maintained a self-insurance reserve for workers' compensation and other damages, but in view of the 1940 explosion, this would no longer do, especially with a war looming. If the blast on November 12 was not due to sabotage, who could predict the future? Indeed, after Pearl Harbor, which followed little more than a year later, roughly half of the general public fully expected enemy attacks on America's eastern cities. Consequently, after talking with John Hancock, Inc., which had expressed concern that the property securing its bonds at least have insurance coverage, Speer and Mundy arranged for a policy to cover war-related damages.[24] In a sense, the war had come quite close to home for the water company.

When the United States entered the shooting war in December 1941, Middlesex Water's participation in the conflict became visible in a variety of large and small ways. Following the Pearl Harbor attack, for example, the company quickly moved to comply with Defense Council of New Jersey black-out regulations and with a municipal request to install an air raid siren atop the Park Avenue pumping station. The board of directors also took steps to allow certain employees leave for military service, and to bring working hours in line with those of most defense industries. After June 1942, Middlesex employees worked a standard week of forty hours, earning time and a half for overtime hours. Of greater significance, however, were company efforts to keep pace with virtually continuous requests to extend service to the burgeoning defense plants, especially those along Staten Island Sound. A contract with the Army also increased the flow of water to Raritan Arsenal, a major military supply center.[25] A productive industrial base was central to the waging of modern warfare, and in supporting regional industry, Middlesex Water was an integral part of the war effort. Indeed, the rapid build-up of regional war industries would have been impossible without a sufficient water supply.

The war emergency, however, compelled the company to concentrate on expanding the distribution system rather than developing new sources of supply. In fact, by mid-1944 water use

117

at Raritan Arsenal, Camp Kilmer, and in the factories along Staten Island Sound was so heavy that the company could barely keep up with demand. The mains were working to capacity, and an engineering report warned that a breakdown at any critical point in the system could lead to a regional water crisis. The company needed at least a new sixteen-inch main and an additional source of supply.

Work began quickly on the new projects. Before the end of the year, Middlesex had contracted with A. Stanley Mundy & Co., of Woodbridge, to lay a two-mile reinforcing main between Woodbridge and one of the distribution mains in Raritan Township (now Edison). Over the years, the Mundy company would be closely associated with Middlesex Water. Founded in 1928, the firm was a Mundy family concern which specialized in contracting work for utilities. Started with assistance from Ambrose by his son, Albert Carmen Mundy (later a member of the Middlesex Water Company Board of Directors), later generations of the family expanded the business.[26] Not surprisingly, the two companies worked well together, the job went smoothly, and the new reinforcing main was soon on line.

The Middlesex Company also found a supplementary water supply. After failing to conclude a contract for an additional supply from the city of Perth Amboy, the company negotiated a major purchase from the Elizabethtown Water Company (the first of several over the years). The arrangement marked a new relationship between the two water companies. Prior to this, Middlesex had sold to Elizabethtown, which had been a good wholesale customer. But the development of the Raritan-Millstone plant after World War I eventually met all of Elizabethtown's needs; and now Middlesex Water was a customer instead of a supplier.

The completion of the new reinforcing main and the contract with Elizabethtown saw the Middlesex Company through the war. It was clear, however, that the system remained overburdened and that any further demands on it could easily lead to major difficulties.[27]

PEACE BROUGHT LITTLE RESPITE to the Middlesex Water Company. The war had generated a virtual population explosion in Middlesex County with business and real estate development to match, and the company found itself almost constantly on the brink of crisis as it marshalled its resources to keep water in the mains. In fact, the postwar years placed demands on the distribution system that were every bit as severe as the requirements of the Home Front.

The development of the service area over the 1940s and 1950s was genuinely astonishing. The birthrate soared—these were the years of the "Baby Boom"—and industrial prosperity continued to attract new workers. Between 1940 and 1950, New Jersey gained some 680,000 new residents, and the upward trend was even more pronounced in Middlesex County. Census figures placed the county population at 217,077 in 1940; this had grown to 264,872 by 1950, and the count was almost 434,000 by the early 1960s. Population growth in some of the towns served by Middlesex Water was especially pronounced. Carteret, for example, grew by a modest 10 percent between 1940 and 1950; but the increase in Woodbridge was almost 32 percent, while Metuchen added 50 percent. The surging population increases that followed the war were unprecedented in national and state history.[28]

The bulk of the population increase was suburban and urban, and, moreover, it was relatively affluent. For decades, Middlesex County had urbanized steadily, but the postwar economic boom accelerated the process. At the end of World War II, Middlesex County had some 1,300 farms; but by the late 1950s a survey counted well under 600 farms as agricultural acreage gave way to new housing tracts. Measured in terms of family purchasing power, Middlesex County ranked among the top fifty counties in the nation, and thousands of county residents could afford new homes during the 1940s and 1950s. This general prosperity, plus the availability of Veterans Administration mortgages, a central facet of the GI Bill of Rights, stimulated residential construction. In the fifteen years after the war, Middlesex County ranked second in the state in housing construction starts, which posted a nearly 101 percent increase over the levels of 1940. Where there were 55,948 dwellings in 1940, there were almost 112,400 in 1955; and even at this rate of building, housing failed to keep up with demand. For some twenty years after 1945, the New Jersey "home construction industry set new annual records,"[29] and for real estate agents and developers it was a golden age.

As it frequently was for Middlesex Water, however, regional economic and population growth was not an unalloyed benefit. While new customers were always welcome in theory, in practice it was difficult to provide them all with a satisfactory level of service. The same crews that had put in mains during the war years worked overtime connecting new homes to the system in the later 1940s. But regional growth was simply too fast, and the problem went beyond the matter of providing new homes with water (which was difficult enough). The fact was that water consumption in new and existing homes was growing enormously, a phenomenon attributable in large measure to improving lifestyles. As in the rest of the nation, Middlesex County residents generally prospered in the postwar years, and among other things, they spent their money on an array of home improvements and appliances. Swimming pools, automatic washers, dishwashers, garbage disposals, and extra bathrooms, all so much a part of modern life, sent residential water use to unprecedented—and unpredicted—heights. Average New Jersey per capita use stood at sixty gallons per day, although this figure was certainly higher in quickly developing Middlesex County.[30]

Industrial water needs were equally pressing. By the mid-1950s, New Jersey's industrial output ranked seventh in the nation; and of the state's twenty-one counties, the value of Middlesex County manufactures stood fifth. Clay and stone products continued to employ over 2,600 workers, while chemical production and metal refining, long important Middlesex industries, supported ten times that number. These businesses required huge quantities of water. The production of a single ton of chemicals, for instance, could use as much as 220,000 gallons of water; a ton of steel required 65,000 gallons; and the processing of other chemicals could involve 250,000 gallons for each finished ton. By 1955, industrial use of potable water in New Jersey stood at over 300 million gallons per day, with Middlesex County alone accounting for some 10 percent of this.[31] Thus, to a greater extent than ever before, the prosperity of the region depended upon reliable water supplies.

The demands on the distribution system grew rapidly. From a base of some 11,000 industrial, residential, and municipal customers in January of 1949, by May of 1952 the company served 16,500 accounts in Woodbridge, Metuchen, Clark, Carteret, South Plainfield, and Edison (formerly Raritan) Township, as well as providing fire protection service for part of Rahway. Only five years later, the company had fully 30,000 customers. This growth was so sustained and extensive that Middlesex Water had little opportunity to bring new supplies on line gradually or to accumulate capital for long-range planning and improvements to the system. Rather, circumstances compelled the commitment of most existing water resources, capital, and personnel to deal with short-term problems. It was never easy.

In fact, as basic and crucial a matter as extending the mains became a constant and pressing task. As new housing, industry, and municipal facilities proliferated, the company laid new pipe virtually every working day. Between 1945 and 1959, Middlesex Water laid over 112 miles of new mains, even as it repaired or replaced several miles of damaged or substandard pipe. These additions gave the system a total of over 60 miles of transmission mains and 255 miles of distribution mains.[32] The company usually kept up with the demands for new mains, but only barely.

What the company could not do was keep water in all of the mains, or maintain adequate water pressure. Problems that were only becoming apparent or were left unresolved during the war years now assumed a more serious guise. Low water pres-

Company repair crew, 1950s. Left to right: Andy Pogon, Bob Pittenger, Steve Tartza, George McLoughlin, and Tony Ferraro.

sure, for example, which had been an intermittent difficulty in certain residential areas during the early 1940s, brought little response from the BPUC as long as water continued to flow to the vital war industries. But during the 1950s it was impossible to ignore the matter. From time to time, pressure was too low to get water to homes on higher ground, and the Clara Barton, Fords, and Hopelawn sections of Edison and Woodbridge Townships were especially vulnerable to service interruptions. The situation in the Clara Barton area alone affected some eight hundred families, and in nearby Menlo Park, a large public hospital, a summer camp for poor and disabled children, and the state home for disabled veterans also experienced problems.[33] The inconveniences, as well as the dangers to health and fire protection, were all too real, and the BPUC did not overlook them.

Neither did the company. Immediately after the war, Judge Speer explained to local officials and the Utility Commissioners that the company needed to improve the system. He actively sought new financing to keep water flowing to customers, to extend the mains, and to maintain water pressure. As early as 1946, the company undertook an expensive series of renovations and improvements to the facilities at Robinsons Branch in order to meet increased consumer demand. Over the late 1940s and early 1950s, considerable effort also went into developing new sources of supply. At Park Avenue and elsewhere crews actively prospected for new wells, and in 1957, after lengthy negotiations, the Middlesex directors once more agreed to purchase a major daily supply from the Elizabethtown Company.[34] One way or another, Middlesex personnel kept water in the mains, but the situation had become precarious as best.

By the late 1950s, with its immediate service area thirsty for every gallon, Middlesex also was compelled to give up the wholesale water business. Its last wholesale customer had been Plainfield-Union, of which Speer was also president. Unable to buy from the water-starved Middlesex Company, Plainfield-Union increasingly turned to Elizabethtown, which had ample supplies. Eventually, in 1961, the Elizabethtown Company acquired struggling Plainfield-Union.[35] Even before the companies merged, however, as Plainfield-Union slid deeper into trouble, more than a few people at the Middlesex Company nervously watched the dilemma of their erstwhile customer. Would supply problems force Middlesex Water out of independent existence too?

For the time being, however, short-term remedies staved off the worst. Yet stop-gap measures and the renovation of aging facilities, no matter how necessary for immediate company operations, could not continue indefinitely. What the company needed was a long-range strategy that encompassed major improvements to the system, new sources of supply, and the financing necessary to support ventures of this scope. The almost continuous threat of water shortages and pressure problems made planning on this scale difficult; but if the system was to remain viable, Middlesex Water had to deal with the matter sooner rather than later.

AS DIFFICULT AS MATTERS WERE, Middlesex Water Company had some key assets. These were its personnel resources, many of the employees with the firm for years, others hired just prior to and after the war. Their skills and jobs reflected the growing diversity of the company and of the consumer base it served; they also offered a human perspective on the evolution of the water business, which was no longer the relatively uncomplicated affair it had been five decades past.[36]

Ambrose Mundy felt an acute sense of responsibility toward the company he had done so much to build. Since the death of Frank Bergen, he was its most visible employee, and even some of the regional media mistakenly thought he was president.[37] It was Mundy who bore the brunt of complaints about service problems, who dealt with local political officials, who handled routine contacts with the Utility Commissioners, and, on occasion, who personally tried to placate irate consumers. At one point, a delegation of residential customers actually descended en masse on his home to voice their complaints about low water pressure. The superintendent bore all of this philosophically, and even managed to keep his sense of humor. He had a novel response to one angry telephone caller who felt that company rates were too high: Water was cheap, Mundy patiently explained, but distributing water cost a great deal more. Under the circumstances, why didn't the caller bring a few buckets down to the water company office? Mundy cheerfully promised all of the free water the buckets could hold.

Generally, however, there was little room for levity. Mundy poured most of his waking hours into Middlesex Water, and he was in the field checking the status of various projects virtually every day. On his few days off, he still hunted occasionally, and he developed a passionate interest in flowers; but he took no real vacations. Once, in fifty years, he and his wife went to

Bermuda; the rest of the time he drove down to meet his family at the New Jersey shore on summer weekends. Family members recalled that he loved his work even during these difficult years; this was just as well, as he considered that the state of the system was such that he could spend little time without his finger directly on the pulse of company operations. In turn, employees remembered him as decisive and willing to make decisions under pressure, characteristics they felt were essential in seeing Middlesex Water through hard times.

Fortunately, one of Mundy's chief contributions to the company was in assembling a first-rate professional staff. Among his closest associates was Carl J. Olsen, the company's mechanical engineer. Olsen, the son of a Danish carpenter, had grown up in New Jersey, earning his degree from Steven's Institute of Technology in 1922. He worked in various engineering jobs, including a short period with A. Stanley Mundy, Inc. In 1926, however, Olsen had just left a company in western New Jersey when Mary Yost, Mundy's secretary, let her boss know that the young engineer was available. This was typical of the word-of-mouth hiring practices the company had depended upon for years, and this time it worked out particularly well: Olsen got the job as the company's first formally-trained civil engineer—and, some years later, he married Mary Yost.[38]

The steady growth of the system kept Olsen busy, and over the years he gradually emerged as Mundy's right hand. Mundy appreciated the younger man's technical skills, and the engineer found himself consulted on most important matters. Olsen dealt often with A. Stanley Mundy, Inc., which frequently won Middlesex construction bids as the water company's mains expanded, and Mundy and Bergen (and later Judge Speer) trusted Olsen's judgment in dealing with many of the system's supply and distribution problems. By the 1930s, Olsen's grasp of over-all company operations was second to none, and he was easily one of the most accomplished utility engineers in the state. By the 1930s, he was also the company's general manager.

The company hired other key personnel as well, and their jobs also reflected the growing complexity of the company. In 1939, for example, when the BPUC mandated that water companies retain trained chemists to monitor water quality, Mundy and Olsen found and hired George Devlin away from the state Department of Health. Whatever other problems the company faced during its postwar expansion, Devlin's testing and quality control efforts at Robinsons Branch always assured the potability and safety of the water. Given the thousands of people dependent on the company for drinking water, any contamination problem would have been a genuine calamity. Even with company finances strained, Devlin was able to wrangle the necessary resources to keep the water supply healthy; and, frequently on his own initiative, he experimented with some of the most advanced water testing procedures in the business.

Even junior employees found themselves involved in significant projects during these years. Henry T. (Ted) Grundmann joined the company in 1947 as a draftsman, and on his first day on the job he discovered a huge back-log of work left over from the war. Part of his new job was to maintain detailed maps of the water mains. The maps were vital: Olsen and others needed them to chart the expansion of the system and to assist with isolating sections of the service area in the event of an emergency. But during the war, it had been all the company could do to lay new mains, and record keeping got short shrift. It was a major task to bring the maps up to date, but essential if the company was to guarantee the long-term efficiency of the system. Grundmann (who learned fast and ultimately moved into engineering management) also recalled that construction costs, loosely estimated in his first years at the company, soon came under closer scrutiny. By 1948, Speer, Mundy, and Olsen were using more precise cost analyses in system planning as they tried to make every dollar count.

Like the young Ted Grundmann, Louis Plisko also found the pace hectic after the war. He started in meter repair in 1947 and subsequently moved into yard operations, where he too quickly appreciated the importance of better planning. As the number of customers climbed, he recalled, equipment breakdowns were potentially too disruptive to tolerate. These concerns virtually compelled the establishment of preventive maintenance and safety programs, in which Plisko eventually took a leading role. Adversity can breed efficiency, and company personnel contributed vitally to getting the most out of limited resources.

Office operations also evolved as the customer base expanded. Arline Rask, who also started in the company office in 1947, helped do most record keeping by hand, a task that became increasingly difficult as the system reached more consumers. Even so, office automation came slowly. Payrolls were still paid in cash, there was no accountant on staff to handle financial records, and even basic banking relationships were still quite informal. Most stock transfers and dividend disbursements, for example, still took place without the assistance of a regular banking agent. Clearly, the state of business operations invited major reform.

The appointment of a new secretary-treasurer was a major step in this direction. In 1948, Judge Speer persuaded Carolina M. Schneider to leave Public Service and accept a position at Middlesex Water Company. A native of Newark, Schneider was offered a scholarship at Columbia University upon graduation from high school in 1936. But as the oldest of five children, and with the nation still deep in the Great Depression, she declined the offer to attend Columbia; instead, she went to work as a secretary to help support her family. By 1943, Schneider was Speer's secretary at Public Service, Inc., where she came to respect the intelligence and energy of the seventy-four year-old judge. Flattered at his offer of the post at Middlesex Water, she did not accept immediately. While she had learned a great deal about the utilities business at Public Service, she had no legal or accounting background; the appointment would also make her the youngest Middlesex officer, and one of the first women officers of any substantial New Jersey corporation. Even with an offer of $5,000 per year and a company car, it was a lot to consider. At Speer's continued urging, however, she took the job.

Previous secretary-treasurers had not been especially visible, few of them having taken active roles in corporate life. Schneider's impact, however, was quick and significant. Operating with the support of Speer and Mundy, with whom she sometimes worked hundred-hour weeks, she overhauled accounts

payable and payroll operations, switching disbursements from cash to checks. She successfully urged Mundy to raise clerical salaries, found a bank to handle stock transfers and dividend payments, and worked to improve communications with stockholders. While it took considerably longer, she also helped persuade the directors to hire an accountant and a comptroller, and (even later) to retain a data processing firm to handle the payroll. Significantly, Schneider also took the first steps to establish a formal fringe benefits program. Sharing the costs with participating employees, she brought in Blue Cross

Carolina M. Schneider, company secretary-treasurer. Recruited by Judge Speer in 1948, Schneider was one of the first women to become an officer of a significant New Jersey corporation.

and Blue Shield health and hospitalization coverage. It was an immediate success, and laid the foundation for the modern company benefits package which, over the years, gradually offered group insurance, paid vacations, and an employee stock purchase plan. If times were difficult over the late 1940s and 1950s, Schneider's work clearly led to greater company efficiency and better morale.

Thus the work force at Middlesex Water diversified, with employees holding a range of more specific and highly skilled jobs. Hiring could still be a fairly informal business, with personal recommendations and family connections carrying considerable weight; but the need to acquire particular skills for the company's growing and increasingly complex operations made it necessary for Speer and Mundy to look for the best possible people. In large part, they found them, which said a great deal about the company's ability to look to the future, even in the face of the problems of the 1950s.

THE WATER COMPANY TOOK ITS first steps toward serious long-range planning in the late 1950s. After an especially serious low pressure incident in 1953, the Board of Public Utility Commissioners insisted that the company develop a comprehensive solution to its distribution and supply problems. There was really no other choice at this point, although the company eventually concluded that it could not undertake the necessary planning tasks alone. Consequently, in 1957, the directors gave a planning contract to the New York consulting engineer firm of Buck, Seifert and Jost.[39] The engineering company had dealt with similar water utility problems in the past, and its record inspired a needed degree of confidence at Middlesex. Personnel from the two companies got along well, and Carl Olsen was particularly pleased with the arrangements. He knew several Buck, Seifert and Jost engineers professionally and personally, and his contacts facilitated arrangements at Middlesex Water. As events developed, the relationship between the companies was long and productive.

Middlesex Water personnel had no difficulty in explaining the magnitude of the problems experienced with the distribution system. In response, the lengthy Buck, Seifert and Jost engineering report called for a major construction program. Indeed, it detailed an effort of sufficient scope to resolve immediate pressure and supply difficulties and to provide a capacity to deal with the continuing expansion of the consumer base. Central to the plan was the installation of a series of sixteen, twenty, and thirty-inch transmission mains; the construction of a new office and maintenance complex; the drilling of two new wells; and the construction of a large new standpipe. Initial capital requirements would be in excess of $1,310,000.

Actual construction began slowly during the mid-1950s, with the distribution mains and standpipe receiving priority. At forty-eight feet high and with a capacity of five million gallons, the standpipe was the largest the company had ever built. Situated on high ground in Edison Township, it served a dual purpose in helping maintain water "pressure in the system and providing a high volume flow during periods of maximum demand."[40] The new facility came on line early in 1958, and while it served much of its intended purpose, the system was still prone to periodic episodes of low pressure. The fact was that the Middlesex Company had virtually exhausted the ground and surface water resources then available to it, and keeping water in the mains now depended on the careful management of the water supplies already at hand. It was a perilous way to do business and, obviously, more work and a search for new sources of supply lay ahead.

More work, however, meant more money, and there was not a great deal to spare. While inflation stood at one of the lowest levels in history during the 1950s, key costs did continue to rise. The company granted sizable wage increases over the decade, and maintaining standard operations, as well as work on the new distribution mains and standpipe, were expensive propositions. At the same time, the expanding customer base did not generate revenues sufficient to complete the company's capital projects. Carl Olsen now estimated that some residential areas could take longer than fifteen years to repay the initial costs of connecting them to the system. The situation contributed to a cash-flow problem and lower than expected profits, and for the first time in decades, banks were reluctant to loan the company badly needed construction funds. Consequently, improvements to the system lagged and in late 1958, in an extraordinary action, the board of directors voted not to pay quarterly dividends. Speer felt compelled to explain the matter in a special letter to the stockholders, noting that the state of corporate finances had made certain painful "economies" necessary.[41] He was right, and he could have added that things were going to get worse for Middlesex Water before they got better.

At this point, Judge Speer considered that the company's fortunes had reached a critical juncture. The missed dividend, Speer held, was only indicative of a broader malaise. Until the company could arrange a comprehensive solution to its financial dilemma, it could not come to grips in any definitive way with its supply and other system problems. Certainly the program outlined by Buck, Seifert and Jost would never get fully off the drawing board without adequate funding. What the judge wanted was a financial plan that would address, once and for all, the long-term requirements of the distribution system.

In fact, by early 1958 he already had begun the process. For years, the judge had tried to avoid raising water rates, asking only for a slight increase in 1943 in order to facilitate service to war industries. Over 1957 and the spring of 1958, however, he allowed Mundy to pursue a filing for a major increase; and while the BPUC granted only part of it, the settlement promised to boost annual revenues an additional $194,500. It was a start, and Speer fully intended to ask for even higher rates the following year. In addition, he initiated a review of other means of financing capital projects, including the issue of new stocks and bonds. Plans called for the retirement of a substantial share of the company's old debt while at the same time raising $2,300,000 of new capital.[42] By the middle of 1959, plans were well under way to make the necessary applications to the Utility Commissioners, and talks had begun with companies interested in marketing Middlesex Water commercial paper. Speer, at 90 years old, was still very much at the helm.

Having set the new financial wheels in motion, however, the Middlesex president never saw his plans bear fruit. He died on July 8, 1959 after a ten-day illness, only months before the new stock and other fiscal arrangements began to yield tangible results. In fact, the pieces started to come together within the year. Over

131

fall and winter, Middlesex Water was able to place new bonds on the market, prepare a new stock issue, declare a three-for-one split of existing stock shares, begin paying off outstanding indebtedness, and put more money into planning and system improvements.[43] Speer had loved his work, and the effort to improve the company's fiscal outlook was testimony to the fact that, even near the end, the judge had never lost his touch.

Speer's death was a blow to his wide circle of friends and professional associates. The judge was still a popular public speaker, and he was recognized particularly for his advocacy of continuing education for lawyers. His civic contributions brought accolades from colleagues in industry, the law, and philanthropy. He looked constantly for new pursuits. He was a noted hiker of the rugged trails of northwestern New Jersey, which he proclaimed "one of the most beautiful parts of the country." Late in life, he developed a keen interest in banking, noting, on his ninetieth birthday, that he was "immersed" in it. He never thought seriously of retirement and told one reporter that he was "not an early to bed person."[44] Thus, while at an advanced age, and sick for over a week, his energy and influence had been such that news of his death still caught people by surprise.

No one was more stunned than Ambrose Mundy. Family members later recalled his shocked reaction when he learned of the judge's death. The men had worked closely for years, and both were devoting particular effort to resolving the company's recent fiscal problems. The long-time superintendent, quickly promoted as the company's third president, inherited not only Speer's responsibilities, but also all of the challenges confronting the distribution system. Fortunately, Mundy needed no real transition period as he assumed his new office. He already knew the job and he was committed to the agreed upon financial plans and system improvements. Consequently, Middlesex employees saw little immediate change in routine as Mundy took over, save only the fact that board meetings now convened in the Woodbridge offices (Speer generally had met with the directors at his bank office in

Elizabeth). What no one could have predicted, however, was that company routine was on the eve of dramatic change, triggered by a series of events that threatened the viability of the company as nothing had before.

CHAPTER
6

The 1960s: Drought, Reconstruction, and Recovery

AMBROSE MUNDY'S PRESIDENCY began in the middle of a growing statewide concern over water resources and planning policies. The explosion of population growth and economic development that characterized the postwar generation was hardly confined to Middlesex County. It was a national issue, and New Jersey, with its large urban and industrial regions, was among the states most affected. Water resources across the Garden State were coming under considerable pressure, especially in the areas of heaviest growth. There were more residential, business, and municipal consumers than ever before, and their rates of consumption rose steadily. Water use was climbing to such an extent that some commentators warned of a "binge" that threatened to "dry up" the country. Over the late 1950s and early 1960s, predictions of future water requirements were alarming and ran far beyond estimates of anticipated supplies. One study concluded that northern New Jersey—including industrial Essex, Union, Middlesex, Hudson, Passaic, and Bergen Counties—were using about 420 million gallons per day, while ground and surface water sources could safely yield "only 415 million gallons." Other studies warned that worse was yet to come, and that during the 1960s there would be a real possibility of conflict between industry and

the public over available water supplies.[1] The issue received careful and regular attention from the media, and never before in state
history had water resources been such a compelling public issue.

    Several years of unusually dry weather further complicat-
ed the situation. By the early 1960s, rainfall in the American
northeast had
been substan-
tially below
normal for sev-
eral years; the
only better than
average years
had been 1958
and 1960, but
these afforded
only temporary
r e s p i t e s .
Periodically,
surface and
ground water
supplies fell to
particularly low
levels, and
heavily devel-

Company dinner, 1961.

oped New Jersey felt the pressure keenly. Governor Robert B.
Meyner warned that "the shortage of water in New Jersey repre-
sents, in my judgment, the gravest threat to the future of this state.
Every expert and authority on the subject agrees," he continued,
"that we stand at the threshold of a crisis in water supply which is
as serious as anything which has ever confronted the economic life
and welfare of the residents of the state."[2] A less ambiguous
warning would have been difficult to imagine.

    While virtually everyone recognized the problem, there
was no consensus on how to deal with the matter. By the early
1960s, New Jersey had 156 water systems, including 63 municipal

water works, 93 private companies, and the state-owned Delaware and Raritan Canal, which sold raw water to other water systems. With the exception of the canal, all of these systems had to consider local interests in their planning, and the needs and circumstances of individual companies or public systems could vary appreciably. Studies aimed at reconciling differences yielded little. Any number of government, civic, industry, and labor reports endorsed the need for comprehensive long-range planning, and some of these suggested means of facilitating cooperation among or the consolidation of systems. In the end, however, agreement on specifics proved illusive. The most ambitious look at the issue came in 1955, when a special Legislative Commission on Water Supply retained the consulting firm of Tippetts Abbett McCarthy Stratton, Engineers (TAMS). The firm was to prepare a plan for the development and coordination of all New Jersey water resources. But the so-called TAMS Report, while offering a wealth of information on water supplies and use patterns, could identify no single approach to over-all water policy. Suggestions for the formation of some sort of umbrella state water resources control agency, perhaps akin to the independent authorities that ran the state's toll highways, received considerable discussion but ultimately came to nothing. The New Jersey Water Supply Law of 1958 was concerned only with the projected Spruce Run and Round Valley Reservoirs, and offered nothing in the way of a state water policy.[3]

In the meantime, it was difficult for state or local authorities to address water-related issues quickly. It could take years of planning and litigation before the state could acquire reservoir sites. Local residents, real estate developers, water companies, anyone with an interest in a tract under consideration, was likely to become involved in the process. And when the state finally bought land for a reservoir, it could take years to actually build it. Moreover, the public, so concerned with adequate water service, was loath to finance it. In 1955, for example, the TAMS Report led to a referendum for an issue of $100 million in state bonds to support reservoir development; but the public was leery of the cost, and on election day the measure failed badly at the polls. Even an especially serious drought episode in the summer of 1957 failed to loosen the public purse strings.

Interior view of company headquarters, Woodbridge, 1960s. Customers could pay their water bills at the old bank teller window.

That same year, the state purchased the site for the planned Round Valley Reservoir in Hunterdon County, but, recalling 1955, the legislature did not dare ask for a new referendum to finance construction costs. (In 1958, the public did approve $45,850,000 in bonds, but only after the state mounted a carefully orchestrated campaign to generate public support for the measure.)[4] In effect, the popular reticence to finance state water projects was a reflection of the local resentments against water rate increases. While everyone needed water, very few were actually willing to pay for it.

Nevertheless, consumer expectations were high. People saw clearly the importance of water for their homes, jobs, health, and recreation; and with or without state or regional water policies, the public wanted water. Moreover, they wanted it reliably and they wanted it cheaply. What the public did not want was excuses, no matter how reasonable, in the event of service failures. Patience has seldom been an attribute of the American public, particularly on issues of vital importance, and by the late 1950s and early 1960s, water was a volatile subject. For water companies, even good intentions were no defense against criticism. A company with a long-range plan to strengthen its system still had to deal with consumer ire over immediate service difficulties. Any service interruption or perceived inconvenience was likely to result in popular protest; and under the circumstances, protest stood a good chance of attracting more media and political attention than ever before. A worst-case scenario, of course, would be a major service failure in the full glare of the media, which in turn provoked a public outcry with a political reaction to match. Unfortunately, this is exactly what happened to the Middlesex Water Company.

THE TROUBLE DEVELOPED IN the summer of 1960. For the past several years the weather had been dry, with rain fall sparse for long periods. While 1960 had seen more rain, water reserves were still low; and in any case, late June of that year had been dry and particularly hot. The heat wave had sent water use soaring throughout the Middlesex Company's service area. Among residential customers, lawn sprinklers and backyard swimming pools had drawn uncounted gallons from the system; industrial air conditioning had done the same. Steadily, the heavier than normal use began to drain the system; instead of providing the normal 20 million gallons of water per day, the mains were supplying roughly double that amount. The worst problem centered around the large and relatively new Grandview Avenue standpipe in Edison Township. The standpipe, forty-eight feet high, had a normal water level of some thirty-five feet, and on Sunday, June 26, the water level began to drop. The small weekend crew failed to notice the worsening situation and, incredibly, the matter also went unchecked through Monday, June 27. By 9:00 P.M. on Monday night the huge standpipe was empty. Had anyone seen the problem, normal procedure would have called for increased pumping from South Plainfield or Robinsons Branch in order to maintain pressure and to keep water in the mains. But no one noticed anything amiss until some 35,000 residents in Woodbridge, Edison, Metuchen, and Carteret found themselves either with no water at all or with only a trickle. There was too little water in the mains even to assure fire protection. The situation was truly dangerous.[5]

Unfortunately, the company reacted slowly to the developing debacle. It was late on the evening of June 27 that residents noticed either the falling water pressure or the fact that their taps had run dry. By then, very few Middlesex employees were still on the job. Working late, Carolina Schneider began receiving calls from irate and perplexed customers, and it was only after she contacted Mundy and Olsen that the company became aware of the gravity of the situation.[6] By then, it was too late to do much of anything, and Carl Olsen was never able to find out why the crews on duty failed to start emergency pumping to counteract the falling pressure. In any event, the local governments reacted to the crisis before they heard from company officials. The mayors and other municipal leaders quickly initiated measures to curtail water use in an effort to restore pressure to the mains. The mayor of South Plainfield, his town relatively unaffected by the turn of events, asked residents to conserve anyway in order to help the rest of the system recover.

Howls of protest from businesses and residents of all of the affected towns soon became a public issue. The distress was pervasive, and over a hundred complaints quickly reached the BPUC demanding action. The Utility Commissioners convened hearings on June 30, during which representatives of the towns and local industry amply expressed their indignation at the water shortage itself and at what they saw as an inadequate company response. Belabored from all sides, Mundy and Olsen pointed out that improvements to the system were in the works. They spoke of the new thirty-inch distribution main to serve Carteret and Woodbridge, another standpipe, and a booster pumping station, and emphasized that they expected all of these new facilities to be operational by the end of the year. The Utility Commissioners, however, were unsatisfied. They concluded that the company had mishandled the events of June 26 and 27, charging dereliction in failing to recognize the developing emergency, in not promptly notifying public officials, and in having insufficient "personnel or communication facilities available to customers in the event of an emergency situation." Even more damning, the BPUC considered that Middlesex had acted too slowly on the original recommendations of Buck, Seifert and Jost. Consequently, there would be no waiting for the company to correct the situation at its own pace; instead, the Commissioners would impose a schedule.

The BPUC orders mandated a series of emergency measures designed to alleviate the immediate crisis. Significantly, within a week the Middlesex Company had to construct an emergency connection with the Elizabethtown Water Company in order to assure an adequate supply. Simultaneously, Middlesex had to rush work on the new standpipe, booster station, and distribution mains, and make assurances that personnel were in place to prevent another drop in water pressure. The BPUC also insisted on receiving daily reports on the status of the system.

To the extent that they could, company officials continued to explain publicly the steps they were taking to alleviate the immediate crisis. Simultaneously, they stressed the need for long-term solutions to the water problem. In the meantime, as ordered, Mundy concluded a contract with Elizabethtown to assure adequate supplies. It was a shot-gun marriage; Middlesex agreed to purchase two million gallons per day for thirty years at a price of about $264 per day. Later, some customers argued that the established price was too high, but at the time Mundy was in no position to haggle. In any event, the water was flowing within days, and an emergency booster pump was in operation at Menlo Park within a week. By July 1, most local officials conceded that service generally was back to normal, although residents in the affected towns were urged to keep water use to a minimum over the Fourth of July weekend.[7]

The most embarrassing and potentially dangerous crisis in company history had passed. The affair had received wide regional press coverage, and it is no exaggeration to term the episode a public relations disaster. As a result, Middlesex Water personnel understood that virtually all aspects of company performance would receive the Utility Commissioners' particular scrutiny, and that regional consumers were going to be especially touchy about the quality of service. The entire business had provided a stormy opening for the presidency of Ambrose Mundy and, in fact, a grim preview of the rest of the decade.

THE DECADE OF THE 1960s WAS ONE OF the most crucial in the company's history. The water crisis of June 1960 was only indicative of the challenges facing the corporation, and the outlook, while not exclusively bleak, had a discouraging caste. Certainly morale was low among some employees, and who could blame them? Many remembered when the Middlesex Water Company was a major water wholesaler; now they saw Carl Olsen quoted in the press to the effect that Middlesex would probably always be dependent on other companies for water supplies.[8] It was the truth at the time, but it was hardly a comment calculated to inspire confidence. Moreover, as events soon demonstrated, company fortunes would ebb and flow as a range of successive difficulties appeared with bewildering regularity.

For the moment, however, matters seemed to improve somewhat as the fall-out from the summer of 1960 dissipated. Ironically, the Board of Public Utility Commissioners, so critical of Middlesex Water operations in June, was helpful in this regard and proved something of an ally in the months ahead. Once satisfied that the company was making a good faith effort to improve service, the Commissioners acted to facilitate matters. Later in 1960, the Board allowed the company to modify the schedule for the installation of the new transmission mains; and, in the face of strenuous objections by local property owners, it sustained a Middlesex effort to build another large standpipe on the

Grandview Avenue site in Edison. Over the next several years, the Commissioners also allowed rate increases aimed at supporting system improvements and long-range planning. None of this is to say that relations were completely cordial with the BPUC. The regulators never granted the full amount of requested rate increases; and in early 1961, in a dispute over the financing of service to a new housing development, the company and the Board still ended up in court.[9] But there was little question that the BPUC was genuinely interested in helping assure reliable water service in Middlesex County. That, at least, was a positive sign, even if the company and the Board failed to see eye-to-eye on every issue.

Slowly, the Middlesex Water Company restored the integrity of the distribution system. The additional standpipe was a major addition. Built adjacent to the already existing 5,000,000 gallon facility, the new standpipe had a capacity of 2,000,000 gallons, stood 82 feet high, and had a diameter of 65 feet. It was intended to assure adequate water pressure and to supply separate storage for a designated "high service area," a locale earlier prone to low pressure and water shortages. It consisted of some 880 acres of high ground—elevations were between 140 and 240 feet—with a projected residential population of 13,000. The pair of standpipes, which Mundy had painted light blue at the request of residents, dominated the hill crest on Grandview Avenue; motorists on the New Jersey Turnpike could see them from miles away. Ultimately, these steel reservoirs did a great deal to alleviate the area's persistent service problems. (We should note that, technically, a "reservoir" is a storage facility with a diameter greater than the height; a "standpipe" has a height greater than the diameter. Thus the new facility actually was a standpipe, while the earlier structure on Grandview Avenue was, by industry definition, a reservoir.)

Other measures also played important roles in restoring confidence in the system. The new transmission mains in South Plainfield and Woodbridge-Carteret were critical in this regard, and, fortunately, the volume of reported service problems

143

decreased substantially. These improvements clearly helped improve the public image of the company and reassured local officials who remembered the problems of the recent past all too well.

Important as they were, however, these steps were only stop-gaps. They improved matters while the company sought a more comprehensive remedy to its supply problems; they even kept Middlesex Water modestly profitable in the short run. Over the early 1960s, common stock prices hovered around $35 per share, and corporate revenues netted about $3 per share. Although, earnings had been higher in the past, this was still a respectable performance under difficult circumstances. In fact, given the recent publicity accorded company operations, its financial performance attracted regular press coverage.[10] But the system remained fragile, and Ambrose Mundy (and for that matter, virtually everyone who knew the water business) was fully aware that Middlesex Water now risked eventual failure unless it found a reliable and affordable new source of new water supply.

By early 1962, Mundy was devoting a great deal of his time to the supply issue. He had in mind, however, considerably more than new sources of water. Now eighty-six years old, Mundy had worked for the company for five decades, and he could remember when, as a young man, he had supervised the installation of some of the equipment still in service at South Plainfield and Robinsons Branch. And unlike the company president, who still ran the company energetically, some of the old facilities were wearing out. The aging steam pumps at the Park Avenue Station were relatively expensive to run, which rendered the station itself

Nixon Eborn, 1963.

144

increasingly inefficient. Robinsons Branch, which silted up almost continuously, was no longer large enough and was expensive to maintain. Thus, what Mundy wanted was a capital program that included a modern, large capacity water treatment plant, pumping stations, transmission mains, and necessary supporting facilities to match. That is, he wanted to end the company's supply and distribution problems once and for all, and to end its dependence on Elizabethtown Water or anyone else. Improvements to this point had merely bought valuable time to plan for future requirements. In the meantime, it was essential that the company avoid any new crisis.

Like Judge Speer before him, Ambrose Mundy did not live to see his plans become operational. He died of a heart attack on May 31, 1962, after a presidency of under two years. He had been a company institution, part of its collective memory stretch-

Night view of company facilities at Robinsons Branch, 1960.

ing back to the days of Frank Bergen. Mundy had run Middlesex Water tightly but never imperiously; he could seem forbidding but quickly revealed an underlying sense of humor and sympathy for others. He was decisive but could, and did, admit mistakes. He was quite literally a father figure to several employees whom he hired as young men, and who stayed with the company for decades themselves. Perhaps that was testament enough for any man.

TO THE SURPRISE OF NO ONE, CARL OLSEN, so long the reliable right arm of Ambrose Mundy, became the next president. An engineer and executive who knew the company intimately, Olsen's election to the presidency assured directors, employees, customers, and regulators of continuity in Middlesex Water's

Carl J. Olsen, fourth president of the Middlesex Water Company, and Andy Dubiel.

effort to improve the system. Unfortunately, neither Carl Olsen nor anyone else was in a position to assure the success of those efforts; for it was his hard luck to take over as one of the worst droughts in memory began to intensify. It would be Olsen's job to see the company through a truly perilous time.

The drought of the 1960s was extraordinary; in fact, it was one of the worst in American history. It struck hard at the entire Northeast, driving state after state to implement emergency conservation measures and to hurriedly adopt plans to construct new water storage and treatment facilities. New Jersey had seen droughts before, and severe ones at that. A long period of spotty rains between 1904 and 1917 had parched the state, and so had a dry spell that lasted on and off from 1929 to 1932. But the situation in the early sixties was unparalleled. Rainfall, as noted earlier, generally had been below normal since 1955, but after 1960 things got much worse. By 1965, northern New Jersey, which in a normal year expected almost 43 inches of rain fall, was receiving only slightly more than 26 inches. Many reservoirs had fallen to 50 percent of capacity, and a newspaper photograph of the "parched bottom" of Robinsons Branch only illustrated a condition typical across much of the state. The federal Department of the Interior weighed in with equally dismal news: Between 1961 and 1965, the department personnel reported that ground water tables had fallen to the lowest levels "ever measured" at the 85 water recording stations scattered around the state.[11] On June 12, 1965, faced with the very real possibility of economic and social disruption, Governor Richard J. Hughes declared a water emergency. His decree severely restricted water use in northern New Jersey in an effort to reserve supplies for the most essential industrial, residential, and governmental purposes. Two months later, President Lyndon Baines Johnson officially designated large parts of New Jersey, New York, and Pennsylvania as Federal Disaster Areas.[12]

As serious as it was, the drought was never uniform in its impact. Some water companies, with access to reserve supplies and with modern treatment and distribution facilities, managed to get through even the toughest years without imposing major inconveniences on their customers. The Hackensack Water Company, having poured its resources into capital development, including reservoir construction, for over a decade, had enough water to keep its mains full. So did Elizabethtown Water, which, in addition to its own extensive supplies, could draw up to ten million gallons per day from the Delaware and Raritan Canal; it also was negotiating an arrangement with the state to tap the new Round Valley Reservoir in western New Jersey.[13] But these were exceptions; most water utilities, private or municipal, had a hard time of it. Robert A. Roe, Commissioner of Conservation and Economic Development, noted this feast or famine situation even as he conferred with Governor Hughes on emergency planning measures. "During dry periods," he told the press, "New Jersey often finds itself in the position of having a drought in one area and plentiful water in another area, but no means of getting the water to where it is needed."[14]

Certainly the Middlesex Water Company had a hard time of it. Middlesex County was not part of the designated federal disaster area, but Commissioner Roe considered it a danger zone in his planning at the state level. This was no news to Olsen, who knew only too well how the low rainfall had contributed to the company's supply difficulties. Ground water levels were down, although flow from the wells in South Plainfield, reinforced by several newer wells in Edison and Woodbridge, remained fairly strong. But there was trouble at Robinsons Branch. Water level in the reservoir fell sharply, and by mid-1966, some five years into the worst of the drought, the new chief engineer Edward Bastian explained to the local press that conditions at the reservoir had become "extreme." The water was over ten feet below the spillway of the dam, and pumping enough water to maintain water pressure in the system had become a problem. Bastian emphasized that a new ban on lawn sprinkling, car washing, and filling swimming pools was intended to help keep pressure up and avoid interruptions of essential water service. "We do need rain," he noted in a considerable understatement.[15]

Bastian had been candid but calm with the press. What he could not reveal, however, was the frantic pace of behind-the-

Robinsons Branch Reservoir during the 1960s drought.

scenes activity to keep water in the mains and the growing sense of desperation among many of the employees. At one point, the water at Robinsons Branch actually dropped too low to allow normal pumping into the transmission lines; only the ingenuity of the crews on the spot allowed a jerry-rigged system of pumps to keep the water flowing until the reservoir rose a few vital feet. It was a close call. Carl Olsen was so alarmed that on several occasions he and Ted Grundmann actually patrolled residential neighborhoods looking for illegal water use. Nocturnal lawn watering, it seems, was all too persistent in several towns. The drought was a critical concern to everyone at the company, some of whom feared lay-offs if matters failed to improve. There never were lay-offs, but perhaps for the first time veteran employees now asked whether Middlesex Water could survive as an independent firm. Speculation suggested a consolidation with Elizabethtown, or per-haps some form of government ownership. All of this, of course, was nothing more than speculation; but it was understandable given the circumstances of the company, and it was clear evidence of the gravity of the situation.

WHILE THE COMPANY FOUGHT THE DROUGHT, it also fought for its future. Before his death, Ambrose Mundy had done a great deal to map out a comprehensive approach to system improvements; and within a year of assuming the presidency, Carl Olsen, who had worked so closely with Mundy, was looking for the means to get the plans off of the drawing boards. In this, Olsen soon had the assistance of Edward Bastian, who joined the Middlesex Company as chief engineer in 1963. Bastian knew company operations well. Earlier, he had been with Buck, Seifert and Jost, and had worked on the planning studies for Middlesex Water during the 1950s. Now he was ready to help Olsen deal with the acquisition of a reliable water supply.

Specifically, Olsen was interested in a long-term arrange-ment with the state to purchase water from the Delaware and Raritan Canal. The company would then build a new pumping station as well as a state-of-the-art treatment plant. If all went well, the new facilities would provide adequate service for the entire region and allow the company to close the old steam pump-ing station at South Plainfield and phase out the veteran Robinsons Branch Reservoir. Its water supply would stand in reserve for extreme emergencies. As it had previously, Middlesex would con-tinue to work with Buck, Seifert and Jost in over-all planning and facilities design. Estimates placed the cost of the venture as high as $10 or $11 million, which was by far the most ambitious undertaking in company history. But Middlesex Water had no real choice; the alternative to modernization was probable failure.

The first major step came in 1963, when the company submitted an application to the State Water Policy and Supply Council (a division of the Department of Conservation and Economic Development) to draw water from the Delaware and Raritan Canal. There was plenty of water available in the canal, and any temporary shortage could be made good by pumping from the Raritan River itself. The canal was a New Jersey landmark; built before the Civil War, for decades it carried freight and passenger traffic across the central part of the state. Abandoned in 1934, the state acquired the waterway as a source of industrial and potable water and placed it under the governance of an independent commission.[16] The Middlesex Company made its application on August 6, expecting that the matter would receive a routine approval. It did not. Instead, the matter took over a year, and served to illustrate how slowly the wheels of water policy could turn, even in the midst of serious drought conditions.

The Supply Council, which was favorably disposed to the Middlesex Company request, had at least two other matters to consider before approving the application. First, the city of New Brunswick, which also had an interest in the canal as a potential water supply, objected to the Middlesex request. The company had tangled with the city over water rights over a generation earlier. This incident occurred during the effort to develop the Millstone-Raritan project with Elizabethtown Water, and New Brunswick had lost that fight. This time, all the city could do was to initiate another delaying action, as the Supply Council eventually found for the company. There remained, however, the matter of the Elizabethtown Water Company. Elizabethtown, now a major supplier of Middlesex Water, held a temporary grant to draw up to 10 million gallons per day from the canal, and could not afford to give up this supply until replacement water became available from the new Round Valley Reservoir. The state, however, was still deciding on a price for Round Valley water, and negotiations dragged on well into 1964. Consequently, after an initial ruling for the Middlesex Company in July, final approval of the application came only in December of 1964.

It was worth the wait. The state grant allowed Middlesex to pump 20 million gallons per day from the canal until December of 1969 (by which time Elizabethtown's rights to canal water would have lapsed), after which it could take 10 million gallons per day for another 20 years.[17] For the first time in decades, the Middlesex Water Company had an adequate and reliable source of water supply.

Aerial view of the Raritan River, showing New Brunswick (left), Piscataway (upper right), and Highland Park (lower right). The Delaware & Raritan Canal runs parallel to the river at left. In order to develop the canal as a source of supply, the company would build a new pumping station on the left bank of the river, just above the bridge connecting New Brunswick to Highland Park. A main laid under the river bed upstream from the bridge carried the water to the new treatment plant in Edison.

With this, what was now termed the "D&R Project" (for Delaware and Raritan) began to move in earnest. The first phase was the construction of a raw water intake and pumping station near the New Brunswick lock (Lock 13) on the canal, behind the offices of Johnson & Johnson, Inc. Once again, the city of New Brunswick voiced concerns, this time objecting that the pumping station would impede improvements to near-by Route 18. But Olsen negotiated a satisfactory compromise on the site, and Vanguard Construction Company, of New York, had the project under way in early 1967. Upon completion, the building was roughly 20 by 30 feet with an exterior styled to compliment the colonial architecture of the nearby J&J structures. The fully automated pumping station was capable of sending 40 million gallons per day through a 54-inch raw water supply main to a new treatment plant to be located in Edison.[18]

A. Stanley Mundy, Inc., so long a mainstay of Middlesex Water construction efforts, built the mile-long raw water main. The huge line, laid under the bed of the Raritan River, connected the pumping station in New Brunswick with the site of the new water treatment plant in Edison. It was installed over the course of several months, its progress charted daily by motorists along Route 18 and by hundreds of Johnson & Johnson employees and Rutgers University students whose offices and dormitories overlooked the river. Later, A. Stanley Mundy also built a 48-inch transmission main of some 6.5 miles to connect the new treatment plant with the existing distribution network.

Construction also began on the new Delaware & Raritan Water Treatment Plant in 1967. The site was located at the end of Fairview Avenue in Edison, on property that was formerly part of the Army's Camp Kilmer. The company had worked closely with the township council in acquiring the necessary property, and the process included vacating seven streets. Events went smoothly, however, as Edison officials readily conceded the benefits of a reliable water supply. They also appreciated the considerable construction permit fees the company paid into the municipal treasury, as well as the prospect of virtually perpetual gross receipts taxes.[19]

The plans called for an impressive modern automated treatment facility, built in a park-like setting and centered around a handsome and spacious control building. The main structure would house the plant offices, a control room capable of directing all operations, a fully equipped laboratory, chemical feed and storage facilities, employee rooms, flash mixer units, and a pump room with three filtered water pumps and switchgear. Outside the control building, designs included coagulation, reclaiming and decanting basins, eight rapid sand filtration units, and a wash water standpipe. The entire facility was designed to treat 20 million gallons per day for delivery into the distribution system, more than enough to service the growing customer base.[20] It would also be enough to free Middlesex Water from dependence on purchased supplies.

As planning and construction acivities became ever more complex, the company added another key management position. In 1965, Olsen hired Ernest (Ernie) Gere as controller to monitor the firm's increasingly complicated budget. Gere stayed until 1970, by which time the D&R Project was well along, and then left for another job in Texas. Yet he had helped the company get a firm grip on its expenditures during a crucial period, and after a call from Olsen in 1972, he agreed to come back. (In 1989, Gere became the company's senior vice president.)

Treatment plant construction relied on the efforts of five contractors, each bringing a different specialty to the job. Koppers Company, Inc., constructed buildings and other structures; the Roberts Filter Manufacturing Company supplied filter, chemical, and flocculating equipment; and the Fisher Tank Company built the standpipe. Control room instrumentation was the responsibility of American Chain & Cable Company, while Molnar Electrical Contractors handled all wiring and electrical equipment. Buck, Seifert and Jost, central to the design effort from the beginning, helped coordinate over-all construction operations. The entire venture spoke volumes on how sophisticated the engineering and technical aspects of the water business had become since Frank Bergen had, in effect, served as his own general contractor.

THE BUSINESS WAS ALSO MUCH more expensive and the company devoted considerable time and energy to raising money for the D&R Project and normal operations. By 1968, D&R construction alone had cost $5.7 million, and the bills kept coming. The costs of financing, however, were heavy. Interest on bank loans and bonds, as well as stock dividend payments, totaled over $1,150,000 annually by 1969, and rising interest rates were taking the figure higher. In fact, rising interest charges became a major consideration in the calculation of company requests for rate increases. Even after the BPUC granted an increase of 15 percent in 1967, Olsen knew that the costs of the D&R Project, as well as other operating expenses, had become a tremendous burden—a challenge the company simply could not face indefinitely without some long-range fiscal assurances.

Realistically, the Middlesex president considered the financial alternatives. While his goal was an independent and prosperous Middlesex Water Company, circumstances compelled Olsen to ponder various means of cooperation with other water companies, and even the possibility of merging with a stronger utility. Certainly he had grounds for pessimism: the bankers, as Ernie Gere recalled, told him bluntly that the Middlesex Company "could not meet debt and interest obligations out of current revenues."[21] Yet, given the effort expended on the D&R Project, Olsen was reluctant to sacrifice company autonomy. There had to be an alternative.

The solution came in 1969. Pressed by mounting expenditures, Middlesex again felt constrained to seek higher rates. The chief reason, Olsen pointed out, was "the high interest costs which we must pay the banks." In February of 1969, he noted, banks were charging the company 7 percent; but as the weeks went by, rates climbed steadily toward 10 percent. The higher interest put company financial planning at risk, and he urged everyone at the company to reduce costs "whenever and wherever we can."[22] Once more, Middlesex Water filed a request to increase its rates with the PUC. This time, however, the request did not follow the usual pattern.

Construction of the Delaware & Raritan Treatment Plant, Edison, 1967. Upon opening, the plant was renamed the Carl J. Olsen Treatment Plant.

The 1969 rate increase followed a series of protracted and important discussions with the Utility Commissioners. Carefully, Olsen, other company officials, and a series of consultants explained the intricacies of financing the D&R Project. Buck, Seifert and Jost again supplied considerable assistance, a fact which further cemented the already strong professional and personal ties between George Buck, Carl Olsen, William Seifert, Carolina Schneider, and other Middlesex personnel. At the same time, new personalities also played a role in events. During the hearings, a young Buck, Seifert and Jost engineer, J. Richard Tompkins, presented testimony on behalf of the company's request. It was his first such appearance—and the company's first real chance to have a look at the man who, a decade later, would come back as its fifth president. Finally, all of the effort paid off:

156

the commissioners agreed that the new treatment plant was the only way to guarantee the region an adequate water supply, and that the company would need revenues sufficient to maintain the construction effort.

The commissioners' decision went further, however. Significantly, they allowed the company a "forward look" in its new rates. That is, the company could set rates to meet the anticipated construction expenses of the D&R Project rather than simply keeping pace with rising operating costs. It was a precedent-setting decision. The PUC never had allowed such a rate calculation in the past, and the consequent new revenues were crucial in obtaining new bank financing and allowing construction to proceed.[23]

It did proceed. Its credit improved by the rate case, Middlesex was able to negotiate a series of loans worth some $10.5 million with Morgan Guarantee Trust Company in New York and a consortium of New Jersey banks. Corporate profits, however, could never cover a loan that large; in fact, planning estimates suggested that by 1972 profits alone would pay for only some 15 percent of D&R construction. The balance would have to come from the proceeds of stock and bond sales; and by 1969, the company had marketed $4.5 million in new bonds and a preferred stock issue of $1.5 million. The securities sold out quickly, a sure sign of investor confidence in the D&R Project and the long-term prospects of Middlesex Water.

Mindful of previous public relations difficulties, Olsen also had the company take its case for responsible financing directly to consumers. "Diplomacy" was a necessity, he insisted, as management tried to "plan for a stable and assured future" while appeasing customers who "feel that water should be free."[24] Significantly, the company made a concerted effort to inform the public of the Delaware and Raritan Project. Newspaper stories and advertisements explained what the new plant was intended to do and how much the company was investing in the new venture. Repeatedly, notices stressed "the vital importance of water" to regional communities and industries, and emphasized that rate increases were not only necessary but modest. With the same purposes in view, Middlesex Water also took a prominent part in local civic functions such as participating in local fairs and parades, and sending representatives to various municipal celebrations. The theme was always the same: water was crucial for prosperity, and the Middlesex Water Company was doing all it could to give the public the water it needed.[25] Never before had the company tried so hard to present a positive public image or to draw the attention of residents to the importance of investing in improved water service. And at least some of the message got through. "No one looks forward to the constant price-rise on every thing," one customer wrote, "but at least the Water Company has given us an explanation and one not hard to understand."[26]

In conjunction with this effort at public relations was a concerted attempt to improve customer services. All employees received periodic reminders that their conduct on the job helped determine what people thought of Middlesex Water. "Remember," one notice read, "To the Customer—YOU are the Company." A Customers' Service Department, planned in the late 1960s and actually established in 1970, now handled inquiries from consumers, and improved billing procedures and data processing made it easier for customers to arrange meter readings and service. There were even some letters of appreciation for jobs well done. When Leon Silakoski, Jim Brady, and Sammie Harrison found and quickly repaired a serious leak for one customer, he noted that all three "were friendly, courteous, and helpful in restoring my water supply with all due speed."[27] At first glance these seem small or routine matters. They were not. In aggregate, customer services, in all of their variety, were (and are) vital aspects of the business, points of contact with the consumers where courtesy and efficiency paid dividends in public satisfaction. It was impossible, of course, to make every customer happy or to satisfy every complaint; but it was equally true that the popular standing of the company had improved remarkably since the dark days of June 1960.

As the company focused on the D&R Project, normal operations maintained an active pace. They also reflected the growing complexity of the water business. In 1964, for instance, a flood in Woodbridge wrecked much of the billing equipment in the company's Main Street office. It was an inconvenience, but the event provided the opportunity to install an up-to-date automated billing and data processing system. A new Data Processing Department (better known as the "IBM Department") took on the enormous task of keeping track of customer records. By 1968, the department dealt annually with 157,873 residential bills, 2,149 industrial bills, 162,207 payments, 28,399 reminders, 10,466 suspension notices, and all meter records. This all happened through the hard work of a department of six employees under the supervision of Arline Rask, by then with the company for almost 20 years, and who had completed special training with IBM, Inc., on the operation of the new equipment.[28]

Other departments and individuals were just as active. George Devlin, journeying down from his post at Robinsons Branch, kept a regular check on the water quality in the Delaware and Raritan Canal; while at the Eborn Pumping Station in Carteret, the company installed a new emergency engine powered by liquid propane gas. James Baskerville and Joseph Baginski were the primary installers of the engine, the first of its kind for the company and designed to maintain service to Woodbridge and Carteret in the event of an electrical power failure.[29] In the shop yards, Louis Rask, the only full-time mechanic, recalled the emphasis on preventive maintenance to keep company vehicles safe and on the road. Policies were strict: No one cut corners on vehicle safety. In the field, Donald G. (Jerry) McCabe and Anthony (Tony) and Angelo Ferraro worked on the various planning and construction projects that kept the distribution system functioning and expanding. Indeed, the combined experience of the McCabe and Ferraro families at Middlesex Water totalled almost two hundred years. This list could go on, although it is clear enough from these few examples that "normal" operations now constituted a wide range of pursuits that kept virtually everyone at the company busy and contributing.

By late 1969, work on the D&R Project was well advanced. The pumping station, raw water, and transmission lines line were finished, and the treatment plant itself was in its final stages. At this point, company personnel worked on the site along with the contractors preparatory to actual start-up operations. It was an exciting time as Middlesex crews learned the fine points of the new equipment and how to keep the various components of the plant working as a unit. Larry Dubiel, whose father and brother had worked at Park Avenue and Robinsons Branch, was instrumental in establishing plant operations and maintenance procedures that became a hallmark for company efficiency and safety for decades.[30] Final work on D&R facilities was also long and difficult, and the plant crew ended up putting in considerable over-

Laying 24" water main near Woodbridge.

160

time hours on unpredictable schedules. The welfare of hundreds of thousands of consumers—not to mention the welfare of the Middlesex Water Company itself—depended on the new plant functioning as intended. This was no small thing, and Carl Olsen, Ed Bastian, and all others on the site took the last stages of preparation seriously indeed.

THE LONG YEARS OF PLANNING AND construction ended in December of 1969. At ten o'clock in the morning on Sunday, December 28, the new facilities came to life as operators started the pumps at the Raw Water Intake and Pumping Station in New Brunswick. Treatment processes began as soon as water reached the now formally-named Delaware and Raritan Canal Water Treatment Plant in Edison; and at 11:30 a.m. the following day, December 29, pure water flowed for the first time into the new transmission main and on into the system. Without any difficulty, the new pumps sent out water at a rate of 10 million gallons per day. The modern era of Middlesex Water Company operations had begun.

Briefly, the D&R Plant was a local phenomenon. Media coverage of the new complex was fairly extensive, and over the spring of 1970 the company held receptions and open houses for employees and regional political and industrial dignitaries. Even groups of school children came through the new facilities. In fact, the gleaming new equipment, the sophisticated control room, the handsome building and large standpipe made for an impressive tour.

While everyone connected with the D&R Project recognized the opening of the plant as a milestone in the company's history, the event was a particular triumph for Carl Olsen. By 1969, he had been with the company for over 40 years, through good times and bad. Olsen had brought the company through the drought and all of the immediate challenges it had presented; while at the same time he had carried on the program of system improvements initiated under Judge Speer and expanded and refined under Ambrose Mundy (whose children and grandchildren were Middlesex stockholders or directors, and who remembered with pride the contributions of Ambrose to what became the D&R Project). It was an accomplishment any utility executive would have envied, and several years later the board of directors formally recognized the fact. On August 29, 1973, they voted to rename the new plant the Carl J. Olsen Water Treatment Plant. And fittingly, it was Edward Bastian, by then vice president, and who had worked so closely with Olsen in bringing the D&R venture to completion, who officially notified employees of the board's action.[31]

All of this, however, was in the future. In the meantime, there was still work to do at the new treatment plant. In addition to monitoring all equipment and systems for early "bugs," laboratory personnel began the critical tasks of water quality analyses. Running the new laboratory was Water Treatment Superintendent Edward D. Mullen, formerly a chemist and assistant superintendent with the Hackensack Water Company. In January of 1970, Mullen and other laboratory personnel moved their operations to Edison from the old facilities at Robinsons Branch. The modern Delaware and Raritan lab was equipped to perform physical, chemical, bacteriological, and microscopical tests, and Mullen and his staff regularly tested some thirty-five water samples drawn weekly from every part of the distribution system. At all times, the company remained in compliance with the Potable Water Quality Standards of the New Jersey State Department of Health.[32] The extensive testing was fully necessary; years of industrial and residential development had made water pollution a regional concern, and company water purification efforts were an essential safeguard of public health.

As the new treatment plant became operational, however, another phase of the firm's history came to a close. Company plans had called for taking older facilities out of service when the D&R plant opened, and events unfolded accordingly. In fact, the process had begun already. Four years before, in 1966, the age of steam power at the company ended as the Park Avenue pumping station in South Plainfield was silenced, replaced by more efficient and smaller electric pumps. Soon after, the old station itself fell to the wreckers ball. Olsen, who years before had helped design the Park Avenue facility, watched the demolition in silence. Tompkins, who was with Olsen that day, remembered the veteran company president as being deeply affected as the venerable station came down.[33]

In 1970, it was the turn of Robinsons Branch. The reservoir, one of Frank Bergen's most ambitious capital projects, and a mainstay of the company's supply for three generations, went into reserve. Within the next decade, the deserted pumping, treatment, and maintenance facilities came down, and the old Corbin

Demolition of the old steam-powered Park Avenue pumping station, 1970.

Reservoir became part of the past. The Garden State Parkway, one of the busiest highways in the nation, now carries thousands of motorists across the water each day, the vast majority of them never knowing that the Robinsons Branch of the Rahway River was anything other than a picturesque lake.

CHAPTER
7

The Mature Utility:
The Middlesex Water Company in the Modern Era

WHEN IT OPENED, THE CARL J. OLSEN Water Treatment Plant was a state-of-the-art facility. Coupled with now adequate sources of water supply, the new treatment and pumping complex easily could handle the needs of the existing distribution system and service area. Yet those who designed and built the Olsen Plant had considerably more in mind than the present, or even the immediate future. Their concerns lay with the long-term needs of the company and the requirements of regional growth; and in fact, the original plant design had incorporated provisions for later expansion, fully anticipating that the system would have to keep pace with the increasing consumer base over the last quarter of the twentieth century. Yet only time could determine the success of a long-range plan, and the following decades would test how well the Middlesex Water Company had charted its course for the future.

THERE IS NO QUESTION THAT MIDDLESEX WATER began the 1970s with good marks from the public. Regional confidence in the company, already vastly improved over the late 1960s, remained high as the quality of service consistently met local residential and commercial needs. The new treatment complex remained something of a popular attraction, and the company ran newspaper advertisements offering tours of the plant through the mid-1970s. The Customer Service Department continued to help polish the company's image as well, although dealing with the public was not always easy. At one point, to cite one thankfully unusual example, a woman called to complain about her bill. It was too high, she said, because she was no longer buying hot water from Middlesex—she was using her own. Another customer argued that she should pay less because her husband had been dead for some months; however, the deceased husband, apparently uninformed of his demise, contacted the company the following day to resolve the matter.[1] A great deal of good will accrued from an arrangement with South Plainfield. In 1973, after years of negotiation with the township, the company agreed to sell and lease part of its Spring Lake property for use as a public park. The park became a heavily-used municipal facility without disrupting the operations of the company's Spring Lake well field.[2] Thus, as the company began operations in its modern era, relations with consumers were improving; and public relations, long a thorn in the company's side, now functioned smoothly.

Within the company, there was optimism about the future. The Olsen Plant had resolved some of the most pressing operational concerns, and fears of water shortages, pressure problems, and related system difficulties largely disappeared. For the first time in decades, company planning could proceed without these traditional bogeys looming in the background. Looking to the future, the company instituted a number of organizational changes, including some key personnel actions. These steps were intended to facilitate expanding service needs, and they reflected the growing importance of engineering to company operations. Less than a year after the Olsen Plant came on line, some familiar names received promotions. Edward Bastian, as noted earlier, became Vice President of Engineering and Operations, responsible for all engineering, water treatment, pumping, and distribution. Ted Grundmann, now a Middlesex veteran, was promoted to Manager

Laboratory personnel, Carl J. Olsen Treatment Plant. Left to right: Robert Petz, Joseph Ritter, Edward Mullin, Raymond Silakoski, and George Devlin.

of the Engineering Department, reporting to Bastian. A new Distribution Division, also under Bastian's supervision, consolidated all distribution system maintenance and construction responsibilities, with Jerry McCabe as Manager. Within the division, Tony Ferraro took over duties as Distribution Maintenance Superintendent, in charge of all system maintenance operations.[3] The new arrangements provided better operational control of the system as well as a more efficient means of allocating company resources. In effect, management structure was evolving to take better advantage of the new facilities and technology.

The reorganization also illustrated a concerted effort to make company operations as cost-effective as possible. In fact, Olsen put a premium on the matter, feeling that Middlesex Water could not afford to waste time or money. The new treatment plant

Aerial view of the completed Carl J. Olsen Treatment Plant.

and the continuing expansion of the system represented the largest
capital expenditure in company history; and while these improvements offered the company a promising future over the long run, it
did not follow automatically that Middlesex Water would have
plenty of money in the short term. Indeed, over the early 1970s,
revenue was in tight supply, a situation with several causes.
Significantly, there was an evolution of the customer base.
Gradually, as the population and development patterns changed in
Middlesex County, residential users steadily increased while
industrial and business customers cut back usage dramatically.
The process was not abrupt, but it seemed inexorable. The old
terra cotta works, for example, and the metal refining and finish-
ing companies, so long mainstays of Middlesex Water revenues,
were passing from the scene over the late 1960s and 1970s.
Worse, the new residential customers did not immediately gener-

ate enough revenue to offset the industrial declines. Olsen reminded all employees, as he had in the past, that it took considerable time—sometimes more than a decade—to repay the investment of adding a home to the distribution system. Finally, the BPUC once again was reluctant to allow the company timely rate increases. Together, these factors made it difficult to meet short-term expenses.

The company president took the situation seriously. At different times, he explained the gravity of the revenue problem to employees and shareholders, noting that it forced the company to borrow to maintain operations, thus further complicating its finances. Everyone, he reminded the entire company, had to be alert to cost savings wherever and whenever they could. In 1975, in a gesture impossible to misunderstand, he resorted to a drastic measure. In order to help alleviate what he termed "our deteriorating financial condition," Olsen announced a postponing of annual wage increases. He was confident, he assured employees, that the Public Utility Commissioners eventually would approve another rate increase, which would allow the company to grant the raises in pay. But for the moment, there was little else anyone could do in the face of "these difficult times."[4]

Olsen was as good as his word. The "difficult times" passed, and after a rate increase—the BPUC had to agree that the company's impressive capital program merited larger revenues—and the promised raises were forthcoming. Indeed, by 1976 most company economic indicators were positive. Plant value moved from under $44 million in 1975 to over $51 million by 1980; at the same time, average book value of Middlesex Water common stock avoided extremes, rising slowly from about $12 to almost $14. Net income rose, sometimes erratically, from $1.8 million in 1976 to over $2.1 million in 1980. Dividends reflected the steady improvement of the company's fiscal performance. Shareholders, who received about $.55 per share in 1976, were getting around $.90 in 1978 and $1.10 in 1980.[5] Thus company growth was gradual and incremental, if unspectacular, and was typical of a well-managed public utility. Investments in utilities companies rarely attracted speculators and seldom yielded large short-term capital gains; rather, utility stocks traditionally were better long-term investments. Such was the Middlesex Water Company over the late 1970s. It was a safe investment and returned a reliable income for shareholders willing to hold onto their stock, but no one got rich quickly. By the end of the decade, financial analysts considered it one of the best water company stocks in the state.[6]

This corporate stability was the legacy of Carl J. Olsen. It was under his leadership that the benefits of the planning and expenditures of the 1960s and early 1970s became evident. Looking back, he saw his efforts on behalf of the company as a "day-to-day grind" with no "outstanding" or startling events. Bringing the company safely into the last quarter of the twentieth century, as Olsen saw it, was an exercise in staying "on top of everything." By 1980, however, the veteran president saw his labors as essentially done. He was eighty, and he had been with Middlesex Water since 1926. Fifty-four years, Olsen concluded was enough. "I think when you are 80 years old it's time to hang up the gloves," he told friends as he announced his retirement.[7] It was the end of an era for the company. In succession, Olsen had known Bergen, Speer, and Mundy; he had seen the most desperate years of the Great Depression and had played a key role as Middlesex Water struggled through the post-war period. As a trained engineer, Olsen had brought a professional dimension to company operations, and over the years he had been instrumental in adding additional professional staff. He had led the Middlesex Water Company for eighteen years, and when he left on December 31, 1980, he was the first president of the company not to have died in office.

Olsen's retirement did not end his relationship with the company. He remained a member of the board of directors until 1983, at which point he moved to Scottsdale, Arizona. The board then named him a director emeritus. Olsen died at 84 years old on February 10, 1985; this was ten years to the day after the death of his wife, the former Mary Yost, also a Middlesex Water Company employee of many years.[8]

WITH THE RETIREMENT OF CARL OLSEN, the company directors faced the task of recruiting a new chief executive officer. The board knew of Olsen's departure well in advance, thus there was time to make a thorough search for his replacement. Fortunately, the job went smoothly, for there was a candidate readily available: in late 1980 the directors selected J. Richard Tompkins. The new president, only the company's fifth, took office on January 1, 1981. At 42 years old, Tompkins was considerably younger than the previous chief executives of the company, but he had compiled an impressive record in the water business, and he brought with him a wealth of experience. An engineering graduate of Villanova University, he had worked for Buck, Seifert & Jost, under the tutelage of George H. Buck. He was familiar with Middlesex Water operations since the early 1970s and had testified in all rate cases since 1969. Later, he joined Associated Utility Services, Inc., of Mount Laurel, New Jersey, a consulting firm in regulatory and management issues. As a consultant, Tompkins worked on various Middlesex planning and development projects for some 14 years, including rate case presentations before the Board of Public Utilities. In bringing Tompkins aboard, the directors got a man who knew the company and the water utility business.

Tompkins maintained the company's momentum, although he did so in the face of an immediate and serious challenge. Once again, rainfall had been scant in New Jersey, and the state faced another major drought. By late 1980, conditions across much of the state were as grim as they had been during the dry spell of the early 1960s. Yet because of the improvements to the Middlesex Water supply and distribution system over the 1970s, the drought of 1980 and 1981 proved a curious affair for the company. In fact, Middlesex customers never faced real water shortages. Nevertheless, as the crisis in other parts of the state deepened, the company fell under the state-wide emergency drought planning and reduced water use mandates. Caught in a developing regulatory web, the impact of the drought on Middlesex Water would be

J. Richard Tompkins, fifth president of the company.

pronounced, but not because of any lack of water. Rather, the company was unable to sell the bountiful supply of water it had.

For much of New Jersey, the situation was genuinely grave by the late summer of 1980. In August, rainfall was only 20 percent of normal, while at the same time the hot summer weather placed heavy demands on the water reserves of the northeastern part of the state. These conditions led steadily to a water crisis. Worse, there were few interconnections between the distribution systems of the parched northeast and water supplies in other parts of New Jersey (some of which were still ample). As the reservoirs dropped, various water supply agencies and experts warned Governor Brendan Byrne of impending disaster, and in response he declared a state of emergency in most of Morris, Hudson, Essex, Bergen, Somerset, Union, and Passaic Counties. Governor Byrne's order restricted nonessential water use for residential customers and asked commercial users to replace potable with non-potable water usage whenever possible. Two additional executive orders subsequently placed restrictions on municipal water use as well; but by late September, it was clear that conservation measures had failed to stem the depletion of the reservoirs. Therefore, the governor ordered water rationing in the most seriously affected northeastern communities. This was the most serious government involvement in a drought situation in state history.[9]

To this point, Middlesex Water customers faced no use restrictions. The company assured regional authorities of the adequacy of supplies, and explained to users that "farsighted planning and management action" of years ago had resulted in "ample" water reserves. A publication sent to all customers reported that Middlesex Water could draw plenty of water from its own wells, and that it had long-term purchase agreements in place with the state-owned Delaware and Raritan Canal and, more recently, the Round Valley-Spruce Run reservoir systems. In addition, the company was still buying water from Elizabethtown. In short, customers had little to worry about, as "the developed supplies" of Middlesex Water, the company concluded, had "a dependable capability well in excess of present requirements."[10]

The company could give these assurances even as the media reported the deepening crisis elsewhere in the state. And it was deepening. Despite stringent emergency management steps, the situation continued to deteriorate as rainfall remained at some of the lowest levels in recorded history. As reservoir levels continued to fall, some estimates predicted the quick exhaustion of water supplies. Consequently, in late January 1981, the governor issued additional emergency orders aimed at cutting residential water use by 25 percent and expanding water rationing to another 187 communities, including those in Middlesex County. With these rules in effect, emergency orders covered 372 municipalities and affected over 5,000,000 people.[11]

Thus, in the midst of plenty, Middlesex Water customers found themselves rationed. As the restrictions took hold, water use fell steadily and residential use within the stricken areas declined the required 25 percent. This was a fine example of conservation, but in the Middlesex Water service area, it was a futile gesture in fighting the drought. In fact, the restrictions in Middlesex County would have made sense only if the company could have pumped water to the distressed parts of the state. Unfortunately, there was no way to get water from Middlesex Water Company supplies to the parched northeast; and local savings in Middlesex County simply flowed into the Atlantic Ocean. The only real effect was on company finances. Revenue fell dramatically as water consumption plummeted over 1981. Net income dropped off some 10 percent from 1980 levels, and earnings per share fell from $3.12 in 1980 to $2.67 in 1981. Even the breaking of the drought in May, and the subsequent end of rationing, failed to alter the situation at first. Customers resumed normal water use patterns very slowly, and consumption levels climbed back to 1980 levels only in late 1983. Once the consumption habits of customers changed, Ernie Gere (by then Vice President and Controller) explained to the press, they did not change back quickly.[12]

In the end, Middlesex Water simply was stuck with its losses. The company argued in state Appellate Court that rationing

174

had been unnecessary in its service area, and that the state should reimburse its lost revenues. But the case made little headway. In July 1983, the court held that while the water restrictions may have been unnecessary, Governor Byrne's emergency orders were still legal and therefore "the type of injury suffered" by the company was "not legally compensable."[13] There was a certain irony in the situation: The drought fully demonstrated the success of well over a decade of company planning and improvements to protect its customers against water shortages. And yet, if only for two years, the company paid a stiff price for its success.

As frustrating as the drought situation was for the company, it did not stop other initiatives. The most immediate concern involved badly needed maintenance and administrative facilities. In Woodbridge, the old corporate headquarters, familiar to so many local residents, were simply too small for vastly expanded company operations. The former bank building could not accommodate new automated and computerized office systems, which required considerable new space. Nor could existing facilities support the efficient maintenance of the growing fleet of company vehicles and other equipment. After weighing alternatives, the company decided to build an entirely new headquarters and maintenance complex. In the spring of 1981, after approval by local planning authorities, construction began on a seven-acre tract on Ronson Road in Iselin. Plans called for two structures. The main office building would provide about 25,000 square feet of office space, while a 22,180 square foot garage and shop would service the twenty-one Middlesex Water trucks. The design contract went to the award-winning firm of Eckert, Morton, Russo & Maggio, Architects and Planners. The resulting brick and glass buildings were stylish and practical; and when they opened in 1984, they allowed the company to combine significant aspects of its field operations with key administrative functions. Within two years, Tompkins was able to note important results. The new facilities supported better computer operations, allowed for centralized maintenance of company equipment, and made it easier to expand

175

The new Middlesex Water Company headquarters building, Iselin, 1980s.

customer services.[14] Until the construction of the headquarters and maintenance complex, most capital expenditures had gone into the system itself; the new buildings, however, served to emphasize the importance of management in the functioning of a modern utility.

This was just as well, because the chief opportunities for the Middlesex Company over the rest of the 1980s, and into the 1990s, would vastly increase the demands on management and on the personnel who kept the distribution system functioning. Perhaps the most pressing matters were the closely related issues of pumpage and revenue. While the company was fiscally stable and returning consistent profits, falling consumption over the first half of the eighties raised a potential threat to revenues. The situation had several roots, including the weather. In 1985, another dry spell gripped much of New Jersey. The state eventually responded as it had during the drought of 1980-81, and once again the governor (this time Thomas Kean) mandated water use restrictions. Again, company water supplies were fully adequate to the situation, but voluntary conservation measures once more cut into revenues.

The most threatening problem, however, was economic. The changing nature of the customer base, already in evidence during the 1970s, became a preeminent concern during the early 1980s. Pumpage for industrial sales continued to decline, as Carl Olsen had noted before his retirement, and now Tompkins had to deal with an even more pronounced trend. Industrial water users, Tompkins told stockholders in 1985, while no longer a majority of the customer base, still had been an important and "stabilizing segment of Middlesex Water Company" revenues. Yet this vital economic sector steadily fell away as regional plant closings accelerated and remaining companies curtailed their operations and implemented water saving measures. The reduction or end of service to large water users such as Fedders, U.S. Metals, Chevron, Tennaco, Public Service Electric and Gas, Reynolds Metals, and other manufacturing companies was particularly damaging. Between 1980 and 1985, Tompkins found, average water pumpage had gradually declined by some 3.5 million gallons per day (mgd)—that is, from 29.0 mgd to 25.5 mgd.[15] Never again could Middlesex Water officials look, as Frank Bergen had, to the regional industrial base as a stable or long-range source of revenue; if the company was to remain profitable in the future, it would have to investigate alternative markets for its water and services.

For almost ninety years, the consolidated water company—that is, the company born of the merged Midland, Middlesex, and Consumers Aqueduct Companies—had concentrated operations in eastern Middlesex County. The only exceptions had been wholesale deliveries to the Elizabethtown and Plainfield-Union Companies in Union County, and several retail connections in Clark (also in Union County). By the early 1980s, however, con-

cern over falling pumpage led Tompkins and other company officers to consider a major expansion of the service area. There were
several opportunities, mostly in residential areas. Continuing
wholesale contracts allowed some sales to Edison Township and
the Borough of Highland Park. But a key step came in early 1985,
when the company signed a special thirty-year contract with East
Brunswick. The arrangement called for the treatment and pumping of 4.0 mgd for that township alone. The agreement was unusual, however, in that no company water reserves were involved; the
contract provided only for the treatment of East Brunswick's raw
water supplies, which came from the Delaware and Raritan
Canal.[16] In April 1985, construction began on a new 2.8-mile
transmission main of 36-inch prestressed concrete cylinder pipe to
connect the East Brunswick distribution system to the Olsen
Treatment Plant. It was a substantial undertaking, with A. Stanley
Mundy Co. and Spiniello Construction Company handling the
three sections of the job, and water began flowing in January of
1986.

This contract, while not replacing all lost industrial business, nevertheless contributed significantly to corporate fiscal stability. Moreover, the wholesale agreement with a large township
was a key sign of things to come. By late 1985 negotiations also
had begun with local authorities in South Amboy, Sayreville, and
Old Bridge. While these contacts did not produce immediate
results, they did reflect the fact that many regional townships and
cities, some of which faced pressing water supply concerns, were
interested in exploring business arrangements with Middlesex
Water.[17] As a result, the company could plan with a degree of confidence as it moved to extend the bounds of its service area.

THE MOST SIGNIFICANT FACTOR IN THIS new-found
confidence, however, derived from a series of important environmental developments. These took place in the South River Basin,
a region of southern Middlesex and northern Monmouth Counties
drained by the South River. For years, townships in the South

River Basin area, which included East Brunswick, Sayreville, Old Bridge, Marlboro and other communities, had drawn their water supplies from a series of underground aquifers. This had sufficed for decades, but over the years, development of the region put considerable stress on the aquifers. By the 1950s, studies and public hearings warned that residential and industrial users were depleting the groundwater, and that salt water consequently was seeping into the aquifers. In some areas, salt water encroachment ruined large numbers of wells. There was considerable public outcry, and a debate raged in the late 1950s and early 1960s over the best means of dealing with the problem. For a time, there was sentiment for building a tidal dam on the South River, which some experts argued would have allowed fresh water to recharge the aquifers.[18] But for all of the discussion, for almost thirty years regional and state authorities took little concrete action. The entire situation was a standing invitation to trouble.

Perhaps the most disturbing aspect of the matter was an almost complete absence of attention to securing supplies to supplement groundwater from the threatened aquifers. In particular, neither the communities nor the state mounted any systematic effort to develop surface water supplies, or to bring in water via transmission lines, in order to reduce local groundwater withdrawals. This was short-sighted, but similar to so much earlier water policy planning in New Jersey. Issues of cost and the inability to conduct effective joint planning among neighboring municipalities fostered the slow growth of a regional water crisis. Many local water officials saw it coming, and said as much. Nevertheless, the crisis came: in 1985, the New Jersey Department of Environmental Protection declared the entire South River Basin a Critical Groundwater Area. The DEP declaration was a serious affair, mandating that local communities drastically reduce their use of groundwater. Now there was no choice; the South River towns had to look elsewhere for much of their water.

Local officials looked in various directions for relief, investigating purchases from private and publicly-owned water suppliers. There were any number of discussions with Middlesex Water, Elizabethtown Water, and the cities of New Brunswick and Perth Amboy, both of which operated large municipal systems. The South River Basin townships made no decisions lightly. The stakes were now too high to allow for mistakes, and much of the region's future prosperity depended upon an effective solution to the water crisis. Population and employment projections in both Middlesex and Monmouth Counties indicated rapid development throughout the South River Basin for the rest of the decade, which made reliable water supplies imperative. In Marlboro Township, for example, located in northern Monmouth County and one of the fastest growing communities in the South River Basin, planning for major residential developments went on hold because of the water shortage. In Sayreville, an already heavily developed Middlesex County municipality, the restrictions on groundwater use raised concerns over the ability to maintain local functions as basic as fire protection and sewer service.[19]   The situation starkly revealed the dependence of economic development and public safety on the presence of reliable water supplies.

Almost uniformly, however, the proposals of the Middlesex Water Company generated considerable interest among the townships. The company had plenty of water, and the Olsen Plant, with appropriate modifications, was capable of handling the necessary treatment and pumping assignments. Indeed, some local water officials commented publicly that Middlesex best "guaranteed a strong and healthy supply of water" for the area.[20] The early phases of these discussions had led to the service agreement with East Brunswick, followed by a subsequent contract to supply Old Bridge; and with the encouragement of the state Department of Environmental Protection, the company began planning to extend its service area even further into the South River Basin.

The key to this task was technical as well as financial. The company needed to transfer millions of gallons of surface water per day from the Raritan River Basin, where Middlesex had plentiful supplies, to the endangered distribution systems in the South River Basin municipalities. In 1985, Middlesex took the initial engineering steps to meet the new challenge. It increased the pumping and treatment capabilities at the Olsen Plant, and then mapped out steps for an even larger expansion of the Olsen Treatment Plant facilities and for a major transmission main extension into the South River Basin. These plans, geared to support a growing service area, were also vital to offering water service at reasonable rates. Expansion, Tompkins explained to the shareholders, would allow "economies of scale in the production and supply of water service that will benefit both existing and prospective customers. Without an expanded sales base," the Middlesex president noted, "the continued decline in usage would require rate increases that would be difficult to impose."[21]

Barring unforeseen complications, however, prospects seemed bright for the continued growth of the service area. The new contracts negotiated through 1985 had begun to replace the revenues lost in former sales to industrial customers, and discussions with other South River Basin water purveyors offered prospects for additional sales. By early 1986, Tompkins was able to assure the directors and shareholders that most plans, including the enhancement of the capabilities of the Olsen Treatment Plant, were well under way. Since 1980, he noted, corporate revenues had climbed by 50 percent and earnings had remained fairly steady at about $2.00 per share. Over the same period, the value of Middlesex Water Company stock had more than doubled, and had done so in the face of new stock issues and a two-for-one split.[22] This was performance any utility could envy, and it had consequences beyond the immediate balance sheet. Indeed, such fiscal reports continued to support strong investor interest, a fact central to the company's ability to finance the expansion of the system.

Fortunately, company operations over the rest of the decade largely measured up to expectations. The expansion into the South River Basin was a virtually unqualified success. In addition to Old Bridge and East Brunswick, by 1990 Sayreville and Marlboro Townships were Middlesex customers, extending the bounds of the service area farther than ever. This expansion, however, required a massive capital program. Projects involving enhancements of treatment, pumping, and transmission facilities continued virtually nonstop throughout the late 1980s and early 1990s, and the price tag was measured in tens of millions of dollars.[23]

Yet the results were impressive. By 1989, work at the Olsen Treatment Plant had added a steel storage reservoir with a capacity of ten million gallons. Contractors also installed a new 15 mgd auxiliary pumping station, as well as a 25 mgd finished water pump. These projects significantly increased the pumping capabilities of the Olsen plant and offered the system considerable flexibility in periods of peak demand. New transmission mains also pushed deep into the South River Basin. By 1990, one segment of 36-inch and 42-inch pipe ran for 6.5 miles, connecting Marlboro with existing mains serving Old Bridge and Sayreville. Another section, completed in 1992, ran for over five miles through the Borough of South River toward the Olsen Plant. These pipeline projects alone cost $13 million. The state Economic Development Authority financed $10 million of this amount, with the rest funded through new stock and bond issues.[24] Again, the company was able to market its debt successfully.

Even as work on the transmission mains pressed ahead, however, equally important concerns kept Middlesex personnel busy. Working with a team of consultants, the Engineering Department prepared designs for even more additions to the Olsen Plant. Between 1988 and 1992, there were improvements in the plant's sedimentation basins and filters. These improvements would increase water treatment and production capabilities by 50 percent, changes essential to operations given the rapid growth of the consumer base. In addition, as it increased its capabilities, the company spared no effort or necessary expense in the acquisition of the best new technology and equipment. What had been a state-of-the-art plant in 1970 remained a state-of-the-art plant in 1992.

Earth boring machine used for laying pipe under roadways.

Safe and dependable service, however, also was predicated on the maintenance of existing plant facilities and distribution mains. During the 1980s, a typical year saw the company install well over 20,000 feet of distribution mains—and this figure was over 35,000 in some years—as well as maintaining hundreds of service lines, water meters, and fire hydrants. Carefully monitored scheduled maintenance kept operating equipment and systems in operation with remarkably few mechanical or other problems.

Generally, maintenance and repair efforts were routine, although there were exceptions. In early 1987, for example, the repair of a 24-inch main running under the Raritan River proved more exciting. The company had leased rights to an unused Perth Amboy pipeline as part of its initial effort to provide service to the South River Basin. The line, however, had been out of service for

183

some time and needed major rehabilitation before carrying water supplies to the thirsty communities south of the Raritan. Divers worked in near-freezing water under conditions of virtually zero visibility. Working by touch, they had to locate the main, find the break, remove layers of silt, and cut away sections of damaged pipe as long as 14 feet. It was exacting and dangerous work, and the rehabilitation of the line was a major engineering achievement completed in a short time and at a reasonable cost.[25] Yet like more mundane repair chores, the underwater work was an integral part of serving the expanding customer base; and however difficult, the company was prepared to do whatever was necessary to keep water flowing uninterrupted.

THE EXPANSION INTO THE SOUTH RIVER BASIN paralleled an increasingly complex regulatory atmosphere. Rate-making remained a critical aspect of the company's agenda with the Board of Public Utilities—the new name, beginning in 1977, for the old State Board of Public Utility Commissioners. In fact, the issue assumed a particularly important guise as the costs inherent in modernizing and maintaining the distribution system escalated. Between 1980 and 1985 alone, for example, Middlesex Water Company operating costs of all kinds increased by some 53 percent, which by itself would have justified rate relief.[26] Costs continued to rise steadily through the early 1990s. As a result, on several occasions the company brought rate cases before the BPU, each of which gradually moved the price of water higher. Still, by the early 1990s, a typical Middlesex Water residential customer paid relatively modest service charges. In Metuchen, for instance, which the company supplies on a retail basis, a household of two or three people paid about $.75 a day, roughly $250 per year, for water service. Charges were similar in municipalities purchasing water wholesale. Under the circumstances, it was a rare rate increase that provoked the heated public reactions of the 1920s, or even of the 1960s.

Yet presenting a rate case to the BPUC was a more complicated business that ever before. In great measure, the process followed outlines familiar to litigants since the 1920s. By the 1980s, however, cases required enormous amounts of documentation, which in turn required enormous amounts of time to compile. The documentation submitted in support of a 1990 rate increase, for example, excluding actual testimony by company officials and consultants, was voluminous.[27] Even so, a final rate was never a precise calculation; BPU hearing officers had to interpret masses of statistics and related evidence, and in the end a decision was as much a matter of judgment as of mathematics or the letter of regulation.

Nor was an agreed-upon rate necessarily final. The federal Tax Reform Act of 1986, for example, demonstrated how unexpected developments could reopen the rate-making process. The new tax law reduced federal corporate taxes appreciably over 1987 and 1988, and the BPU ordered all New Jersey utilities to calculate the effects of the tax savings on their revenue projections. The companies then reduced customer rates accordingly, which saved Middlesex Water consumers $619,000 in 1987 and $497,000 in 1988. The entire affair kept management busy gathering data and calculating the impact of the rate changes, which, in fact, were minimal. But the tax reductions, coupled with lower energy costs in the mid-1980s and increased wholesale contact sales, made it unnecessary for Middlesex Water to seek an immediate rate increase.[28] Thus the regulatory scene was not fiscally dangerous, just extremely complex.

This complexity made in-house counsel a necessity. In 1985, the company hired Dennis G. Sullivan as General Counsel. His immediate task was to help cope with the press of regulatory matters, and he played a critical role in the South River Basin expansion. In addition, Sullivan was also instrumental in the initiation and development of service and other contracts.

Significantly, the rate-making process could now involve parties beyond the companies and the Board of Public Utilities. Since the advent of regulation in New Jersey, the public and other interested groups offered frequent testimony at rate hearings, but

the real combatants were the BPU and the utilities. Yet in the
early 1980s, this mix began to change as other state agencies saw
an increasing stake in water pricing and regulatory procedures.

Two cases in particular illustrated this developing trend. In
1981, in an effort to make its involvement in water supply more
efficient, the state placed water sales from the Delaware & Raritan
Canal and the Spruce Run-Round Valley Reservoir complex under
the control of a new public agency. This was the New Jersey
Water Supply Authority, an independent branch of the state
Department of Environmental Protection.[29] Subsequently, in 1982,
the Water Supply Authority unilaterally, and virtually without
warning, raised the price of supplies it sold to the water companies
by almost 100 percent. While doing so, the authority knew that
state regulatory laws prevented the utilities from immediately
passing any part of the increase along to consumers. Having
negotiated water rates with the BPU on the basis of established
costs of state water supplies, the companies cried foul; like any
other water user, what they wanted was a formal hearing before
the imposition of a rate increase.[30] The utilities had to follow due
process before they could initiate rate increases of their own, and
they expected nothing less from the state.

The issue quickly went into litigation. The Middlesex
Company, which now drew water from the reservoirs as well as
the canal, therefore joined several other utilities in a suit against
the Water Supply Authority. And the companies, allied as the
Water Users Association, did not fight alone. The state
Department of the Public Advocate, arguing that the Water Supply
Authority had violated "fundamental principles" of fairness,
joined in the suit. The case, which dragged on until March of
1983, eventually ended with an uneasy compromise: the Supply
Authority reduced its price increase by some 30 percent, but it
retained the right to impose price increases largely on its own
terms. On the other hand, the companies were allowed to use
these increased costs in calculating new rate charges of their
own.[31] The entire affair was significant beyond the matter of the

final cost of water from the authority; it also signalled that the BPU was no longer the only state agency to figure in setting the price of water.

A second case further illustrated the point, while injecting a certain irony into the situation. In March 1989, Middlesex Water Company filed a rate increase with the BPU for $3.7 million. The case was fully litigated by December, when the company received approval of an increase of $2.4 million, which represented a return of 12.4% on common equity—less than the 13.75% the company had thought was fair. The case had followed all procedures, including the filing of all documentation and a full series of hearings. Yet in early 1990, the company received word that the New Jersey Public Advocate—a former ally against the Water Supply Authority—had filed an appeal. The Public Advocate was protesting certain aspects of the BPU's handling of the case, in essence claiming that established rate-making procedures had given consumers short shrift. The charge was exasperating for the company and irritating to the BPU, which had seen itself as the guardian of the public welfare since its origins under Woodrow Wilson. As a result, the company and the board joined forces in a legal action that eventually fought off the Public Advocate.[32] But the episode had brought a novel twist to the history of state water rates: the regulators and the regulated had teamed up against another public office—one that earlier had allied with the companies against the Water Supply Authority. The regulatory maze was now more convoluted than ever, and on any given occasion any number of interests and agencies could choose to become involved in arguing the price of water. One can only wonder what Frank Bergen would have made of the situation.

YET RATE-MAKING, NO MATTER how important was only one aspect of water regulation. Over the 1980s, water quality and environmental concerns began to demand equal attention. Such issues, of course, were not particularly new; government, the public, and business had long recognized the importance of safe water

187

as a key to maintaining public health and supporting economic development. What had changed, however, was the nature of water pollution itself and popular perceptions of its consequences.

In fact, these changes were profound. By the early twentieth century, water treatment techniques generally had proven effective against the most serious biological contaminants. Historically, various bacteria, fecal matter, and other organic wastes had posed the greatest threats to water purity, especially in heavily populated areas. Filtration and chlorination, however, had eliminated the majority of the gravest problems; sand and charcoal filters also dealt successfully with most inorganic sediments. But if many of these traditional threats were manageable, pollution remained a serious concern as the twentieth century drew to a close.

Growing fears centered on toxic chemical wastes, which added a complex and ominous new dimension to water safety. The chief problems arose from the sheer variety of chemical wastes, some of which posed health threats impervious to traditional water treatment techniques. The list of toxic substances was painfully long: lead, salt, radon, various uranium compounds, pesticides, benzene, vinyl chloride, phosphates, mercury, and many other pollutants all posed threats of varying degrees to water supplies. Some of these dangers were well-known; lead and mercury, for instance, were old adversaries. But toxic pollutants assumed a grim prominence as the public learned of the extent of chemical leaching into water supplies from thousands of waste dumps around the country (and New Jersey had more than its share of such dumps). In addition, the media, as well as more sober research publications, stressed that these contaminants could be lethal. Lead and mercury were poisonous even in relatively low quantities, and many other toxins were carcinogens. Under the circumstances, there was every reason for concern.

Public reaction was strong. Over the 1980s and early 1990s, the press covered toxic threats to drinking water extensively, including the debate over what water quality standards federal and state authorities should adopt to protect the public.[33] Actual incidents involving polluted water usually attracted considerable local attention, although some situations were more serious than others. One rather bizarre experience of Elizabethtown Water offered a case in point: the company found itself in court, sued by an irate owner of pet fish. Too much chlorine and ammonia in the water, he charged, had killed his fish; Elizabethtown denied there was any ammonia in the water, and that chlorine was present because of normal water treatment. The dispute tied up the court-room for two days before the judge threw out the case. Elizabethtown, the court ruled, was responsible for delivering water safe for humans, not for rare breeds of exotic fish.[34] The case was hardly typical, but it did illustrate something of how touchy the public was over the issue of water quality.

Not all incidents had the virtue of fish-story humor, although they spoke volumes about how quickly the public could respond to fears over water quality. Middlesex Water received its share of complaints as it expanded into the South River Basin, and they were not completely unexpected. Concerns about water taste often occur, for example, when introducing a surface supply into a system previously on well supplies. Such difficulties are usually temporary and would have surprised no one in the water business. In January of 1986, with the public aware that Middlesex would be treating East Brunswick water, the township health officer received no fewer than seventeen complaints about the taste of the water. These he dutifully passed on to the company, although he hardly expected the company's response. The complaints, the company told East Brunswick, were a bit premature—Middlesex Water was not scheduled to begin servicing the township for another week.[35]

A second incident was more serious. In July of 1987, a high bacteria count in Old Bridge threw a brief scare into the company. Testing caught the bacteria quickly enough, and efficient remedial action quickly eliminated the problem. Company equipment or procedures had not caused the problem; in fact, the bacteria had been in the Old Bridge system all along and became disturbed when reverse pumping began. But in order to dispel any public misunderstandings, Tompkins immediately explained the matter to the press. His candor was clearly for the best, as the local media in fact reported the prompt actions of the company in correcting the predicament. There was no adverse impact on public health, and concerned citizens in one section of the township were advised for a day to boil drinking water as a precautionary measure.[36] The ready and effective response of Middlesex Water Company emergency procedures was reassuring; but once again, water quality was before the public under graphic and alarming circumstances.

By the late 1980s, federal and state authorities were responding vigorously to public concerns over the safety of water supplies. In 1986, the national Safe Drinking Water Act established federal water purity standards, and made provisions for amending regulations as research and the monitoring of water quality dictated.[37] In New Jersey, a series of major studies of organic and nonorganic pollution threats to drinking water produced legislation on testing, purity standards, pollution controls, and research that governed all water systems in the state. Regulations against the discharge of toxic substances into water supplies tightened up considerably, and official lists of potentially dangerous toxics grew steadily. These various efforts eventually produced the New Jersey State Water Quality Standards, which took effect in 1989.[38] The new rules were the most stringent in state history and, in conjunction with federal regulations, illustrated the extent of public concern—and even distress—over the depth and complexity of water pollution problems. Indeed, at both the state and national levels, there were critics who still believed the new regulations too lax; and perhaps for the first time, at least in the popular mind, environmental concerns and the purity of water had become as important as the price of water.

The advent of these new rules added an increasingly complex dimension to the regulatory scene. Anti-pollution legislation placed additional demands on the entire water industry, sometimes necessitating the installation of additional treatment equipment and experimentation with new purification techniques. But water quality was an age-old concern for most companies anyway, and the majority of them had anticipated at least some of the new requirements.

Certainly this was the case at Middlesex Water. At the Olsen Plant, the Water Quality Department experimented extensively with various new treatment technologies. Over the late 1980s, for example, there was a particular focus on replacing chlorine with ozone as a disinfectant. This project was part of a broad and continuing effort to keep abreast of the most effective, efficient, and economical methods of water treatment consistent with regulatory standards.[39] In late 1989, the company began the installation of new tube settling units in the sedimentation basins at the Olsen facility in order to improve effluent quality. The following year, an air-stripping facility went into operation at the Spring Lake well field, assuring water quality in excess of the stringent New Jersey standards; and by mid-1992, the company had undertaken a similar installation at the Park Avenue well field.[40]

Monitoring the safety of the water supply, then, as well as evaluating and maintaining treatment facilities and procedures, was a continuous and ever increasing operation. The equipment installed over the late 1980s and early 1990s is capable of detecting the most minute traces of volatile organic compounds and other pollutants. And treatment procedures are designed to remove them completely and to assure consumers of fully pure and safe water. While the public was only occasionally aware of any specific activities in these respects, water quality efforts nevertheless have remained the highest operational priority at Middlesex Water.

BY THE EARLY 1990s, TOMPKINS COULD look back on a hectic but productive decade of service at the company. A changing customer base, drought, expansion into the South River Basin, and the pronounced concerns over water quality had left few dull moments. They also had placed considerable pressure on company operations at virtually all levels. Still, corporate activities and plans had proceeded with few significant disappointments or setbacks, and it was clear that Middlesex Water Company personnel were not only working hard, but working effectively.

This record of productivity was never a matter of chance. Rather, it derived from personnel policies that emphasized high standards of performance in all operational areas and at all levels. Virtually all jobs were important. Middlesex Water was never a large company if measured in terms of people: by 1991, there were only 135 employees, not appreciably more than there were 40 years earlier. Thus everyone had a defined role to play, and there was little margin for error; hours and days lost to absenteeism, accidents, mistakes, or indifferent work habits were simply too costly. Under the circumstances, maintaining company morale and loyalty, or fostering good working conditions, was not a luxury or an afterthought; it was a critical operational factor.

Training opportunities constituted a central element in personnel operations. In 1990 alone, for example, fully half of Middlesex employees attended customer service seminars, while most specialized personnel took part in continuing education in pursuit of various water treatment and distribution licenses or certificates. Supervisors were involved as well, with the company arranging a series of training sessions designed to improve performance and productivity. And 1990 was only a typical year, company practice was to maintain continuing education opportunities as a regular aspect of human resource development.

The results of this activity are always difficult to quantify, but anecdotal evidence has indicated considerable success. First, there is the fact that Middlesex Water has maintained increasingly complex operations without adding appreciably to its workforce—a strong indication that existing personnel have maintained and enhanced their skills and abilities to contribute. Job safety is another consideration. Accidents have been few, and over the

1980s the company's internal newsletter noted months without time lost to injuries or other mishaps. Moreover, other than time lost to scheduled maintenance, company equipment failures were few and far between. Finally, as Tompkins emphasized in a report to the shareholders, "the real proof of these extra efforts on the part" of Middlesex Water Company personnel was the "increasing number of compliments received from customers."[41] It would seem that resources invested in "human capital" have repaid themselves handsomely.

In fact, such a record in developing human resources merits comment, for it carries implications reaching beyond the company. At least through the early 1990s, a decade of political and social commentators have lamented the decline of American productivity, and both education and industry have endured astringent criticisms for deficiencies in the training of the American workforce. In this context, the Middlesex Water Company stands as an important example to the contrary. Company practice has illustrated how effectively an American company can function with a relatively small but well-trained staff. Over the balance of the twentieth century, as the nation addresses the problems of its deteriorating infrastructure—including its utilities base—it cannot afford to take such illustrations lightly.

If the company workforce was lean but effective, senior management displayed similar attributes. By the late 1980s, Tompkins had assembled his own management team and, in keeping with practice since the days of Frank Bergen, the number of officers was limited. Ernest C. (Ernie) Gere, the Middlesex Water veteran, now served as Senior Vice President and Controller. Walter J. (Wally) Brady, another long-service officer, who had been Assistant Vice President (as well as Assistant Secretary-Assistant Treasurer), became Vice President for Human Resources in 1987, and latter assumed broader responsibilities as Vice President for Administration. Upon the retirement of Carolina Schneider in 1987, Marion F. Reynolds became Secretary-Treasurer. Reynolds had considerable experience in utilities;

before coming to the Middlesex Water Company, she had been Assistant Corporate Secretary at Public Service Electric & Gas. Schneider herself remained very much on the scene. Already a member of the Board of Directors, she took an active part on Board committees where her detailed knowledge of company operations remained a continuing resource. In 1989, Richard A. Russo, a licensed professional engineer, took over as Vice President for Operations. Russo also came with an extensive background in the water business, having served as head of the City of Trenton Waterworks. The following year, in an action reflecting the continuing importance of legal and regulatory affairs, the directors also promoted General Counsel Dennis G. Sullivan to Vice President. Thus it was a relatively small team of officers serving with Tompkins, but they effectively represented the expertise and experience necessary to map and implement company policy.

At all levels, there was considerable employee stability. There was relatively little turn-over among company personnel, and the pattern of long-term employment, evident as early as the 1920s and 1930s, remained a commonplace into the 1990s. Careers of twenty years were not unusual, and the plaque in the hall of the headquarters building on Ronson Road carries dozens of names with service records extending beyond thirty years. Clearly, the company has generated significant employee loyalty—indeed, many employees are stockholders—and there has been a tradition of participation in corporate social functions. Whether competing in tapping contests, helping to bring out the company newsletter, or attending a summer picnic, the effect of such activities has been to foster a sense of common purpose within company ranks. Moreover, fringe benefits, including health care, kept pace with standards throughout the utilities industry. Thus, while no organization or company can hope to satisfy everyone on the payroll, a majority of the men and women at Middlesex Water have considered it a good place to work.

With a long-term record of employee stability and satisfaction, company labor-management relations generally have functioned smoothly. Controversies arose from time to time, but Middlesex Water employees never have unionized. There was some sentiment for a union in the 1930s, but little came of it. There were far fewer people working at the company then, and with the country still in the grip of the Great Depression, satisfaction with regular employment far outweighed any grievances over long hours and few benefits. Over 1985 and early 1986, however, a more concerted unionization effort grew out of a misunderstanding of the changed work environment and responsibilities at the Olsen Plant. The Utility Workers Union of America campaigned to represent company workers, while the company carefully made the case for not organizing. Writing to a union organizer, Tompkins explained that Middlesex Water already was "a good place to work and to grow, in a friendly atmosphere"; and, ultimately, a majority of employees agreed. In a close vote, the employees rejected the union, while the company undertook efforts to further improve corporate communications and management training in a bid to avoid future difficulties. From time to time after 1985, some employees have expressed honest interest in the benefits of a union. Yet, through the early 1990s, majority opinion still held that a union was not necessary for the success of the company or those working there.[42]

AS THE MIDDLESEX WATER COMPANY MOVED into the final years of the twentieth century, it did so on the basis of two decades of carefully planned and steady growth. With the opening of the Olsen Treatment Plant, the company was able to map a future free of the old fears of supply shortages. The success of the new plant—so much a legacy of Ambose Mundy, Carl Olsen, and those who worked with them—enabled Tompkins and his team to lead the company into a virtually new era. The move into the South River Basin, so painstakingly calculated, expanded the company service dramatically. In turn, the new customer base sustained the ability of the company to provide meaningful jobs for its employees and reasonable returns for its investors. Moreover, all of this occurred in a period when, all too frequently, drought and threats of water pollution reminded the public that reliable and safe water service could never be taken for granted. Those who worked at Middlesex Water never took it for granted either, but their collective efforts, day in and day out, all but assured it for hundreds of thousands of New Jersey residents. The company, a confident and mature utility after a century of operations, was an integral and central part of the infrastructure of one of the most populous and prosperous regions of the United States.

EPILOGUE

Toward a Second Century

IN JULY 1988, THE MIDDLESEX WATER COMPANY *Newsletter* announced an impending management audit. Periodically, the article explained, the New Jersey Board of Public Utilities required such reviews of management operations, and over the past several years other water companies had gone through the process. Now it was the turn of Middlesex Water. The exercise would allow the company an opportunity, the writer noted, to "demonstrate to our regulators and our customers our positive accomplishments." The results, reported in early 1989, were not disappointing. The audit described a well-managed and highly productive company. Middlesex Water, the report stated, provided "its customers with high quality potable water service. The Company's personnel are dedicated to the water business. There is a strong executive financial and operational management within Middlesex."[1] In short, this was a company that knew what it was doing.

Subsequent events quickly confirmed these complimentary observations. In late 1990, Tompkins wrote a memorandum for the Executive Committee of the Board of Directors in which he raised the possibility of a major step for the company. Preliminary contacts with John F. Alexander, the president and majority stock-

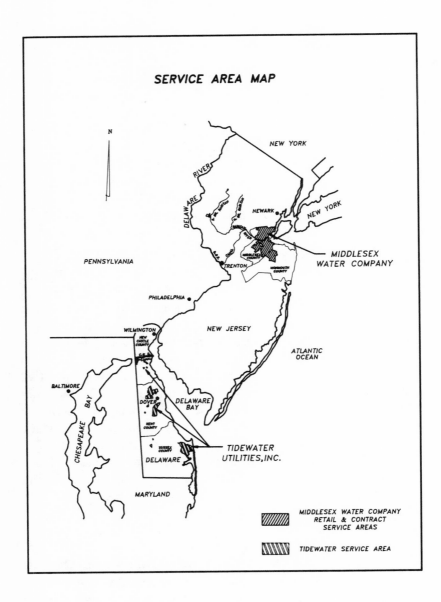

Middlesex Water Company service area, 1990s.

holder of Tidewater Utilities, Inc., of the state of Delaware, had raised some interesting possibilities. Tidewater served over three thousand customers in some sixty communities in Sussex, New Castle, and Kent Counties, and there was real potential for the expansion of the customer base. Alexander, chiefly responsible for the founding of the company, was interested in becoming part of a larger organization; and Tompkins saw an opportunity to improve Middlesex Water's financial position through an advantageous acquisition.[2]

The deal came together slowly but steadily. It took almost another two years to work out the details of the purchase and to secure the necessary regulatory approvals. Considerable time went into setting the price and terms of payment to Alexander, satisfying a minority Tidewater stockholder, working out arrangements for Tidewater employees, and presenting the case for the purchase to Delaware and New Jersey authorities. In the end, Middlesex Water issued preferred stock to acquire Tidewater, and the sale finally closed on October 20, 1992.[3] The effort proved its worth as the Delaware customer base developed as predicted—and the Middlesex Water Company was now a major utility in two states.

Naturally, the company was pleased with the results of the Tidewater acquisition—just as it had been pleased with the results of the BPU management audit. Yet these developments surprised no one familiar with the men and women who worked at Middlesex Water. Unstated, however, but inherent in the Tidewater acquisition and the BPU report was another crucial matter. There was also a clear recognition that Middlesex Water was a vital part of the region it served. Over a hundred years before, Frank Bergen, William Corbin, and other early investors had recognized the signal relationships between economic growth, the public welfare, and an adequate regional utilities base. They built the Middlesex Water Company on those relationships, which, as the BPU audit implied, remained as vital as they ever had been. Safe and reliable water service was no less important to society in the 1990s than it was in the 1890s.

In their century of service, the men and women who worked at Middlesex Water also made another point. Even in a regulated industry, a well-managed investor-owned company could operate effectively. It was possible to balance the needs of

Park Avenue treatment plant.

shareholders with the requirements of customers, and to marshal the capital necessary to maintain the most advanced technology in the industry. This had been the case since the founding of the company; and at no time, even during the early controversies with the old Board of Public Utilities Commissioners, did anyone seriously suggest that public ownership of the distribution system could better serve the region. Private enterprise had founded the company, and management and employees since the days of Frank Bergen had maintained its independence and profitability while serving the public welfare. The Middlesex Water Company is, at its centennial, one of the largest investor-owned water utilities in New Jersey, and one of the most successful.

Middlesex Water Company Board of Directors, 1990. Standing, left to right: Stephen H. Mundy, Ernest C. Gere, Joseph S. Yewaisis, Edward D. Bastian, and Jeffries Shein. Front row, left to right: J. Richard Tompkins, William E. Scott, Carolina M. Schneider, and John P. Molnar.

In a sense, the history of Middlesex Water has been a collective biography. Over four generations of men and women have worked for the company, many of them devoting entire careers. Brothers, fathers, sons, husbands and wives have worked together in offices, maintenance buildings, pumping stations, storage and treatment facilities, and in the field. During the 1890s, they did pick and shovel work, laid and caulked miles of cast iron pipe, fed coal-fired steam pumps, and operated some of the earliest treatment equipment in the country. Over time, their skills and activities changed as the needs of the public compelled changes in the system. There is still some pick and shovel work, but Middlesex employees are now among the best trained and experienced people in an industry reliant on advanced engineering and technology,

Company officers, 1994. Left to right: Ernest C. Gere, Richard Russo, Dennis Sullivan, J. Richard Tompkins, Walter Brady, and Marion Reynolds.

automated systems, and exacting standards of quality. The success of the Middlesex Water Company during its first century has come from their common effort. It will be their efforts that will see the company safely into its second century.

ENDNOTES

Notes to Chapter 1

1   For a contemporary survey of New Jersey economic activity, see *Industries of New Jersey* (Newark and Philadelphia: Historical Publishing Co., 1883); on agriculture, see Hubert G. Schmidt, *Agriculture in New Jersey: A Three-Hundred-Year History* (New Brunswick: Rutgers Univ. Press, 1973).

2   Federal Writers' Project, *The WPA Guide to 1930s New Jersey* (New Brunswick: Rutgers University Press, 1986; orig. 1939), 320, 352-53 .

3   *Ibid.*, 46; Wheaton J. Lane, *From Indian Trail to Iron Horse: Travel and Transportation in New Jersey, 1620-1869* (Princeton: Princeton Univ. Press, 1939), deals with the rise of improved transportation and related industries.

4   On the impact of the Civil War on New Jersey industry, see Jeannette Paddock Nichols, "The Industrial History of New Jersey Since 1861," Chapt. 43, in Irving S. Kull, ed., *New Jersey: A History* (4 vols., New York: American Historical Society, 1930), Vol. 3: 896-98; see also Mark Edward Lender, *One State in Arms: A Short Military History of New Jersey* (Trenton: N.J. Historical Commission, 1992); *WPA Guide to New Jersey*, 47-50.

5   Nichols, "Industrial History of New Jersey, " 897-98.

6   Leo Marx, *The Machine in the Garden: Technology and the Pastoral Ideal in America* (New York: Oxford Univ. Press, 1964).

7   Richard P. McCormick, *New Jersey From Colony to State, 1609- 1789* (rev. ed., Newark:N.J. Historical Society, 1981; orig. 1964), Chapt. 2.

8   For the history of county boundaries, see John Parr Snyder, *The Story of New Jersey's Civil Boundaries, 1609-1968* (Trenton: Bureau of Geology and Topography, 1969); John P. Wall and Harold E. Pickersgill, eds., *History of Middlesex County, New Jersey, 1664-1920* (3 vols., New York: Lewis Publishing Co., 1921), I:49-55.

9   For information on the early towns, see *ibid.*, 19-24, 401-402, 416; see also the *WPA Guide to New Jersey*, 299, 362-63; Steele Mabon Kennedy et al., *The New Jersey Almanac, 1964-1965* (Upper Montclair: N.J. Almanac, 1963), 489.

10   For general descriptions of early county economic activity, see W. Woodford Clayton, ed., *History of Middlesex and Union Counties...* (Philadelphia: Everts & Peck, 1882), 422-586; *Industries of New Jersey*, 33.

11   On the economic effects of the Revolutionary War, see McCormick, *From Colony to State*, 154, 161-63.

THE MIDDLESEX WATER COMPANY

12   Wall and Pickersgill, eds., *History of Middlesex County*, 271-74, 472-73; for a typical list-ing of county businesses (which were overwhelmingly small in scale), see various town entries in *Boyd's New Jersey State Business Directory* (Washington, D.C.: Wm H. Boyd, 1878), *passim*; see also *Industries of New Jersey*, 33; *New Jersey Almanac 1964-1965*, 492.

13   *WPA Guide to New Jersey*, 299; *New Jersey Almanac, 1964-1965*, 489.

14   *New Jersey Almanac, 1964-1965*, 491; see the various references to Middlesex County in Lane, *From Indian Trail to Iron Horse, passim.*

15   *The New Jersey Almanac*, 1964-1965, 488-91.

16   *WPA Guide to New Jersey*, 552. A few ocean-going vessels did put in at Woodbridge docks until slit from the claypits blocked the narrow channel.

17   *Industries of New Jersey*, 33; *WPA Guide to New Jersey*, 301; *New Jersey Almanac, 1964-1965*, 491.

18   Clayton, ed., *History of Union and Middlesex Counties*, 424-25, 554.

19   William Stainsby, comp., *The Industrial Directory of New Jersey* (Trenton: Bureau of Statistics, 1901), 49-50, 233; *Industries of New Jersey*, 33; Clayton, ed., History of Union and *Middlesex Counties*, 554.

20   Stainsby, comp., *Industrial Directory of New Jersey*, 130, 188-89, 208.

21   *WPA Guide to New Jersey*, 299, 362.

22   State of New Jersey, Dept. of State, Census Bureau [S.D. Dickinson], *Compendium of Censuses, 1726-1905* (Trenton: Murphy Publishing Co., 1906), 28-29; State of New Jersey, Census Bureau, *Census of 1910* (Trenton: N.J. Dept. of State, 1911), 86.

23   For data on precipitation, geology, and the water supplying central New Jersey, see Cornelius C. Vermeule, *Report on Water Supply*. Vol. III of *The Final Report of the State Geologist* (Trenton: Geological Survey of New Jersey, 1984), 13-17, 207-208; *New Jersey Almanac, 1964-1965*, 112; Clayton, comp., *History of Union and Middlesex Counties*, 423.

24   *New Jersey Almanac, 1964-1965*, 114-15.

25   Geological Survey of New Jersey, *Annual Report of the State Geologist for the Year 1901* (Trenton: MacCrellish & Quigley, 1902), 119.

26   *Ibid.*, 114-15; Robert D.B. Carlisle, *Water Ways: A History of the Elizabethtown Water Company* (Elizabeth: Elizabethtown Water Company, 1982), 17-18; Clayton, comp., History of Union *and Middlesex Counties*, 429; Wall and Pickersgill, eds., *History of Middlesex County*, 69.

27   The Geological Survey as of 1893 listed only three Middlesex County towns with water systems: New Brunswick, which pumped water from Lawrence Brook, and Perth Amboy and South Amboy, which both pumped water from Tennent's Brook; see Vermeule, *Report on Water Supply*, 315-17.

28   For a survey of the claypit companies, see Clayton, ed., *History of Union and Middlesex Counties*, 424-25, 554.

29   Vermeule, *Report on Water Supply*, 319-20.

30   On the water use involved in different production processes, see Saloman J. Flink, "Water Resources," in Saloman J. Flink, ed., *The Economy of New Jersey* (New Brunswick: Rutgers University Press, 1958), 102-103.

31   David L. Cowen, *Medicine in New Jersey* (Princeton: D. Van Nostrand Co., Inc., 1964), 83.

32   Vermeule, *Report on Water Supply*, 314-15.

33   Vermeule's discussion of pollution and water treatment is in his 1894 *Report on Water Supply*, 298-99.

34   Stainsby, ed., *Industrial Directory of New Jersey [1901]*, 50.

35   Frank Bergen, "Memo relating to the origin and development of Middlesex Water Company," c. 1924, Middlesex Water Company Records, Book 1, Iselin, N.J.

36   Stainsby, ed., *Industrial Directory of New Jersey [1901]*, 50; Lewis T. Bryant, ed., *The Industrial Directory of New Jersey, 1918* (Paterson: N.J. Bureau of Industrial Statistics, 1918), 104.

206

37   Vermeule, *Report on Water Supply*, 320.

38   *Ibid.*, 316-18.

39   See the various references in Mary Murrin, ed., *New Jersey Historical Manuscripts: A Guide to Collections in the State* (Trenton: N.J. Historical Commission, 1987), 24, 42, 47, 79, 108.

40   Adrian C. Leiby, *The Hackensack Water Company, 1869-1969* (River Edge: Bergen County Historical Society, 1969), Capts. 2 and 3; Carlisle, *Water Ways*, Chapter 4.

41   Many stock holders owned only a single share. Stock records are in Newark Aqueduct Company, Book of Transfers, 1803-60, MG 278, New Jersey Historical Society [NJHS], Newark.

42   The various water companies of the S.U.M. can be traced in the business records held in the Passaic County Historical Society, Paterson, N.J. The records include: East Jersey Water Co., 1889-1923; Montclair Water Co., 1887-1923, Passaic Water Co., 1857-1923. In 1923, these companies were merged to form the Passaic Consolidated Water Co.

43   Murrin, ed., *New Jersey Manuscripts*, 58 .

44   The new law was "An Act for the Construction, Maintenance and operation of water works for the purpose of supplying cities, towns and villages in this state with water," April 21, 1876, Com. Stat., 3635.

45   On the growth and importance of utilities generally, see Thomas N. McCarter, "Public Utilities in New Jersey [1907]," pp. 16-27, in *One Phase of a Jerseyman's Activities* (Garden City, N.Y.: Country Life Press, 1933), 16-20; on Public Service, see James C.G. Conniff and Richard Conniff, *The Energy People: A History of PSE&G* (Newark: PSE&G, 1978).

46   See the tables listing New Jersey supply systems to 1893 in Vermeule, *Report on Water Supply*, 315-18

Notes to Chapter 2

1   On the founding of the original company, see Frank Bergen, Memo relating to the origin and development of the Middlesex Water Company, c. 1924, Middlesex Water Company Records, Book 1, Iselin, N.J., 1; New Jersey Secretary of State, *Corporations of New Jersey: List of Certificates to December 31, 1911* (Trenton: MacCrellish & Quigley, 1914), 425; biographical information on Corbin is in Daniel Van Winkle, ed., *History of the Municipalities of Hudson County, New Jersey, 1630-1923* (3 vols., New York: Lewis Historical Publishing Company, 1924), III: 696-97.

2   *Ibid.*, 697; William H. Corbin, comp., *The Act Concerning Corporations in New Jersey. . .* (8th edn, Trenton: Naar, Day & Naar, 1894); N.J. Commissioners to Care for the Gettysburg Battle Monument, *Report* (Trenton: Naar, Day & Naar, 1893). Corbin was also something of a local historian of the American Revolution; see his *The Battle of Elizabethtown. . .* (Elizabethtown: Journal Press, 1905?), and *Connecticut Farms: An Address. . .* (Elizabethtown: Journal Press, 1905).

3   Van Winkle, ed., *Hudson County*, III: 697.

4   On the depression of the 1890s in New Jersey, see Jeanette Paddock Nichols, "The Industrial History of New Jersey Since 1861," Chapt. 43, in Irving S. Kull, ed., *New Jersey: A History* (4 vols., New York: American Historical Society, 1930), Vol. 3: 920-24.

5   John P. Wall and Harold E. Pickersgill, eds., *History of Middlesex County, New Jersey, 1664-1920* (3 vols., New York: Lewis Historical Publishing Company, 1921), II: 472-73; N.J. Labor and Industry Department, *Fifth Annual Report of the Inspector of Factories and Workshops of the State of New Jersey, 1887* (Trenton, John L. Murphy Publishing Co., 1887), 72-73; water use figures are based on data in Report of the Superintendent [of the] Middlesex Water Company. . ., July 1907, MWCR, Book 1.

6   Wall and Pickersgill, eds., *Middlesex County*, 473.

7   *Ibid.*, II: 473; N.J. Labor and Industry Dept., *Fifth Annual Report. . .Factories and Workshops*, 72-73; water consumption estimates are calculated from the Report of the Superintendent. . .1907, MWCR. Later information on some of these companies is available in N.J. Bureau of Industrial Statistics, Dept. of Labor, *The Industrial Directory of New Jersey. . .1918* (Paterson: News Printing Company, 1918), 105, 653.

8   For a list of early Middlesex Water Company contracts, see Minutes of Directors Meeting, June 23, 1897, Midland Water Company Minute Book, June 12 1896-July 17, 1897, p. 31, Middlesex Water Company Records, Middlesex Water Company, Iselin, N.J.

9   Bergen, Memo relating to the origin and development of Middlesex Water Company, MWCR, 1.

10   N.J. Sec. of State, *Corporations of New Jersey*, 425.

11   *Ibid.*, 426; Meeting of Incorporators, June 12, 1896, Midland Water Company Minute Book, June 12, 1896 to July 17, 1897, p. 3, Middlesex Water Company Records, Iselin, N.J. The Midland Company also considered going into the electricity generating business and amended its charter accordingly (see the minutes of the June 17, 1896 meeting, *ibid.*, 19); nothing came of the idea.

12   *Ibid.*, 16. Unless otherwise noted, the Midland Water Company Minute Book, in the MWCR, is the source for the following discussion of the early growth of the Midland Company and its subsequent merger with Corbin's Middlesex Water Company.

13   *Ibid.*, 33; Minutes of Meeting of Directors of Middlesex Water Company (the consolidated company), July 22, 1897, MWCR; N.J. Secretary of State, *Corporations of New Jersey*, 426.

14   Biographical information on Bergen is from Edward Quinton Keasbey, *The Lawyers and Courts of New Jersey, 1616-1912* (3 vols., New York: Lewis Historical Publishing Co., 1912), III: 232-33; a detailed obituary is in the *Newark Evening News*, Nov. 12, 1934. The account over the next several paragraphs is based on these sources.

15   Robert D.B. Carlisle, *Water Ways: A History of the Elizabethtown Water Company* (Elizabeth: Elizabethtown Water Company, 1982), 80-87.

16   "McCarter Again President of P.S.," *Newark Evening News*, Apr. 19, 1933.

ENDNOTES

17   Some of Bergen's interests and activities are noted in: "Historic Park Is Dedicated in Morristown," *Newark Evening News*, July 5, 1933; "At Banquet in Celebration of Billboard Bill Victor," *ibid.*, Apr. 2, 1930; "Scholarship Shown In Dr. Bergen's Books," *ibid.*, June 7, 1931; "Frank Bergen Lauds Works Board," *ibid.*, Jan. 15, 1915; Frank Bergen to William T. Hunt, Apr. 1, 1897, MG 22, Hunt Autograph Collection, A-B File, New Jersey Historical Society, Newark, N.J. Bergen's essays are collected in Essays and Speeches of Frank Bergen (2 vols., Newark: Privately Printed, 1931).
18   "Frank Bergen Is Dead at 82," *Newark Evening News*, Nov. 12, 1934; "Declined Seat on the Bench," *ibid.*, June 8, 1906.
19   The above account was compiled from the following: "Frank Bergen Again Will Make His Home In Elizabethtown," *Newark Evening News*, Dec. 30, 1923; "Mrs. Frank Bergen of Bernardsville," *ibid.*, Feb. 27, 1948; "Bergen Gives Yale $20,000 for Memorial to His Son," *ibid.*, May 19, 1919; "A Bank's Unusual Philanthropical Venture," *Metro Newark*, Spring 1987, 11-12; interview with Theodore Grundmann, Metuchen, N.J., Oct. 13, 1989.
20   The various aspects of McCarter's career can be traced in his collected essays and papers, *One Phase of a Jerseyman's Activities* (Garden City, N.Y.: Country Life Press, 1933).
21   On the Keans, see Carlisle, *Water Ways, passim*; Adrian C. Leiby, *The Hackensack Water Company, 1869-1969* (River Edge: Bergen County Historical Society, 1969), Chaps. 2 - 3; Paul A. Stellhorn and Michael J. Birkner, eds., *The Governors of New Jersey, 1664-1974: Biographical Essays* (Trenton: New Jersey Historical Commission, 1982), 165-68.
22   On the rise of professional managers, see C. Joseph Pusateri, *A History of American Business* (Arlington Heights, Ill.: Harlan Davidson, 1984), Chapt. 12.
23   "Midland Water Company Minute Book, June 12, 1896 - July 17, 1897," MWCR, pp. 25, 26, 29, 32.
24   Frank Bergen to Robert M. Kellogg, Aug. 12, 1897, p. 2, *ibid.*
25   Frank Bergen to Thomas Doud, Oct. 14, 1897, Middlesex Water Company Letterbook, p. 52, MWC.
26   Bergen, "Memo relating to. . .Middlesex Water Company," MWCR.
27   Midland Water Company Minute Book, June 12, 1896 - July 17, 1897, MWC, p. 31; "Report of the Superintendent of the Middlesex Water Company [1907], MWCR. Unless otherwise noted, discussion of customers and extension of the water mains is based on these two sources.
28   Frank Bergen to R.M. Kellogg, Apr. 7, 1903, Middlesex Water Company Letterbook, p. 300, MWC.
29   Details on the company's first decade are traced in the "Minutes of Meetings of Directors of the Middlesex Water Company," July 22, 1897 - Oct. 3, 1907, pp. 25, 26, 36, 64, 82. Hereafter cited as "MWC Minutes of Meetings."
30   Bergen to P.H. and J. Conlan, Sept. 14, 1900, MWC Letterbook, 229; Bergen to R.M. Kellogg, Jan. 22, 1901, *ibid.*, 238.
31   *Ibid., passim*; income and asset figures are listed in the June and December meetings of each year. "Report of Superintendent of the Middlesex water Company. . .," 1907, MWCR.
32   Frank Bergen to Amos Andrews, Oct. 13, 1897, Middlesex Water Company Letterbook, MWC; Bergen to Wheeler Condenser & Engineering Company, [Oct. 7], 1902, *ibid.*; "MWC Minutes of Meetings," Feb. 6, May 29, 1903, 36, 51.
33   The growth of corporate concerns over the water supply is traced in "MWC Minutes of Meetings," July 28, 1903, p. 56, Oct. 17, 1904, p. 75-76, and *passim*.
34   Bergen, "Memo relating to the origin. . .of [the] Middlesex Water Company," MWCR.
35   The geology and hydrology of the Rahway River water shed, including Robinsons Branch, are discussed in Henry R. Anderson, *Geology and Ground-Water Resources of the Rahway Area, New Jersey*, New Jersey State Water Policy and Supply Commission Special Report No. 27 ([Trenton]: U.S. Geological Survey, 1968), 6-7, 31-32.
36   "Minutes of a Meeting of the Directors of the Consumers Aqueduct Company," Sept. 10, 1907, pp. 53-54, MWC; "Minutes of Meetings," Dec. 16, 1905, p. 95, MWC; *ibid.*, Mar. 9, 1906, pp. 103-105.

37   Unless noted otherwise, the following account of the construction of the reservoir at Robinsons Branch, as well as the Consumer Aqueduct Company, is based on "Minutes of Meetings," Mar. 9, Mar. 24, Apr. 5, Dec. 11, 1906, Jan. 20, Feb. 13, Apr. 5, July 23, Sept. 10, Oct. 7, 1907, pp. 103-107, 130, 138, 162, 168-69, 180, MWC; "Certificate of Incorporation of Consumers Aqueduct Company," Mar. 25, 1907, MWC; "Minutes of the First Meeting of Directors of Consumers Aqueduct Company [and of subsequent meetings]," Mar. 25-Oct. 3, 1907, pp. 23, 25-26, 37, 39, 41-45, 48-55, 75-78, MWC.

38   "Minutes of Meetings," June 30, 1907, p. 113, MWC; *ibid.*, July 23, 1907, p. 162.

39   The contract negotiations had stalled as early as April 1906, and Bergen was never able to get them back on track; see *Ibid.*, Apr. 5, 1906, p. 107, MWC.

40   "Minutes of Meetings. . .Consumers Aqueduct Company," May 28, June 19, Sept. 10, 1907, pp. 25-26, 37, 41, 48-54, MWC.

41   The above account of the completion of the reservoir is from Bergen, "Memo relating to the origin. . .of the Middlesex Water Company," c. 1927, MWCR; and "Minutes of Meetings," May 13, 1908, p. 29, MWC. The consolidation of the companies is traced in "Minutes of Meetings. . .Consumers Aqueduct Company," Oct. 3, 1907, pp. 75-78, MWC.

42   The customer base is derived from figures in "Report of the Superintendent [of the] Middlesex Water Company. . .," 1907, MWCR; financial and dividend information is in "Minutes of Meetings," July 27, 1907, p. 162; June 30, 1908, p. 72.

Notes to Chapter 3

1   Statistics on the growth of the water mains were drawn from information in the "Annual Report of the Middlesex Water Company as Corrected by the Commissioners to the Board of Public Utility Commissioners of the State of New Jersey. . .1911" [title varies by year; hereafter cited by year as BPUC Report], MWCR; "Middlesex Water Company Income & Loss Account From January 1st 1908 to December 31st 1911," MWC Minutes of Meetings, 1911, pp. 186-87; "Valuation of Middlesex Water Company Property as of Dec. 31, 1919," MWCR, Old Files, Folder 2, Box 94.

2   Interview with Leon Silakoski, Woodbridge, NJ, 5 Oct. 1989.

3   *Ibid.*, interview of 13 May 1991.

4   "Water Co. in Role of Turning Worm," *Newark Evening News*, 15 Sept. 1915.

5   Herbert B. Baldwin to Frank Bergen, 22 May 1908, in MWC Minutes of Meetings, 1908, p. 32-33, MWCR.

6   MWC Minutes of Meetings, 10 June 1908, p. 34, MWCR; "Valuation of Middlesex Water Company Property as of Dec. 31, 1919," MWCR; MWC Minutes of Meetings, 23 Dec. 1920, MWCR.

7   Geological Survey of New Jersey, *Annual Report of the State Geologist for the Year 1901* (Trenton: MacCrellish & Quigley, 1902), 132.

8   David L. Cowen, *Medicine and Health in New Jersey: A History*. New Jersey Historical Series, No. 16 (Princeton: Van Nostrand, 1964), 83; on filtration in Europe and America, see N.M. Baker, *The Quest for Pure Water: The History of Water Purification from the Earliest Records to the Twentieth Century* (New York: American Water Works Association, 1948), Chapters 6 & 7.

9   *Ibid.*, 136-41, 148-51, 158-60; Adrian C. Leiby, *The Hackensack Water Company, 1869-1969* (River Edge: Bergen County Historical Society, 1969), 95-97, 110-111.

10   George W. Fuller, "Report on Water Supply" [prepared for Conference of Municipalities Served by Elizabethtown, Plainfield-Union, and Middlesex Water Companies], 5 Aug. 1922, p. 8, MWCR; Baker, *Quest for Pure Water*, 217-28.

11   BPUC Report for 1911, MWCR.

12   MWC Minutes of Meetings, 14 April 1916, pp. 30-32, MWCR; George W. Fuller, "Report on Water Supply" [report for Conference of Municipalities Served by Elizabethtown, Plainfield-Union, and Middlesex Water Companies], 5 Aug. 1922, pp. 9-10, MWCR.

13   MWC Minutes of Meetings, 14 April 1916, pp. 30-32; Frank H. Sommer, "In the matter of proposed increases in the rates of Middlesex Water Company, etc.: Memorandum on behalf of municipalities and other users," 1924 [brief for New Jersey State BPUC hearing, Frank H. Sommer, counsel], 45.

14   MWC Minutes of Meetings, 14 April 1916, p. 30-32, MWCR; "Valuation of. . .Property as of Dec. 31, 1919," MWCR.

15   The above account of MWC supply sources and pumping activities was based on information in *ibid*.; in Fuller, "Report on Water Supply," pp. 8-11, MWCR; and in Sommer, "In the matter Middlesex Water Company," pp. 46-47, 49.

16   On Kellogg, see "Minutes of a Meeting of the Directors of Consumers Aqueduct Company, 10 Sept. 1907, p. 50, 76, MWCR; MWC Minutes of Meetings, 16 Dec. 1905, p. 114; correspondence from Bergen is in Middlesex Water Co., Letter Book # 1, 11 Aug. 1897-5 June 1903, MWCR; Kellogg's resignation is noted in MWC Minutes of Meetings, 12 Aug. 1908, p. 39-40.

17   *Ibid.*, 14 Oct. 1908, p. 47.

18   Information on Mundy's background came from interviews with his children, Barbara Reusmann and Albert C. Mundy, Scotch Plains, NJ, 5 Sept. 1989; interview with Ms. Marion Sanborn [daughter of Ambrose Mundy], Scotch Plains, NJ, 6 May 1990; interview with Leon Silakowski, Woodbridge, NJ, 20 May 1991.

19   Records are scant on the number of employees before 1915; I estimated based on random notes in company records. After 1915, the the BPUC Annual Reports note the number of employees for given years. Additional information on early employees and work at the company came from an interview with Barbara Reusmann of Scotch Plains, NJ, 5 Sept. 1990.

20   On the Panic of 1907 in New Jersey, see Jeannette Paddock Nichols, "The Industrial History of New Jersey Since 1861," Chapt. 43, in Irving S. Kull, ed., *New Jersey: A History* (4 vols., New York: American Historical Society, 1930), Vol. 3: 929-31.

21   Statistics on profits and dividends were drawn from information in: "Annual Report of the Middlesex Water Company as Corrected by the Commissioners to the Board of Public Utility Commissioners of the State of New Jersey. . .1911" [hereafter cited by year as BPUC Report], MWCR; "Middlesex Water Company Income & Loss Account From January 1st 1908 to December 31st, 1911," MWC Minutes of Meetings, 1911, pp. 186-87.

22   On the lack of standardized accounting in the company's early years, see Arnold B. Rosenthal, "Investigation of the Middlesex Water Company, Woodbridge, New Jersey," 1938, MWC Records, Iselin, N.J.

23   Sommer, "In the matter of. . .Middlesex Water Company," 22-23.

24   Rosenthal, "Investigation of Middlesex Water Company," 68-86; Sommer, "In the matter of. . .Middlesex Water Company," 22-23.

25   BPUC Report for 1911, MWCR; MWC Minutes of Meetings, 28 Dec. 1917, p. 50.

26   Fuller, "Report on Water Supply," i-ii; Frank Bergen, "The Water Situation in Union, Middlesex and Somerset Counties," *Elizabeth Daily Journal*, 6 Aug. 1923 [reprint of Bergen speech of 10 Sept. 1919]; NJ Board of Public Utility Commissioners, "Memorandum by Board: In re failure of Middlesex Water Company, Elizabethtown Water Company and Plainfield-Union Water Company to comply with order of the Board dated June 8th, 1920," 15 May 1923, MWCR.

27   Sommer, "In the matter of. . .Middlesex Water Company," 51.

28   Various complaints about service were detailed in *ibid.*, pp. 2-5, 20; "Shaving Hindered by Low Water Pressure," *Newark Evening News*, 8 Jan. 1925.

29   Percentage drawn from data in *ibid.*

30   For pipe sizes, see "Valuation of Middlesex Water Company Property. . .1919," MWCR; engineering reports and comments on the standpipes are quoted in Frank H. Sommer, "Supplementary Memorandum on behalf of municipalities and other users" [addendum to brief for BPUC regarding MWC rate request], July 1924, pp. 2-3, 8-9; and Sommer, "In the matter of. . .Middlesex Water Company," pp. 52-53, MWCR.

31   *Ibid.*, 44-45.

32   Company responses to complaints are noted in *Ibid.*, 44-45.

33   Sommer, "Supplementary Memorandum," 4.

34   For overview of the Raritan-Millstone venture from the perspective of the Elizabethtown Company, see Robert D.B. Carlisle, *Water Ways: A History of the Elizabethtown Water Company* (Elizabeth, N.J.: Elizabethtown Water Company, 1982), 110, 118-130. The Piscataway and Raritan Water Companies, Elizabethtown subsidiaries, had figured in the 1918 planning, but the Board of Conservation and Economic development ruled that only the larger companies should be principals. MWC and Bergen's action are noted in MWC Minutes of Meetings, 29 Aug. 1918, p. 54; "Mr. Bergen's

Reply to Plainfield," 28 Sept. 1925 [reprint of letter from Bergen to Common Council of the City of Plainfield], MWCR.

35   *Ibid.*, 4; "Menace of Water Famine," 7-8; Bergen, "Water Situation," 7-8.

36   Fuller, "Report on Water Supply"; *The Menace of a Water Famine*, 1-3.

37   The memorandum of 8 June 1920 is excerpted in N.J. BPUC, "Memorandum: In re failure. . .to comply with order of the Board dated June 8th, 1920," 15 May 1923.

38   "The Menace of a Water Famine," *Magazine of the Chamber of Commerce of the Plainfields*, Supplement, April 1923, 4; "Frank Bergen Is Critic Of State Utilities Board," *Newark Evening News*, 20 June 1922; "Argues Board Rule Halts Water Work Completion," *ibid.*, 4 May 1923; Frank Bergen, "The Water Situation in Union, Middlesex and Somerset Counties," *Elizabeth Daily Journal*, 6 Aug. 1923.

39   Bergen, "The Water Situation," 11-13.

40   "In the matter of the filing by Middlesex Water Company of increased rates" [Middlesex Water Company petition to the BPUC], 15 July 1920, MWCR; "Lacked Income for Water Development," *Newark Evening News*, 24 June 1924; Board of Public Utility Commissioners, "Memorandum by Board: In re failure of Middlesex Water Company, Elizabethtown Water Company and Plainfield-Union Water Company to comply with order of the Board dated June 8th, 1920," 15 May 1923, MWCR.

41   BPUC, "In re failure of Middlesex Water Company. . .to comply with order of the Board dated June 8th, 1920," 5-6; "Argues Board Rule Halts Water Work Completion," *Newark Evening News*, 4 May 1923.

42   *The Menace of a Water Famine*, 4; BPUC, "In re failure. . .to comply with order of the Board dated June 8th, 1920," p. 1; Bergen, *The Water Situation*, 13-14.

43   For examples in this regard, see "Water Crisis Near, Sanitarians Told," *Newark Evening News*, 4 Dec. 1920; Frank Bergen, "The Water Situation in Union, Middlesex and Somerset Counties," *Elizabeth Daily Journal*, 6 Aug. 1923; "Constructive Program Only Method to Solve Water Problem," *New Evening News*, 4 Sept. 1924; Frank Bergen, *The Chimney Rock Project: A Statement* (1928).

44   The above account was drawn from Bergen, *The Water Situation*, 6-7; "The Menace of a Water Famine," 4-7; BPUC, "In re failure. . .to comply with order of the Board dated June 8th, 1920," 7-8.

45   BPUC, *Financial and Miscellaneous Statistics Compiled from the Annual Reports made by Public Utilities to the Board of Public Utility Commissioners for the Year 1913* (Union Hill, NJ: Dispatch Printing Co., 1915), 7-9.

Notes to Chapter 4

1   This survey of progressive concerns comes from Arthur S. Link and Richard L. McCormick, *Progressivism* (Arlington Heights, Ill.: Harlan Davidson, 1983), esp. Chapts. 1, 2, and 3; the quotation is from p. 21.

2   Ransom E. Noble, Jr., *New Jersey Progressivism before Wilson* (Princeton: Princeton Univ. Press, 1946), 4-6; Frank Bergen, *Essays and Speeches of Frank Bergen*, Vol. 2 (Newark: Privately Printed, 1931), 209-10; Thomas N. McCarter, *One Phase of a Jerseyman's Activities* (Garden City, N.Y.: Country Life Press, 1933), 17.

3   Noble, *New Jersey Progressivism*, 4.

4   The above treatment of New Jersey progressivism comes from ibid., 4-11, 68-71, 100-103. Ransom's perspective is openly sympathetic with the reformers and hostile to business, but his is the best single overview of early New Jersey progressive motivations and concerns. Unless noted otherwise, the following account is based on Ransom.

5   McCarter, *A Jerseyman's Activities*, 17.

6   Bergen, *Essays and Speeches*, 213; see also James C.G. Conniff and Richard Conniff, *The Energy People: A History of PES&G* (Newark: PSE&G, 1978), 195-96.

7   Arthur S. Link *et al.*, eds., *The Papers of Woodrow Wilson* (Princeton: Princeton Univ. Press, 1966-), 21:311, 316, 341-42; 22:11; David W. Hirst, *Woodrow Wilson: Reform Governor; A Documentary Narrative* (Princeton: Van Nostrand, 1965), 88-90, 170-71, 218-19; Bergen, *Essays and Speeches*, 229.

8   William Henry Speer, "Political Panaceas and the People," *American Industries*, (June 1911):30-31.

9   Link, ed., *Papers of Woodrow Wilson*, 22:579-80.

10   George H. Dietz, "Public Utility Regulation in New Jersey, 1938 to 1949" (M.A. thesis, Rutgers Univ., New Brunswick, N.J., 1949), 3, 11, 87; Adrian C. Leiby, *The Hackensack Water Company, 1869-1969: A Centennial History* (River Edge, N.J.: Bergen County Historical Society, 1969), 155-56.

11   *Reports of the Board of Public Utility Commissioners*, Vol. II, June 9, 1913 to May 12, 1914 (Union Hill, N.J.: Dispatch Printing Co., 1915), 213-15; ibid., Vol. IV, March 11, 1918 to Feb. 9, 1919 (Trenton: State Gazette Publishing, 1919), 416-20.

12   Frank Bergen, "Going Value," *Proceedings of the Seventeenth Annual Convention of the New Jersey Utilities Association* (1932), 36-58.

13   On the Public Service case, see "Middlesex Water and Public Service Cases," *Newark Evening News*, 16 Aug. 1924.

14   For the development of Bergen's constitutional argument, see "Middlesex Company Asks Injunction on New Water Rates," *ibid.*, 13 Aug 1924; "What Is Equity's Essence In Middlesex Water Issue," *ibid.*, 19 Aug. 1924.

15   Unless noted otherwise, this following account comes from the *Reports of the Board of Public Utility Commissioners*, Vols. VIII [16 Mar. 1920 to 21 Dec. 1920] to XIV [12 July 1928 to 8 Apr. 1930], passim.

16   "Middlesex Water Company and Agent arraigned in Brief," *Newark Evening News*, 19 June 1924.

17   *Ibid.*, XII:426.

18   "Middlesex Company Gets Increase...," *Newark Evening News*, 1 Aug. 1924; "May Start Over in Water Case," *ibid.*, 11 Oct. 1927.

19   The company's appeal to the federal court is noted in: "Middlesex Company Asks Injunction on New Water Rates," *Newark Evening News*, 13 Aug. 1924; "Master to Sit in Water Rate Appeal," *ibid.*, 30 Sept. 1924; "Finds Water Rates Fixed Too Low for Middlesex Company," *ibid.*, 26 May 1925.

20   "Challenges Order For Water Rebate," *ibid.*, 3 Feb. 1925; Frank Bergen, *The Water Situation in Union, Middlesex, and Somerset Counties* (Elizabeth: *Daily Journal*, 1923), 10-11; "What Is Equity's Essence In Middlesex Water Issue," *Newark Evening News*, 19 Aug. 1924.

21   "Finds Water Rates Too Low For Middlesex Company," *ibid.*, 26 May 1925; "Court Upholds Ban On Utilities Board In Water Co. Suit," *ibid.*, 7 Jan. 1926.

22   "Chance to Escape State Loss of Rate Control," *ibid.*, 8 Jan. 1926.

23   For *Times* coverage, see stories on 1, 21, 29 Aug. 1926. There were also follow-up stories on 27 Mar. 1927 and 17 Jan. 1928.

24   "Master's View on Middlesex's Rates Attacked by Board," *ibid.*, 5 June 1925. There was another District Court hearing in June, which also went against the BPUC on grounds of timeliness and because the Board's appeal to the Supreme Court already was in progress; see "Utilities Board Plea Is Denied," *ibid.*, 19 June 1926; "Peace Sought In Water Suit," *ibid.*, 25 June 1926; "Sommer, Angry At Bergen, Out Of Water Case," *ibid.*, 12 Oct. 1926.

25   "Middlesex rate On Water Up to Supreme Court," *ibid.*, 6 Apr. 1926; "Having Appealed to Caesar...," *ibid.*, 9 Apr. 1926; "May Start Over In Water Case," *ibid.*, 11 Oct. 1927.

26   "Peace Sought In Water Suit," *ibid.*, 25 June 1926; "Water Problems Nearer Solution," *ibid.*, 9 July 1926; "Seek to End Water Fuss," *ibid.*, 14 July 1926; Minutes of Meetings, 14 Apr. 1925, Middlesex Water Company, Iselin, New Jersey; "Approve Bond Issue," *Newark Evening News*, 26 Mar. 1927.

27   Frank Bergen to Joseph F. Autenreith, 10 Feb. 1926, in *The Water Situation: Correspondence between the President of Middlesex Water Company and the President of the Board of Public Utility Commissioners* [pamphlet] (1926), Middlesex Water Company, Iselin, N.J.

28 "In the Matter of the Application of the Middlesex Water Company...," *Reports of the Board of Public Utility Commissioners*, XIV [12 July 1928 to 8 Apr. 1930]:411-15.
29 MWC Minutes of Meetings, 14 Apr. 1925; "In re - Consolidation of Plainfield-Union Water Company and Middlesex Water Company," 25 Feb. 1929, MWCR, file 216.

30 A copy of the draft contract for the formation of the Somerset Water Company, dated only 1927, is in MWCR, file 216; Robert D.B. Carlisle, *Water Ways: A History of the Elizabethtown Water Company* (Elizabeth: Elizabethtown Water Company, 1982), 125-130.

Notes to Chapter 5

1 This picture of Middlesex County economic activity is based on James A.T. Gribbin, comp., *The Industrial Directory of New Jersey, 1938* (Trenton: Norris W. Brown, N.J. Dept. of Labor, 1938), 14-15, 20-21, 23, 29.
2 *Ibid.*, 29; William E. Ohland, comp., *Report of the Activities of the Civil Works Administration in Middlesex County, New Jersey (November 16, 1933 to March 1934)* (Perth Amboy: Civil Works Admin., 1934), 1-15.
3 Arnold B. Rosenthal, "Investigation of Middlesex Water Company, Woodbridge, New Jersey" (CPA Report, prepared for the Middlesex County Board of Chosen Freeholders, 23 March 1938), 105.
4 Figures are drawn from company statistics from the early 1930s and compiled for yearly filings with the state in the *Annual Report of the Middlesex Water Co. as corrected by the Commissioners to the Board of Public Utility Commissioners of the State of New Jersey.*
5 For information on work and workers during the Great Depression, I relied on interviews with Theodore Grundmann, 13 October 1989, Metuchen, New Jersey; and with Leon Silakoski, 5 October and 7 November 1989, 13 May 1991, Woodbridge, New Jersey.
6 "Frank Bergen Seriously Ill at Bernards Home," *Newark Evening News*, 12 Apr. 1932; "McCarter Again President of P.S.," *ibid.*, 18 Apr. 1933.
7 "Anarchy Looms Unless People Back Constitution, Bergen Says," *ibid.*, 19 Nov. 1933; Frank Bergen, "Prosperity Plundered By Long Term Bonds," *ibid.*, 8 Jan. 1933; "Historic Park Is Dedicated In Morristown," *ibid.*, 5 July 1933; "Urges More Respect Paid to Constitution," *ibid.*, 17 Feb. 1934.
8 "Frank Bergen Is Dead at 82," *ibid.*, 12 Nov. 1934; "Frank Bergen Will Is Filed," *ibid.*, 23 Nov. 1934; "To Perpetuate Bergen Memory," *ibid.*, 24 Nov. 1934; "Mrs. Frank Bergen of Bernardsville," *ibid.*, 27 Feb. 1948; "A Bank's Unusual Philanthropical Venture," *Metro Newark* (Spring 1987):10-12.
9 For biographical information on Speer, I relied on an interview with Carolina M. Schneider, 24 July 1987, Middlesex Water Company, Iselin, N.J.; *Who Was Who in America*, III (Chicago: A.N. Marquis Co., 1960), 807; "Judge Speer, 90, Enjoys Full Life," *Newark Evening News*, 21 Oct. 1958; "W.H. Speer Dies at 90," *ibid.*, 8 July 1958.
10 "Judge Speer Resigns To Join Public Service," *ibid.*, 17 June 1922; "Judge Speer's Retirement From Morris Canal Body" [Editorial], *ibid.*, 19 June 1922.
11 "What Depression?, Middlesex Water Co. Asked With Dividends At 12 Per Cent," *Perth Amboy Evening News*, 2 July 1937.
12 Julian Mason, "The New Deal," *Riverton [N.N.] New Era*, 3 Jan. 1935.
13 Federal Writers' Project, *The WPA Guide to 1930s New Jersey* (New Brunswick: Rutgers Univ. Press, 1986; orig. 1939), 76, 108, 577.
14 "Authorized to Investigate Water Rates in Middlesex," *Newark Evening News*, 23 Nov. 1936; "Middlesex Water Rates Under Fire," *ibid.*, 18 Dec. 1936.
15 Arnold B. Rosenthal to Edmund A. Hayes, 23 Mar. 1938, Middlesex Water Co. Records, Iselin, N.J.; "Middlesex May Ask Cut in Water Rate," *Newark Evening News*, 11 May 1937.

16   Rosenthal, "Middlesex Water Company," 1; "Water Rate Data Given Middlesex," *Newark Evening News*, 2 July 1937; "To Report on Water Co.," ibid., 7 Apr. 1938.
17   Memorandum on Report of Arnold B. Rosenthal, Esq., Accountant for Middlesex County, New Jersey, Board of Chosen Freeholders, on Middlesex Water Company, [1938], MWCR.
18   "Water Rates," *ibid.*, 21 Apr. 1939; "Middlesex Company Cuts Rates," 26 May 1939.
19   Minutes of Meetings, Middlesex Water Company, 6 June, 11 July, 10 Aug., 3 Oct. 1939, MWC.
20   On New Jersey's industrial build-up, see Mark Edward Lender, *One State in Arms: A Short Military History of New Jersey* (Trenton: N.J. Historical Commission, 1991), 82-84.
21   BPUC Reports for 1939 to 1941; MWC Minutes of Directors Meetings, 6 June 1939; Superintendent's Report, *ibid.*, Dec. 1939.
22   Unless noted otherwise, this account of the 1940 explosion and its aftermath is based on Ray Doyle and Arnold Prince, "Probe Nationwide Sabotage After 3 Explosions Kill 15," *Daily Mirror* (N.Y.), 13 Nov. 1940; *New York Herald Tribune*, 13 Nov. 1940; and interviews with Leon Silakoski, 5 Oct. 1989 and 7 Nov. 1989, Woodbridge, N.J.
23   George B. Woodruff to William H. Speer, 25 Nov. 1940, File 208 ["Woodbridge Explosion"], MWCR.
24   MWC Minutes of Directors Meetings, 20 Nov. 1940; Lender, *One State in Arms*, 87; Ambrose Mundy to Edward S. Atwater, Jr., 27 Oct. 1942, MWCR File 226 (War Damage Insurance); Mundy to William H. Speer, *ibid.*
25   The war-time activities of the company are traced in MWC Minutes of Directors Meetings, 16 July 1941 - 15 Nov. 1944.
26   Interview with Barbara Reusmann and Albert C. Mundy, 5 Sept. 1989.
27   MWC Minutes of Directors Meetings, 19 July - 7 Sept. 1944.
28   Donald J. Bogue, *The Population of the United States* (New York: Macmillan, 1959), 9; Steele Maron Kennedy *et al.*, eds., *The New Jersey Almanac, 1964-1965* (Upper Montclair: N.J. Almanac, Inc., 1963), 489; *New Jersey Industrial Directory, 1956-57 Edition* (Union City, 1956), xxii.
29   Bruce R. French, "Housing," 491-501, in Salomon J. Flink, *The Economy of New Jersey* (New Brunswick: Rutgers Univ. Press, 1958); *New Jersey Industrial Directory, 1956-57*, xvi; *New Jersey Almanac*, 395.
30   *Ibid.*, 116.
31   Flink., ed., *Economy of New Jersey*, 102-104; *New Jersey Almanac*, 339, 342.
32   MWCR, *BPUC Annual Reports*, 1945-59, *passim*; "In the Matter of the Revision in Rates Filed by Middlesex Water...," Docket No. 10241, *Reports of the Board of Public Utility Commissioners*, Vol.1, 2nd Ser., 1 Jan. 1957-31 Dec. 1964, 166.
33   *Ibid.*, 166-67; "Dry Raritan Area Raps Water Co.," *Newark Evening News*, 24 June 1954; "Woodbridge Asks Probe of Water Co.," *ibid.*, 17 Aug. 1955.
34   *Reports of the BPUC*, 1957-64, 166; "Weighing Bond Plan Of Middlesex Water," *Newark Evening News*, 19 June 1946; "Plan $400,000 Issue Of Water Co. Bonds," *ibid.*, 26 May 1949; "Weighs Stock Sale By Water Company," *ibid.*, 20 May 1952.
35   Carlisle, *Water Ways*, 170-78, 208-212.
36   Unless noted otherwise, the following section on company personnel during the 1940s and 1950s derives from a series of interviews with Carolina M. Schneider, 24 July 1987; Henry T. (Ted) Grundmann, 13 Oct. 1989; Arline J. Rask and Louis H. Rask, 12 Nov. 1987; Louis Plisko, 19 Nov. 1987; Anthony (Tony) Ferraro, 24 Oct. 1987; George Devlin, 29 Oct. 1989; Barbara Reusmann, 22 Mar. 1989; Stephen Higham Mundy, 22 Mar. 1989; and written notes from Marian Mundy Sanborn [1989] and Albert C. Mundy [1989].
37   "Dry Raritan Area Raps Water Co.," *Newark Evening News*, 24 June 1954.
38   "Carl J. Losen, 84: Was Water Company Chief," *News Tribune* (Woodbridge), 11 Feb. 1985.
39   *Reports of the BPUC*, 1957-64, 167.
40   *Reports of the BPUC*, 1957-61, 128.
41   "Water Firm Denied Loans," *Newark Evening News*, 22 Feb. 1958; "Middlesex Water Dividend Passed," *ibid.*, 21 Nov. 1958; "Utility Pays No Dividend," *ibid.*, 9 Nov. 1958.

42   *Reports of the BPUC, 1957-64*, 164-79; "Firm Plans Stock Split," *Newark Evening News*, 3 Oct. 1959.
43   "Water Firm Dividend Set," *Newark Evening News*, 6 Nov. 1959; "Firm Plans Stock Split," *ibid.*, 3 Oct. 1959; "Water Company Offering Stock," *ibid.*, 3 Dec. 1959; "Water Deal Is Approved," *ibid.*, 2 Dec. 1959.
44   Josephine Bonomo, "Judge Speer, 90, Enjoys Full Life," *Newark Evening News*, 21 Oct. 1958; "W.H. Speer Dies at 90," *ibid.*, 8 July 1959.

Notes to Chapter 6

1   Charles Schaeffer, "America on a Binge That Threatens to Dry Us Up," *Newark Star Ledger*, 22 May 1963; Solomon J. Flink, "Water Resources," in Flink, ed., *Economy of New Jersey*, 99-115; Max Grossman and Arthur L. Sherman, "Present and Prospective Use of Water by the Manufacturing Industries of New Jersey" (Consultant Report, New Jersey Dept. of Conservation and Economic Development, Div. of Water Policy and Supply, 14 June 1963), 3.
2   "Drought Warning," *Evening News* (Perth Amboy), 11 Aug. 1965.
3   *Ibid.*, 114-15; New Jersey County and Municipal Government Study Commission, *The New Jersey Water Supply Handbook* (Trenton: State of New Jersey, 1983), 36-37.
4   Flink, "Water Resources," 113-14; *N.J. Water Supply Handbook*, 36-37.
5   Unless otherwise noted, the story of the 1960 water emergency is drawn from State of New Jersey, Dept. of Public Utilities, Board of Public Utility Commissioners, "In the Matter of Board's Investigation of Safe, Adequate and Proper Service of the Middlesex Water Company," Decision and Order, Docket No. 606-437, 1 July 1960; "Middlesex Water Firm Reprimanded," *Newark Evening News*, 2 July 1960; "Help on the Way," *ibid.*, 30 June 1960; "Water Lack Reason Asked," *ibid.*, 29 June 1960.
6   Interview with Carolina Schneider, 24 July 1987, Middlesex Water Company.
7   "Metuchen Mayor Asks: Go Easy on Water," *ibid.*, 2 July 1960.
8   "Doubts Middlesex Water Getting Contract Volume," *ibid.*, 10 Dec. 1960.
9   *Reports of the BPUC, 1961*, 180-86; "Water Plan Is Offered," *Newark Evening News*, 10 Aug. 1960; "Water Rate Hike Upheld," *ibid.*, 28 Sept. 1962.
10   "Water Utility Hikes Dividend," *Newark Evening News*, 15 Nov. 1962; "Water Company To Sell Stock," *ibid.*, 10 June 1963; "Water Company Reports Gains," *ibid.*, 15 Aug. 1963; "Middlesex Water Sales, Income Up," *ibid.*, 20 Nov. 1963; "Water Utility's Stocks on Market," *ibid.*, 11 Dec. 1963; "Water Utility Ups Income," *ibid.*, 24 Mar. 1964.
11   Paul Zumbo, "Arid N.J. in a Spring Fever," *The Daily News* (New York), 4 Apr. 1965.
12   "Drought Warning," *Evening News* (Perth Amboy), 11 Aug. 1965; Adrian C. Leiby, *The Hackensack Water Company: 1869-1969* (River Edge, N.J.: Bergen County Historical Society, 1969), 219-21.
13   *Ibid.*, 220-21; "Water A'Plenty In 1964 Says Elizabethtown," *Westfield Suburban News*, 8 Jan. 1964; Robert D.B. Carlisle, *Water Ways: A History of the Elizabethtown Water Company* Elizabeth: Elizabethtown Water Co., 1982), Chapt. 7.
14   "Officials Mapping Action on Drought," *Evening News* (Perth Amboy), 6 Apr. 1965.
15   James W. Sullivan, "Warning on New Jersey Water Shortage," *Hearld Tribune* (New York), 6 Apr. 1965; "Middlesex Water Level Drops," *Evening News* (Perth Amboy), 23 July 1966.
16   *New Jersey Water Supply Handbook*, 7-8.
17   "State Approves Canal Water Use," *Newark Evening News*, 23 Dec. 1964; "Paulus Promises City Fight for Water," *Daily Home News* (New Brunswick), 10 July 1964; "Horvath Objects to Pumping Station Site," *ibid.*, 3 Jan. 1965.
18   "New Brunswick Freeway Plan," *Star Ledger* (Newark), 16 Apr. 1964; Ian McNett, "Utility Mapping $6 Million Project," *Evening News* (Perth Amboy), 16 Dec. 1964; Charles Dustow, "Water Supply Safeguard Seen," *Courier News* (Somerville), 17 Mar. 1965; "Our Company Means Business," *Waterways* (Middlesex Water Company), Winter 1968/1969, 1-2. Unless noted otherwise, this account of the building of the D&R Project is based on the above sources.

19   "Water Plant a Boon to Edison," *The Evening News* (Perth Amboy), 7 Apr. 1967.
20   Buck, Seifert and Jost, D&R Project Brochure [1967], Middlesex Water Company Records, Iselin, N.J.
21   Ernest C. Gere, Memorandum, Doc-1658D [comments on book MS], 15 Jan. 1993, MWCR.
22   Peter W. Yaremko, "Smaller Water Rate Increase Proposed," *The Evening News* (Perth Amboy), 9 May 1967; "PUC Grants 15% Water Rate Hike," *ibid.*, 1 July 1967; "Our Company," *Waterways* (1968/1969), 2; Carl J. Olsen to Middlesex Water Company Employees, 8 Dec. 1969, MWCR.
23   *Ibid.*; J. Richard Tompkins to W.J. Brady, Memorandum, Doc-2157B [comments on book MS], 18 Mar. 1993, MWCR.
24   *Ibid.*, 2.
25   See company advertisements in the *Independent Leader* (Woodbridge), 14 Jan. 1965; *Newark Sunday News*, 23 Jan. 1966; *Evening News*, 11 Feb. 1966. "The Bottle Burst!" Middlesex Water Company rates brochure [1969], MWCR; "Newspaper Clippings on Woodbridge 300th Anniversary," File 473, MWCR; "Fairs, Celebrations, Observances, Parades, Etc.," File 533, MWCR.
26   "The Mailbag," *Waterways* (Summer 1970), 3.
27   *Ibid.*, 2-3.
28   "Water Company Employees Wind Up New Course," *Independent Leader* (Woodbridge), 18 Feb. 1965.
29   *Waterways* (1969-69), 1-3.
30   Tompkins to Brady, Doc-2157B, 18 Mar. 1993, MWCR.
31   Edward D. Bastian, Memorandum to Middlesex Water Company Employees, 4 Sept. 1973, MWCR.
32   "The D&R Water Treatment Plant," *Waterways* (Summer 1970), 2-3.
33   Tompkins to Brady, Doc-2157B, 18 Mar. 1993, MWCR.

Notes for Chapter 7

1   "The Customer Service Department," *Waterways*, Winter 1969/1970, p.1.
2   Marc B. Leavitt, "Middlesex Acquiring Land," *News Tribune* (Woodbridge), 2 Nov. 1973.
3   Carl J. Olsen, Inter-Office Memorandum, 1 Sept. 1970, MWCR.
4   Carl J. Olsen to Middlesex Water Company employees, 17 Apr. 1975, MWCR.
5   Middlesex Water Company, *1985 Annual Report*, 7.
6   Michael A. Taylor, "Middlesex Water long haul prospect," *Asbury Park Press*, Sec. D, 4 Dec. 1983.
7   "Olsen to Retire from Middlesex Water," *News Tribune* (Woodbridge), 2 dec. 1980.
8   "Carl J. Olsen, 84, was water company chief," *News Tribune* (Woodbridge), 11 Feb. 1985.
9   Water Emergency Task Force, *New Jersey's Water Emergency: September 1980-April 1982* (Trenton: New Jersey Department of Environmental Protection, Division of Water Resources, 1983), xi-xii.
10   MWC, *Facts About Your Water Supply*, [May 1982].
11   *Ibid.*, xii.
12   MWC *1985 Annual Report*, 7; Kathy Barrett Carter, "Middlesex water firm loses bid to sue state for drought losses," *Star-Ledger* (Newark), 28 July 1983; Taylor, "Middlesex Water long haul prospect," *Asbury Park Press*, 4 Dec. 1983.
13   Carter, "Middlesex water firm losses bid," *Star-Ledger*, 28 July 1983.
14   "Middlesex Water Co. HQs given tentative OK," *News Tribune* (Woodbridge), 19 Feb. 1981; "Office Profile," *Architecture New Jersey*, July/Aug./Sept. 1984, 28; MWC, *1985 Annual Report*, 2.
15   *Ibid.*, 1.

16   "Water pipeline project starts," *News Tribune* (Woodbridge), 23. Apr. 1985; MWC *1985 Annual Report*, 3.

17   These negotiations are noted in the *Annual Reports of the Middlesex Water Company* over the early and mid-1980s.

18   Charles A. Appel, *Salt-Water Encroachment Into Aquifers of the Raritan Formation in the Sayreville Area, Middlesex County, New Jersey, with a section on a proposed Tidal Dam on the South River* (Trenton: U.S. Geological Survey & N.J. Dept. of Conservation and Economic Development, 1962), vii, 10, 27-29.

19   Port Authority of New York and New Jersey, *The Regional Economy: Review 1988, Outlook 1989 for the New York-New Jersey Metropolitan Region* (New York, 1989), 16, 19, 31; "Middlesex County," *Regional Labor Market Review*, Aug. 1988, 57-68; N.J. Dept. of Labor, *Employment Projections* (Trenton, 1989), 46-50; MWC *1988 Annual Report*, 7-9.

20   "Water authority official hails pipeline project," *News Tribune* (Woodbridge), 14 Aug. 1984; Suzanne Russel, "S. Amboy negotiating for water service," *ibid.*, 2 May 1985; K.J. Cocuzzo, "Perth Amboy water unavailable to Old Bridge," *ibid.*, 13 Apr. 1988.

21   MWC *1985 Annual Report*, 1-2.

22   *Ibid.*

23   Unless noted otherwise, the following account of system improvements is based on information found in the *Annual Reports of the Middlesex Water Company*, 1985-91.

24   MWC *1988 Annual Report*, 1; *Middlesex Water Company Newsletter*, July 1988, 1.

25   "Rehabilitation of Perth Amboy 24" Main," *Middlesex Water Company Newsletter*, Mar. 1987, 1.

26   *New Jersey Water Supply Handbook* (Trenton: County and Municipal Gov't Study Comm, 1985), 44; MWC *1985 Annual Report*, 1.

27   MWC, "In the Matter of Middlesex Water Company For Approval of An Increase in its Rates for Water Service and A Change in Depreciation Rates," 30 Aug. 1990.

28   MWC, *1987 Annual Report*, 7.

29   *New Jersey Water Supply Handbook*, 7.

30   Water Users Association and N.J. Public Advocate *v.* New Jersey Water Supply Authority, 3 Mar. 1983 (Aa 180), 1-2.

31   *Ibid.*, 18; In the Matter of the Petition of Middlesex Water Company. . ., 23 Oct. 1989, OAL DKT. NO. PUC 1742-89, Agency DKT. NO. WR89030266J, 6.

32   MWC, *1989 Annual Report*, 7.

33   Robert Cohen, "U.S. faulted on water safeguards," *Star-Ledger* (Newark), 19 June 1987; Philip Shabecoff, "U.S. Sets Rules On 8 Chemicals In Public Water," *New York Times*, 25 June 1987; Carol Kocheisen, "Lead contamination bill revised on drinking water at the tap," *Nation's Cities Weekly*, 3 Oct. 1988, 10.

34   Lisa Peterson, "Water company cleared in fish death," *Star-Ledger* (Newark), 10 July 1991.

35   Tompkins to Brady, 18 Mar. 1993, 10.

36   K.J. Cocuzzo, "Bacteria taints Old Bridge water," *News Tribune*, 3 July 1987.

37   40 *CFR* Parts 141, 142, National Primary Drinking Water Regulations; Environmental Protection Agency, "National Primary Drinking Water Regulations," *Federal Register*, 18 July 1991, 33050-33127; "Water Quality," *Federal Research Report*, 6 Dec. 1991, 1-2.

38   New Jersey Division of Environmental Protection, Division of Water Resources, *New Jersey Special Water Treatment Study, Phase II: Final Report*, prepared by Camp Dresser & McKee, Inc. (Trenton, 1988); *NJR*, 58:10-22, 58:10-23, 160-93; *NJR*, 58:11-71, 6-19.

39   MWC, *1989 Annual Report*, 3.

40   MWC, *1990 Annual Report*, 1.

41   "Safety On The Job," *Middlesex Water Company Newsletter*, Mar. 1987, 1; MWC *1990 Annual Report*, 1.

42   Utility Workers Union of America, Meeting Announcements [four circulars], Aug. 1985, Leon Silakowski, Woodbridge, NJ; J. Richard Tompkins, Open letters to Middlesex Water Company employees, 7 & 12 Aug, 1985, 5 Mar. 1986, MWCR.

ENDNOTES

Notes for the Epilogue

1   "Management Audit," *Middlesex Water Company Newsletter*, July 1988, 1; MWC, *1989 Annual Report*, 9.

2   J. Richard Tompkins to Executive Committee, 7 Dec. 1991, Acquisition of Tidewater Utilities—Delaware, Tidewater Utilities Record Group, Vol. 1, MWCR.

3   The full course of the Tidewater acquisitions can be traced through correspondence and related legal and fiscal documents in the three volumes of the Tidewater Utilities Record Group, 1990-92, MWCR.

A NOTE ON SOURCES

I list here only the most important and helpful sources consulted during the research and writing of this study. Yet if this listing is not complete, it does indicate the range of materials upon which I formed my views of the Middlesex Water Company. It should also serve as a guide for those who wish to push further into the history of the company or the histories of utilities businesses generally. Those wishing to trace the precise documentation for the present book should refer to the notes to each chapter.

It is worth noting, however, that anyone pursuing additional research will have their work cut out for them. The historical literature does not offer an especially broad context for important aspects of the narrative. In particular, there have been few studies of the water industry as a whole. The best is N.M. Baker's *The Quest For Pure Water* (1948), which offers an excellent source for the history of water treatment technology; but it is dated now, and in any case Baker said little about the water business as a commercial enterprise. General histories of American business barely mention most utilities, let alone water companies. On the other hand, there are some helpful local studies, with New Jersey companies being the subjects of two very good ones. In fact, Adrian Leiby's, *The Hackensack Water Company, 1867-1967: A Centennial History* (1969), and Robert D.B. Carlisle's *Water Ways: A History of the Elizabethtown Water Company* (1982), are models of their type. Still, no study has used individual corporate histories in any comprehensive study of the water industry. Thus I had to construct much of the industrial context for the Middlesex Company from primary sources.

1. Corporate Record Groups and Related Company Sources

All Middlesex Water Company records, as well as the records of predecessor companies, used in this study are housed in the company headquarters
building on Ronson Road, Iselin, New Jersey. They consist of published and
unpublished sources, including well-organized files and notebooks containing fiscal, technical, and operational records, correspondence, reports to regulatory bodies and shareholders, and minutes of directors and shareholders meetings. The
most helpful were:

Bergen, Frank. Middlesex Water Company Letterbook, 1897-1902. Bound MS.
Copies of Bergen's business correspondence.
Consumers Aqueduct Company. Minutes of Directors and Shareholders
Meetings, 1906-1907. Bound MS.
Middlesex Water Company. Annual Reports. Published prior to each annual
shareholders meeting since the 1980s; previous annual reports are unpublished
and included with Minutes of Directors and Shareholders Meetings.
Middlesex Water Company. Annual Report of the Middlesex Water Company to
the Commissioners of Board of Public Utility Commissioners of the State of
New Jersey, 1911 to present. Title varies slightly from year to year; cited as
BPUC Report in the notes.
Middlesex Water Company. Minutes of Directors and Shareholders Meetings,
1896-1897. Bound MS.
Middlesex Water Company [the consolidated company]. Minutes of Directors
and Shareholders Meetings, 1897 to present. Bound MS and looseleaf
notebooks.
Middlesex Water Company. Miscellaneous Publications. Pamphlets, notices,
quarterly reports, etc., published occasionally and frequently undated. These
publications were often included with customers' bills to communicate
information about rates, water use, and consumer information. They are cited
by title in the notes and scattered throughout the company records files
(below).
Middlesex Water Company. Records, 1897 to present. General company archives
in numbered files, containing original technical reports on the distribution
system, business operations, legal and business correspondence, internal
communications and memoranda, rate case filings and related documents,
early fiscal reports. Cited as MWCR in the notes.

Middlesex Water Company Newsletter, 1986-1987.

Midland Water Company. Minutes of Directors and Shareholders Meetings, 1896-1897. Bound MS.

Waterways [Middlesex Water Company newsletter], 1968-1971.

2. Interviews

The identities of all individuals interviewed as part of the research for this book are noted in the Acknowledgements; thus only names and dates of interviews are noted here.

Bastian, Edward. 28 Oct. 1987.

Brady, Walter. Periodically, 1987-1993.

Devlin, George. 29 Sept. 1989.

Ferraro, Anthony. 29 Oct. 1987.

Gere, Ernest C. Periodically, 1987-1993.

Grundmann, Theodore. 13 Oct. 1989.

Mundy, Stephen Higham. 22 Mar. 1989.

Plisko, Louis. 19 Nov. 1987.

Rask, Arline. 12 Nov. 1987.

Rask, Louis H. 12 Nov. 1987.

Reusmann, Barbara. 22 Mar. 1989.

Sanborn, Marian Mundy. 22 Mar. 1989.

Schneider, Carolina M. 24 July 1987.

Silakoski, Leon. 5 Oct. 1989; 7 Nov. 1989; 13 May 1991.

Tompkins, J. Richard. Periodically, 1987-1993.

3. Government Documents and Reports

Anderson, Henry R. *Geology and Ground-Water Resources of the Rahway Area, New Jersey.* Division of Water Supply Special Report 27. Prepared by the U.S. Geological Survey, N.J. Dept. of Conservation and Economic Development. Trenton, 1968.

Appel, Charles A. *Salt-Water Encroachment Into Aquifers of the Raritan Formation in the Sayreville Area, Middlesex County, New Jersey, with a Section on a Proposed Tidal Dam on the South River.* Division of Water Supply Special Report 17. Prepared by the U.S. Geological Survey, N.J. Dept.

of Conservation and Economic Development. Trenton, 1962.

N.J. Board of Public Utilities. "Small Water Company Takeover Act Regulations." *New Jersey Register* 15 Apr. 1990 [17 N.J.R. 910].

N.J. Board of Public Utility Commissioners. *Reports of the Board of Public Utility Commissioners*. Newark, 1911 to present [published annually].

N.J. Board of Public Utility Commissioners. *Financial and Miscellaneous Statistics Compiled from the Annual Reports made by Public Utilities to the Board of Public Utility Commissioners for the Year 1913*. Union Hill, N.J.: Dispatch Printing Co., 1915.

N.J. County and Municipal Government Study Commission. *The New Jersey Water Supply Handbook*. Trenton, 1983.

N.J. Dept. of Environmental Protection, Division of Water Resources. *New Jersey Special Water Treatment Study, Phase II: Final Report*. Prepared by Camp Dresser & McKee Inc. Edison, 1988.

N.J. Dept. of Environmental Protection, Division of Water Resources. *New Jersey's Water Emergency, September 1980-April 1982: A Report from the Water Emergency Task Force*. Trenton, 1983.

N.J. Dept. of Labor. *Regional Labor Market Review: Northern New Jersey Region*. Trenton, 1988.

N.J. Dept. of Labor, Bureau of Occupational Research. *Employment Projections. I. Industry Outlook for New Jersey & Selected Areas, 1986-2000*. Trenton, 1989.

N.J. Dept. of Labor, Bureau of Occupational Research. *Employment Projections. II. Occupational Outlook for New Jersey & Selected Areas, 1986-2000*. Trenton, 1988.

N.J. Dept. of Labor and Industry. *Fifth Annual Report of the Inspector of Factories and Workshops of the State of New Jersey, 1887*. Trenton: John L. Murphy Publishing Co., 1887.

N.J. Dept. of State. *Corporations of New Jersey: List of Certificates to December 31, 1911*. Trenton: MacCrellish & Quigley, 1914.

N.J. Dept. of State. NJR 58:10-58:13, Waters and Water Supply.

N.J. Dept. of State, Census Bureau. *Compendium of Censuses, 1726-1905*. Trenton, N.J.: John L. Murphy Publishing Co., 1906.

N.J. Geological Survey. *Annual Report of the State Geologist for the Year 1901*. Trenton: MacCrellish & Quigley, 1902.

N.J. Study Commission on Regulatory Efficiency. *Study Commission Narrative Report*. Trenton, 1988.

Ohland, William E., comp. *Report of the activities of the Civil Works Administration in Middlesex County, New Jersey (November 16, 1933 to March 1934)*. Perth Amboy: Civil Works Admin., 1934.

Port Authority of New York and New Jersey, Regional Economic Analysis Group. *The Regional Economy: Review 1988, Outlook 1989 for the New York-New Jersey Metropolitan Area*. New York, 1989.

Seaber, Paul R. *Chlorine Concentrations of Water from Wells in the Atlantic Coastal Plain of New Jersey, 1923-61*. Division of Water Supply Special Report 22. Prepared by the U.S. Geological Survey, N.J. Dept. of Conservation and Economic Development. Trenton, 1963.

U.S. Environment Protection Agency. 40 CFR Parts 141 and 142. National Primary Drinking Water Regulations; Radionuclides; Proposed Rule. *Federal Register*, Part II. 18 July 1991, 33050-33127.

Vermeule, Cornelius C. *Report on Water Supply*. The Final Report of the State Geologist, Vol. III. Trenton: Geological Survey of New Jersey, 1884.

4. Newspapers

Asbury Park Press
Christian Science Monitor (Boston)
Daily Mirror (New York)
Courier News (Somerville, N.J.)
Elizabeth Daily Journal
Herald Tribune (New York)
Home News (New Brunswick, N.J.)
Independent Leader (Woodbridge, N.J.)
Nation's Cities Weekly (National League of Cities)
Newark Evening News; Newark Sunday News The most convenient access to the *Newark News* is through the morgue files held at the Newark Public Library.
New York Hearld Tribune
New York Times
News Tribune (Woodbridge, N.J.)
Perth Amboy Evening News
Riverton New Era (Riverton, N.J.)
Star-Ledger (Newark)
Suburban News (Westfield, N.J.)

5. Books

American Water Works Association. *Water Works Practice: A Manual.*
Baltimore: Williams & Wilkens, Co., 1925.

Baker, M.N. *The Quest for Pure Water: The History of Water Purification from
the Earliest Records to the Twentieth Century.* New York: American Water
Works Association, 1948.

Baker, M.N., ed. *The Manual of American Water-Works.* New York:
Engineering News, 1889.

Bergen, Frank. *The Water Situation: Correspondence between the President of
Middlesex Water Company and the President of the Board of Public Utility
Commissioners.* N.p.: Privately Published, 1926.

Bergen, Frank. *The Chimney Rock Project: A Statement.* N.p.: Privately
Published, 1928.

Bergen, Frank. *Essays and Speeches of Frank Bergen.* 2 vols. Newark: Privately\
Published, 1931.

Biographic Encyclopedia of New Jersey of the Nineteenth Century. Philadelphia:
Galaxy Publishing Co., 1887.

Carey, George W., Leonard Zobler, Michael R. Greenberg and Robert M.
Hordon. *Urbanization, Water Pollution, and Public Policy.* New Brunswick:
Center for Urban Policy Research, 1972.

Carlisle, Robert D.B. *Water Ways: A History of the Elizabethtown Water
Company.* Elizabeth: Elizabethtown Water Co., 1982.

Clayton, W. Woodford, ed. *History of Middlesex and Union Counties.*
Philadelphia: Everts & Peck, 1882.

Conniff, James C.G. and Richard Conniff. *The Energy People: A History of
PSE&G.* Newark: PSE&G, 1978.

Corbin, William H., comp. *The Act Concerning Corporations in New Jersey.* 8th
ed. Trenton: Naar, Day & Naar, 1894.

Cowen, David L. *Medicine and Health in New Jersey: A History.* New Jersey
Historical Series, Vol. 16. Princeton: D. Van Nostrand Co., 1964.

Croes, J.J.R. *The History and Statistics of American Water Works.* New York:
Engineering News, 1885.

Cyclopedia of New Jersey Biography. New York: American Historical Society,
1923.

Draffin, Jasper Owen. *The Story of Man's Quest for Water.* Champaign, Ill.:
Garrard Press, 1939.

Federal Writers Project. *The WPA Guide to 1930s New Jersey.* New Brunswick:
Rutgers Univ. Press, 1986; orig. 1939.

Flink, Solomon J. *The Economy of New Jersey*. New Brunswick: Rutgers Univ. Press, 1958.

Fuller, George W. *Report on Water Supply*. n.p.: Conference of Municipalities, 1922.

Halasi-Kun, George J., ed. *Pollution and Water Resources: Columbia University Seminar Series*. Vol. XIV, Pt 2. *Pollution, Coastal Biology and Water Resources Selected Reports*. New York: Pergamon Press, 1981.

Hirst, David W. *Woodrow Wilson: Reform Governor; A Documentary Narrative*. Princeton: D. Van Nostrand Co., 1965.

Honeyman, A. Van Doren. *History of Union County, New Jersey, 1664-1923*. New York: Lewis Publishing Co., 1923.

Industries of New Jersey. Newark: Historical Publishing Co., 1883.

Keasbey, Edward Quinton. *The Lawyers and Courts of New Jersey, 1616-1912*. 3 vols. New York: Lewis Publishing Co., 1912.

Kennedy, Steele Mabon and Bertrand P. Boucher, eds. *The New Jersey Almanac*. Upper Monclair: N.J. Almanac, Inc., 1963.

Kroll, Richard L. and James O. Brown. *Aspects of Groundwater in New Jersey*. Seventh Annual Meeting of the Geological Association of New Jersey. Union: Kean College, 1990.

Kull, Irving S., ed. *New Jersey: A History*. 4 vols. New York: American Historical Society, 1930.

Lane, Wheaton J. *From Indian Trail to Iron Horse: Travel and Transportation in New Jersey, 1620-1869*. Princeton: Princeton Univ. Press, 1939.

Leiby, Adrian C. *The Hackensack Water Company, 1869-1969: A Centennial History*. River Edge, N.J.: Bergen County Historical Society, 1969.

Link, Arthur, *et al.*, eds. *The Papers of Woodrow Wilson*. 21 vols. Princeton: Princeton Univ. Press, 1966-.

Link, Arthur and Richard L. McCormick. *Progressivism*. Arlington Heights, Ill.: Harlan Davidson, 1983.

McCarter, Thomas N. *One Phase of a Jerseyman's Activities*. Garden City, N.Y.: Country Life Press, 1933.

McCormick, Richard P. *New Jersey From Colony to State, 1609-1789*. Rev. Ed. Newark: N.J. Historical Society, 1981; orig. 1964.

McKelvey, William J., Jr. *The Delaware & Raritan Canal: A Pictorial History*. York, Pa.: Canal Press, 1975.

Marx, Leo. *The Machine in the Garden: Technology and the Pastoral Ideal in America*. New York: Oxford Univ. Press, 1964.

Menzies, Elizabeth G.C. *Passage Between Rivers: A Portfolio of Photographs with a History of the Delaware and Raritan Canal*. New Brunswick: Rutgers Univ. Press, 1976.

Michaelson, Connie O. and Michael R. Greenberg. *New Jersey toward the Year 2000: Employment Projections*. New Brunswick: Center for Urban Policy Research, 1980.

Murrin, Mary, ed. *New Jersey Historical Manuscripts: A Guide to Collections in the State*. Trenton: New Jersey Historical Commission, 1987.

National Research Council. *Drinking Water and Health: A Report on the Safe Drinking Water Committee*. Washington, D.C.: National Academy of Sciences, 1977.

Noble, Ransom E., Jr. *New Jersey Progressivism before Wilson*. Princeton: Princeton Univ. Press, 1946.

The New Jersey Industrial Directory [title varies]. Union City: N.J. Industrial Directory Publishing Co. [various publishers], annual editions since 1901.

New Jersey Utilities Association. *Minutes, 1915*. Trenton, 1915.

New Jersey Utilities Association. *Proceedings* [Annual Meetings]. Trenton, 1915 to present.

Pusateri, C. Joseph. *A History of American Business*. Arlington Heights, Ill.: Harlan Davidson, 1984.

Schmidt, Hubert G. *Agriculture in New Jersey: A Three-Hundred-Year History*. New Brunswick: Rutgers Univ. Press, 1973.

Snyder, John Parr. *The Story of New Jersey's Civil Boundaries, 1609-1968*. Trenton: N.J. Bureau of Geology and Topography, 1969.

Stellhorn, Paul A. and Michael J. Birkner, eds. *The Governors of New Jersey, 1664-1974: Biographical Essays*. Trenton: New Jersey Historical Commission, 1982.

The Story of Drinking Water. Denver: American Water Works Association, n.d.

The Story of Water Supply. New York: American Water Works Association, 1969.

Turneaure, F.E. and H.L. Russell. *Public Water Supplies: Requirements, Resources, and the Construction of Works*. New York: John Wiley & Sons, c. 1900.

Wall, John P. and Harold E. Pickersgill, eds. *History of Middlesex County, New Jersey, 1664-1920*. 3 vols. New York: Lewis Publishing Co., 1921.

Who Was Who in America. 3 vols. Chicago: A.N. Marquis Co., 1960.

Van Winkle, Daniel, ed. *History of the Municipalities of Hudson County, New Jersey, 1630-1923*. 3 vols. New York: Lewis Publishing Co., 1924.

6. Articles

"A Bank's Unusual Philanthropical Venture." *Metro Newark* Spring 1987, 11-12.
Cross, Robert F. "Water, Water, Everywhere?" *The Conservationist* 36, No. 2 (1981): 2-7.
"The Menace of a Water Famine." *Magazine of the Chamber of Commerce of the Plainfields,* Supplement. April 1924, 4.
Speer, William Henry. "Political Panaceas and the People." *American Industries* (1911): 30-31.
"Water Quality." *Federal Research Report* 27, No. 48 (1991): 377-378.

7. Unpublished Materials

Chowdhury, Faruque. Small Water Company Takeover Act Regulations. Public Administration Seminar Paper, Kean College, 1990.
Chowdhury, Faruque. Small Water Company Takeover Act: A Case History. Public Administration Independent Study Paper, Kean College, 1990.
Dietz, George H. Public Utility Regulation in New Jersey, 1938 to 1949. M.A. Thesis, Rutgers Univ., 1949.
Newark Aqueduct Company. Book of Transfers, 1803-1860. MG 278. New Jersey Historical Society. Newark, N.J.
N.J. Board of Public Utilities. The Matter of the Petition of Middlesex Water Company for an Increase in Rates and Changes in Its Tariff, BPU Docket No. WR89030266J. 1989.
N.J. Bureau of Water Quality Standards and Analysis, Division of Water Resources. Development of the Final 304(1) Short List. 1989.
N.J. Office of Administrative Law. Initial Decision Re: Middlesex Water Company. OAL DKT No. PUC 1742-89. 1989.
Rosenthal, Arnold B. Investigation of Middlesex Water Company. Audit pre pared for Middlesex County Board of Chosen Freeholders, New Brunswick, 1938.
Sommer, Frank H. In the Matter of Proposed Increases in the Rates of Middlesex Water Company, etc: Memorandum on Behalf of Municipalities and Other Users. Brief for N.J. BPUC. 1924
Utility Workers Union of America (A.F.L.-C.I.O.), Organizing Committee for Middlesex Water Company. Broadsides and leaflets. 1985.

INDEX

Metuchen, N.J., 10, 19, 36—37, 47,
63, 88, 119, 121, 184; water
emergency (1960), 140
Meyner, Robert B., 136
Middlesex County, history, 3—8;
Freeholders,
109, 111, 112; industry, 8—
10, 23—24, 36, 59, 100,
120—121; population, 10,
47, 100, 119—120
Middlesex Water Co., consolidated
company, 29; customers,
23—24, 36—37, 47—48, 61,
113, 121, 177, 178, 195—
196; consumer relations, 63,
66, 73—74, 89, 157—158,
166; departments, 166—167,
182, 191; distribution
systems, 54—56, 63—66,
101, 102, 113—115, 120—
122, 123, 129—132, 143,
171, 178, 183; drought,
171—173; employees
& benefits, 102— 103, 128,
130, 192; finances, 40, 43—
44, 52, 59, 60, 69, 101, 108,
111—112, 127, 130—131,
144, 155, 168—169, 174,
181, 199; meter shop
explosion, 114—117;
officers & directors, 26, 118,
127, 128, 170, 174, 185,
193—194, 197, 201, 202;
offices, 97, 102, 127, 138,
159, 175—176; origins,
21, 25; pumpage, 53, 55—
56, 113—114, 117; pumping
facilities, 38, 54—55, 59;

service area, 21, 198; South
River Basin project, 180;
water rates, 61, 70—71, 88,
93—94, 109, 111, 185; water
shortages, 121— 123, 129,
138—142; water supplies,
118, 130, 151—152, 173,
195; water treatment, 52, 95,
153, 191; wholesale sales, 62,
123, 177; Midland Water
Co., 26, 29, 35, 177
Millstone River, 5, 67
Molnar Electrical Contractors, 154
Molnar, John P., 201
Morgan Guarantee Trust Co., 157
Mullin, Edward D., 162, 167
Mundy, Albert Carmen, 118
Mundy, Ambrose, 57—58, 66, 86, 92,
102—103, 116, 126, 128,
142, 144—145; background &
family, 58, 124—125;
becomes president, 131; and
Frank Bergen, 96; consumer
relations, 143; death, 145
Mundy, Carmen, xiii
Mundy, Stephen H., xiii, 201
Mutual Benefit Life, 112

Newark Aqueduct Co., 17
New Brunswick, N.J., 6—8, 153
New Deal, 103—104, 108
New Idea, 82—83
New Jersey State Geologist, 16, 18, 51
New Jersey Utilities Association, 86
North Jersey Water Supply
Commission, 67

Old Bridge, N.J., 178, 189

232